Should I "Go Walkabout" in Australia

A MOTORHOME ADVENTURE

JOHN TIMMS

AuthorHouse™ UK
1663 Liberty Drive
Bloomington, IN 47403 USA
www.authorhouse.co.uk
Phone: 0800.197.4150

Published by AuthorHouse 11/08/2018

ISBN: 978-1-7283-8068-1 (sc)
ISBN: 978-1-7283-8080-3 (e)

authorHOUSE®

INTRODUCTION

This is not a travel documentary although you will get a lot of information about Australia and a great deal of detail about a few places. This book is more about being confused, the things that went wrong, the things or places that surprised us and those that disappointed us. It also touches on living with your partner twenty-four seven, along with two dogs and what joy those two dogs gave us when we arrived at, for example, a deserted beach. Sometimes when things went wrong I cried and so did my friends but their tears were those of laughter as I continued to send them out our weekly diary via email. It's about the accidents that happened to our vehicles to us and the dogs, unusual physical ailments and boredom which is not what you see on the television when you listen to travel shows. Here in Australia the interviewers always seem to find happy travellers who are sitting on the edge of beautiful beaches with close friends, sipping wine as they watch the sun sink over the horizon and they are all such happy campers. I haven't yet met these people and if I ever try to sit near the beach at sunset, in a warm climate, my only companions are mosquitoes and sandflies! I could spray myself all over with some sort of near lethal mosquito repellent of course but I hate the smell and can't get away from myself quickly enough. So, this is what happened to us (me and my partner) on our first trip which lasted nine months, which was when we realised that we had no hope of getting right around Australia in that time if we wanted to see the coastal areas properly. We started from the Gold Coast in Queensland, travelled the coastline of New South Wales (well the majority of it) visited the Southern Highlands of New South Wales and on to Melbourne. It was so damned cold by then that we turned inland to retreat north again meandering back down to the coastline when we hit a snowstorm, returning to the Gold Coast and then on to Cairns and Cooktown. We returned very slowly down the Queensland coastline discovering isolated seaside hamlets and off road sites.

It took a second, year long trip for us to get around the rest of Australia which is in another book. Am I glad I did it? Yes but there is a lot more behind that answer as you will find out because there were times when I nearly ran away – to catch the nearest plane back home!

Should I Tour Australia?

By

Lisa (Elizabeth) Timms

DEDICATED TO MY DEAR WIFE
WHO SHARED THESE MEMORIES WITH ME
BUT WHO DIED SUDDENLY
ON 5th November 2015.

CHAPTER ONE

31/1/2004- CURRUMBIN, GOLD COAST.

I stood in the middle of the road, immune to the passing traffic, incredulous that my husband, in his haste to start our trip around Australia, had driven off without me. He had left in our 35ft, 16 year old American motor home as our new tenants were moving into our house and whilst I was saying goodbye to my son. He hadn't only left me but also our two dogs behind! Now this wasn't necessarily a bad thing as I was still asking myself if I wanted to leave home at all but with tenants happily placing their furniture into my house, the dogs and I were now homeless.

I knew he was off to buy petrol and I was to follow him in our 'dogmobile'(A double-cab covered Toyota) and he had told me which garage he was going to, so I hurtled off down the road to try and catch up with him. I couldn't understand why I couldn't see him as you can't hide a motor home of that size but he was nowhere in sight and he wasn't at the garage. Totally perplexed, I returned to our house and asked the male tenant if he knew where John had gone.

He looked at me in amazement and asked 'Have you lost him already?'

'Yes, but you were talking to him so I'm asking you if you know which garage he might have gone to?'

'If you've lost him outside the house how on earth are you going to follow him around Australia?' he answered. He appeared to be choking for some reason and coughed to clear his throat.

'Has he got a mobile phone?'

'Yes, we've each got a mobile' I said as I held up both phones.

He bent forwards and I then realised that he couldn't speak for laughing. I got back in the car. I was failing to find anything funny with the situation and felt humiliated and ridiculous so drove a few yards down the road and stopped outside the park. I felt too embarrassed to stay where he could see me! I got the dogs out of the back of the vehicle, gave them a drink of water and waited. I had absolutely no idea what to do. What I did know was that I had made a huge mistake in having agreed to accompany John on a trip around Australia.

About twenty minutes later John came back to find me and I mutely handed him his mobile phone.

'I decided to go to that other garage.' I nodded still mute and close to tears.

I managed to whisper 'You didn't even give me the chance to say goodbye and get into the car and get my seatbelt on and you'd gone! Why didn't you phone me from the garage?'

'Oh, I didn't think of that. That's far too sensible. Come on let's go'.

Thus started our first trip and it was a sign of things to come.

Having gone through months of anguish about this proposed trip I had come to the conclusion that I should accommodate my husband's wish to do so as each of us only has one life and it is important to fulfil your dreams. I had kept telling myself that thousands of people come from all over the world and travel right around this vast land and many thousands of Australians have either done it or are still doing it. Many have found it so enjoyable that they've gone around more than once or have continued to do so for many years. Personally, I am quite happy at home and don't feel the need to rush about exploring unless it means we are going to a nice apartment or hotel for a couple of weeks and are going to get there by plane.

Have you toured all the way around your country? Let's take the U.K. as an example. England, Scotland and Wales combined are not that big (that land mass could be swallowed up inside one of our States and in the case of Western Australia you can add Texas to the U.K. and still have oodles of room left over for a few other countries, so I ask this question. Have you even considered getting into a motor home and calling in on every available seaside town, village and port in the U.K. in a single trip? You probably don't want to but do you feel the need to say that you have done so? I doubt it and I personally think it's quite insane, with one exception and that is a story I read about a man who had arthritis and decided to 'walk it off' by walking around England, Scotland and Wales. I believe he started with only a few paces at a time as he had been mainly bound to a wheelchair and he ended up as fit as a fiddle having accomplished his ambition, minus the pain of his arthritis.

John and I were born in England and neither of us ever considered doing it over there, yet over here in Australia it is becoming the 'norm'. I have no idea why but I blame the tourists because they look at you in amazement if you say you have never seen Uluru (Ayers Rock) or The Northern Territory or Perth because they've been there and as an Aussie it can be quite embarrassing. Actually I'm obviously not an Aussie but nor am I a Pommy as I've been here too long and not only speak a different language, I say and act in ways that startle my family back in the U.K. so I call myself a Possie. That's beside the point and what I am getting at is that many tourists arrive at some major city, purchase an old vehicle or rent one and hurtle around this vast Continent and not satisfied with that they continue onto New Zealand or Thailand and as many other countries that they can fit into their time limit and do the same thing in those countries. It sounds so simple. How come I couldn't get my head around the idea?

Many of the Australians we have met on our travels have taken several years to traverse Australia and when we decided to do a bit of travelling we were continually being asked 'Doing the big trip are you?'

'No, we're just going touring'.

'But you are going to go all the way around aren't you?'

'We have no idea but I very much doubt it' was my usual response.

When I lived in England and Wales it was a treat to take a two week package deal to some Mediterranean country where we would lie on the beach all day to get suitably sunburnt to prove that we had been abroad and we partied all night, with the odd sight-seeing trip thrown in. We'd fly home with our duty free booze and some cheap trinkets as gifts for our friends, exit Heathrow airport with a big sombrero on our heads and that was that for another year. Now the world has shrunk and I'm afraid to admit that I haven't yet been to South America, Peru, bungee jumped in New Zealand, travelled through India or Africa let alone Canada or America and I haven't even been on a cruise ship yet! I've been bringing up kids, working and paying off the mortgage instead.

Finding the right van, preparing it for our use (which required many extra dollars), packing it up and packing up our home took us about ten months and by the time we left I was exhausted. I had good reason to be.

CHAPTER TWO

Two days before departure:

You've heard of Murphy's Law - well Murphy has been up to his tricks this week. A hail storm five months previously had damaged our house and van so badly that it had held up our departure but that wasn't enough for Murphy who had great fun this week! The swimming pool has turned green because the bougainvillea that we were cutting down was bigger than we realised and ended up falling into the pool and covered more than the length and the full depth. In the middle was a baby dove in its nest and the mother, who had fled to the wall, was obviously frantic as her baby could not fly. I was determined to rescue the nest but it took us three hours of standing in the water before we had cut our way through to it. Mother and baby are fine but John and a wonderful friend who helped us are covered with scratches from the thorns. The skip we ordered to put it in has overflowed with branches so we'll have to get the rest of it to the Council dump ourselves.

Now the motor home fridge won't work on gas. The cable for my new mobile phone (to connect it to my laptop computer) also wouldn't work and I had to urgently get hold of the manufacturer. Then I couldn't get my email account to work and the girl at the phone company got so fed up with trying to fix it last night that she told me she was going home! All my friends are waiting for my new email address and I haven't yet cancelled my home internet account. As for the fridge, I've decided we'll go without any food if necessary!

The pergola roof repair still isn't right and as the repairers have been paid, we are having trouble getting them back. Then there have been the endless evening storms which now make me nervous as we have had some hail again and I have visions of us spending the next three months parked in a truck repair car park with two dogs whilst we wait for yet another new roof! The tenants are moving into our house in two days time.

We're getting used to coming down in size as we're now sleeping downstairs in the dining area! Upstairs is empty and clean. It will be odd with no gardening to do and no big house to clean and no patio to constantly sweep (because of dog hairs) and no pool to check - sounds like bliss at the moment as we're amidst turmoil, with papers and underwear and fresh ironing everywhere! It's going to be a very odd feeling when we take off and I'm just starting to realise it's actually going to happen!

CHAPTER THREE

Whilst we were preparing for the trip I made the mistake of reading Bill Bryson's book called 'Down Under'.

By the time I had finished reading about all the creatures that might kill me and my husband during our journey I had already decided to sell the van. It didn't matter that the preparations had so far taken us so many months and had caused endless headaches and many squabbles such as John asking 'Why do you need a washing machine?'

'I won't if you do all the washing'.

'Why do we need a pure sine wave inverter instead of the cheaper type?' (Once an accountant always an accountant and he hadn't long retired).

'Because it says in the books that you must have one for laptops, unless you want to leave your brand new laptop at home which cost us three times as much as the washing machine.'

So having spent months telling friends that I had been on a university course learning about 12v versus 240v (and in our case 110v as the mobile home had been brought in from America), generators, inverters, solar panels and researching water purifiers, communications and how to test that our toilet paper is suitable for our waste system, this dear Bill Bryson had managed to flatten me to the point that I was too scared to go down the road to get my Christmas shopping from the local supermarket. I may have lived in Australia for years but I had not realised how lucky I am to still be alive.

In the years I have lived here I have encountered a crocodile once at close quarters in the wild. That was in north Queensland when I was on a medium-sized boat on the Daintree River with other tourists. We got very close to the bank and the crocodile took offence. I thought it was asleep. It looked as though it was asleep. Before we had the time to register that it was moving it had attacked the boat, which rocked violently. It was obvious that everyone had been as frightened as me because we all laughed! An American tourist was delighted that his cap had got soaked in muddy water and said he would never wash it and would keep it to remind him of this experience. I don't need a cap to remind me that crocodiles can move very fast.

I also had an encounter with a brown snake a few weeks after arriving in Australia. I didn't realise it was dangerous and was amused by the antics of my neighbour who was screaming at my window, with her baby in her arms and her toddler clutched to her side. Being a typical new Pommy immigrant, I asked her if she wanted a cup of tea as she was obviously upset about something. I calmly re-boiled the kettle and heard her scream to me to pour the boiling water over the snake and kill it, so I did. Naturally the poor thing went berserk. Then she told me to get the garden hoe and to chop off its head. I grabbed her baby and told her to do it! Later she came around again and told me that they come in pairs and asked me if I could keep an eye out for its partner. By this time I had studied the headless corpse and had phoned the Brisbane museum to ask them what it could be. Fully informed, I was now petrified to think another could be on the loose somewhere between our two houses, a distance of approximately ten feet. The dead snake was approximately the same length.

I have also seen red back spiders, both dead and alive. We have our homes sprayed internally each year so that if one were to decide to explore inside the house it would drop dead. We have ours done with a product that is harmless to humans and pets, made from a dandelion extract. Luckily they are very shy and keep out of our way. Oddly enough it's the big spiders that terrify me, namely the Huntsmen Spiders which are not lethal. Having said that, I believe all spiders do bite. Anything uninvited that crawls into my house doesn't last long. I ensure it ends up on the floor and I put a glass over the top of it so that it cannot escape and I leave it for my husband to deal with! If he were to go away for six months he would return to find the floor littered with glasses, mugs and jars!

A friend's daughter was boxed in the face by a kangaroo at a wildlife park in Brisbane once and we've often laughed about it, although we couldn't at the time of course because the poor kid was freaked out. I can assure you that this must be a very unusual occurrence, particularly in a wildlife park where the kangaroos just love coming up to you for a feed. The parks that still allow you to have a photo taken with a koala also have an expert handler who explains to you how to hold the koalas as they have very sharp claws so if you ever see an injured one in the wild call a wild life officer rather than moving it yourself. If you have to move it, wrap it up in something very thick – don't suffocate it though!

I have never seen a shark in their natural environment and have only once heard the warning siren at the beach. I was telling my friend who had just arrived from England that she had no need to worry about sharks when what sounded like an air-raid siren went off. It was a false alarm but what fascinated both of us is that no-one took any notice! Not one swimmer or surfer came out of the water. We get constant warnings about water rips at the Gold Coast, which can sweep people out into deep water but it seems that no-one recognises the shark siren!

You can perhaps now understand that I was not unduly worried about the dangers of our wildlife before I read this book. I simply hadn't given the subject any thought. Now it was on my mind. Fish that look like stones until you step on them, snakes (I'd never heard of most of them) and Funnel Web spiders and many of their relatives whose names I've already forgotten. I have apparently been living in blissful ignorance for all these years in the deadliest country in the world, according to that book.

If all this is not enough to put me off my travels there is the apparent boredom of the outback roads. We belong to a motor home club which now has approximately 45,000 happy wanderers as members. I have spoken to a fair few of them and in every case they have told me that I will want to stay 'off-site' (meaning not in a caravan park) more than 'on-site'. I have heard that I simply must visit the outback. A trip around Australia is not a real trip unless we venture inland. I have been assured that I will love it!

Is that so? Having read a few paragraphs in this same book about the endless kilometres of nothingness between Darwin and Alice Springs, I reread them aloud to my husband who promptly suggested that we fly there from Adelaide. He reckons it would be cheaper too.

I found the book utterly depressing and it would certainly have put me off coming to Australia for a holiday if I hadn't emigrated here and it really is so beautiful that I could rave on for hours about it. I did finish the book. I had to in order to find out if the author is still alive and it seems he did survive!

We have previously hired vans and have spent ten days travelling around Tasmania which is stunningly beautiful and a week driving along the Great Ocean Road in Victoria. We had previously owned a van when the children were little and we'd taken them for holidays to various coastal caravan parks in New South Wales and we thought we knew the New South Wales coastline. Another big mistake, as we were to find out on this trip. Anyway, we had loved every minute of our little trips and I kept telling myself that this big trip would be just like those little trips but just strung together over a period of about ten months. One lovely, long holiday was what I had tried to envisage but having read that book it now it seemed more like a 'challenge' - something to be faced with trepidation. I obviously needed a willingness to face adversity and deprivation and this I was definitely not up to.

In fact, I felt exhausted with all the planning and organising and desperately needed a holiday to have a rest. A five star luxury holiday where my bed is made for me and I don't have to shop, cook or wash up! I wanted to laze beside a pool on a sun bed with handsome men offering me fluffy swimming towels and yet another exotic cocktail. The added bonus of a personal masseuse wouldn't have gone amiss either.

CHAPTER FOUR

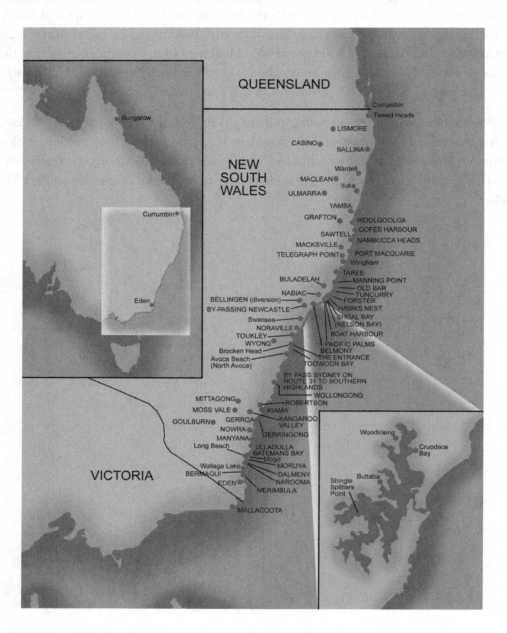

CASINO, N.S.W – our first stop! Yes, we made it. We stopped at a truck stop for a coffee and couldn't get the gas cooker to work to boil the kettle. Now I did tell you that we had read the manuals that had arrived with the bus and had learnt all about the electrical systems and so forth and most sensible people would have read the manuals that would concern them on an every day basis instead of a manual where you need a qualified electrician if you have a problem. We hadn't bothered to read any booklets that covered our basic needs as we had thought that we could handle those items easily. John luckily found a relay under the bonnet and we had power again !

We live in Queensland at the Gold Coast and our home is at Currumbin near the New South Wales border. We intended to cross the New South Wales border and visit all the coastal towns as we headed towards Sydney. However, we had planned to start in Casino which is a little way inland because we had some shares in a new motor home park there and wanted to find out how it was progressing. The northern New South Wales hinterland (countryside) reminds me of the scenery surrounding me when I lived on a mountainside south Wales (U.K) so I always adore visiting the area as it reminds me of 'home'.

We were to keep to the main road, go to Ballina and turn right for Lismore and Casino. Thank goodness I followed John in our Ute because I would have lost him again! He suddenly veered off the main highway, way before Ballina and entered the village of **Bangalow** which is a beautiful tiny village that we have visited before. It is well known for attracting artists and authors as residents and for good coffee. There are many original Queenslanders (houses) with their beautiful wrap-around verandas. He managed to get around the small roundabout in the village centre to turn right and stopped just past it. He expected me to get out and talk to him but he forgot how long the motor home is and I was still stuck on the roundabout, right behind him, holding up the traffic. I thought he'd broken down and I was feeling frantic!

We continued on to the lovely village of **Clunes** (meaning 'pleasant place', which it is) where we stopped for lunch and to give the dogs a run around the pretty park. We talked of the stunningly beautiful scenery we had just passed. We went through **Lismore** next, a University town, with its own airport and at last reached Casino. By the time we had set up camp, had 'drinkies' with fellow campers and had had something to eat, I was bushed. I went to bed at 7.15pm (Queensland time) and woke up at 7.30am New South Wales time, 11 hours sleep! I had had only nine hours sleep in the last two days and I could have slept on a concrete floor by the time we arrived!

Relaxing? Well, water from kitchen sink kept coming up in the bath (again, our mistake as we hadn't read the manual) and that is quite revolting when you've just fried steak and eggs and washed up! One large drawer fell to pieces - now repaired. One cupboard door needs repairing and a piece of wood fell off where the T.V. sits. Now we are trying to understand why the water tank for the hot water is not filling up. A plumber was supposed to visit this morning but he forgot to visit our van and has already left the site. We've sorted the waste water problem out though, thank goodness. We cannot connect to the mains water as the tank keeps overflowing (faulty valve) so are still turning on water pump which is a bit noisy. Apparently it shouldn't be and means a water pressure leak. This is why we planned to come to Casino. This is the new motor home park for club members in Australia. Many people stay for months whilst they redesign the interiors of their vans, do necessary repairs or just have a break from travelling. Being surrounded by people with knowledge of travelling and motor homes can be very useful and in our case it was imperative! In fact, if you want to know anything, just come here as we had a lesson yesterday on the flooding of the Nile Basin which followed a conversation about local weather conditions!

We had been approached when seen struggling with our awning. We'd done something wrong and were scratching our heads. John kept telling me not to talk too loud in case we drew attention to ourselves as we were so green at all this he feels embarrassed! We found out later that several campers had been watching us and we were their afternoon entertainment. Apparently most people struggle the first time if they don't read the instructions like us! We're staying here seven nights to get 'sorted'. I've decided I want my washing machine plumbed in too (but deciding something doesn't mean it gets done in our partnership and it never was installed). I have tried the bucket method (washes while you drive) but inadvertently put in some tie-dye purple trousers and now have several blotchy purple tops!

CHAPTER FIVE

We leave Casino tomorrow and everything that we can repair is done but no sign of the plumber. It's been a week of sleeping very long hours and gradually winding down. Highlights of this week - our day sightseeing in Lismore and finding a street-side van where they made fresh pies. We sat on the sidewalk and enjoyed our pies fresh from the oven and a large mug of coffee for $5. I was amused by the fact that they offered mashed potatoes and mushy peas with thick gravy as an optional extra - reminds me of England. There is some really interesting architecture in Lismore, every shop you could possibly need and acres and acres of parkland as well as the river. We were surprised by the lack of litter bins and yet during our full day's tour we didn't see any rubbish anywhere and everywhere we went was so clean and tidy. I would have liked to have stayed a little longer to visit some of the local Farmer's Markets but John was keen to get back on the road.

We also visited **Ballina** and discovered several beaches and the lighthouse and watched the waves crashing against the rocks below. Callie (one of our two dogs) chased the shadows of Pelicans as they flew back and forth over the beach. When we arrived at one deserted beach, thousands of hermit crabs scampered out of their holes in the sand and trooped towards the waves and did a quick about turn and went back into their holes again! The sight of a mass of blue bobbing tiny crabs absolutely enthralled me. A lovely fish and chip tea at Ballina finished off our tour and we returned across the rolling hills to our temporary home relaxed and exhausted. It is time to leave Casino because Jack (our male Belgium Shepherd) now believes that all the fields around our van are part of his garden which he has to guard and he gets exhausted looking after such a big area. If anyone else tries to walk their dog in the fields or park beyond he gets very irritated.

Callie, his wife, sped off across two fields one morning when I was still half asleep, as she had seen a herd of cows. She thought they were a herd of large dogs to play with and ran straight under the barbed wire fence and chased one so hard I had visions of it collapsing with heat exhaustion. All I could think of at the time was how much does a cow cost to replace? I reckon the farmer would have found curdled cheese coming out of her udders later! Meanwhile, I ran after her, screaming at her in anger and fear, screaming 'John, help' and woke up everyone in the caravan park except John. Luckily I'd managed to get my dressing gown on because I sleep only in my knickers! Jack decided that he obviously needed to do something as he was startled at my reaction, so he rounded up the poor cow and lay down beside it guarding it and looked at me for approval. I felt angry with Callie, proud of Jack and angry with myself as it is the first time I have ever lost control of one of the dogs. A very strict regime has followed and they are now so obedient they won't move from outside our door and have not needed their chains at all.

To stand outside in a large field as the sun goes down and the sky glows red and orange, a full moon rising and a million black bats silently passing overhead is a vision I will never forget. They pass overhead every night but there was that one night when nature's colours provided the perfect setting and the moon looked so near and so round. All that was needed to fulfil a child's picture book would have been a witch on a broomstick.

CHAPTER SIX

WARDELL

Next stop was **Wardell**, south of Ballina which was not a long journey but John wanted to take a short cut and this time I insisted on leading the way. It was an extremely pretty journey but I'm not sure that John actually noticed that. He stopped twice behind me so I spent most of the journey trying to keep him in sight via my rear view mirror and wandering where he was when he wasn't. Apparently the first thing that happened was that the television flew out of the cabinet, over his head and landed on the floor just behind him and no, it doesn't work any more! The next stop was to deal with the fridge door and the contents that spilled out all over the carpet. Jars of jam, bottles of milk, eggs, cheese, sandwich meat, chocolate biscuits, mint sauce and so forth along with apples and oranges and vegetables! I would have been a nervous wreck but he was quite calm on arrival. I had noticed that the road was quite bumpy but as he could not seem to get his head around how to talk to me on the two-way phones, I drove the distance in blissful ignorance (I'll explain our use of the two-way phones later). More to the point is the fact that at least he has agreed to cut out his short cuts!

The park we are at is not large but is very rural and I could happily move here for good. We have so much space overlooking a large grassed area and the horse paddock. Behind us is the pool and one of the owners has brought over a mobile barbecue for our use tonight. The dogs can be off leash but as Jack seems to think that the horses are big dogs, we keep a close eye on him! I took Callie over to see them this morning but she's not interested. However, I was and enjoyed plucking grass and feeding them.

One of my sons came to see us yesterday and ended up staying the night and didn't want to leave! He got along so well with everyone and felt so relaxed. He was allowed to stay free which was nice because he used all the facilities including the laundry! I could not believe that my son had brought 'home' his laundry even when we are on holiday!

It is about 3ks to the most beautiful beach and 16ks to Ballina. The locals mainly shop in Ballina and Lismore has everything (as already mentioned) and that is where the hospital and specialists are. It is a beautiful part of the world here. The journey to Lismore is beautiful and we drove to Evans Head today which is on a fabulous stretch of coastline. We only came to Wardell for one night and have been here two and the residents are already asking us to stay on a while! I fear that if we stay too long I will never want to leave.

Well we did stay on and we will be here tomorrow because we actually have a plumber organised at last for 7.30am - that will make us get up early for a change. It's been a very hot day and all we have done is laze around, eat, swim and read papers with only about two hours of 'work stuff' done. John went to the bank in Ballina, I arranged the plumber, I studied a digital photography book and am more confused than ever and John did a couple of small maintenance items. Bliss!

It seems to me that we have to give up the idea that we can stick to a set itinerary. Other people might be able to but we can't. Plumber turned up and he reckons it's a puzzle! We could have told him that on the phone. There's nothing wrong with the water pump, we have no leaks but water is disappearing somewhere! We now have to take our 'home' and leave it with them at their workshop on Thursday for the day. So all we know so far is that we're not going anywhere until at least Friday.

We took the opportunity to take the T.V in for repair as well. The receptionist told John that if they repair it, it may void the warranty. John pointed out to her that he didn't think that the warranty covered flying TV's that crash to the floor whilst one is driving at 100ks per hour because the stupid owners haven't secured it properly!

Anyway, on our return I promptly broke the bathroom window-winder just to keep John busy because he's fretting as he wants to move on - he's very like Jack our dog. They are both impatient and get restless easily and I wander if perhaps it's a male thing. Callie's a bit more like me as she likes fun but enjoys lying around in the sun and having lots of cuddles and strokes.

Well, we spent over $700 and the pump still cycles off and on. We can connect to mains water now but that still overflows periodically! We gained a new hose though! They had the van for most of what must have been the hottest day of the year and we ended up having to return to the workshop as we were dizzy with the heat, despite having spent many hours in the shade of beautiful trees that line the beach and having had several dips in the sea. The dogs stretched out on the cold concrete floor of the workshop and I suggested to John that I thought I might strip naked and do the same but he told me not to.

CHAPTER SEVEN

YAMBA ROCKS

We arrived at **Iluka** today - a beautiful area but you need spend no more than one day here for there's not much to see! We're at a holiday park and so are countless young mothers and their small children - we found that out when we decided to have a dip in the pool. It's 6.30pm and the pool is still 'standing room only' and it shuts at 8pm so no relief. This is in stark contrast to our last park at Wardell where we could guarantee that no-one was in the pool at 6pm as that is dinner time and time for the news. At Wardell it was mainly adults with a couple of lovely toddlers and a couple of school-age children. We were spoilt at the last park as we felt so at home. The pool was the 'meeting place' and I miss the people there already!

We've booked in for two nights so tomorrow we will go and explore the other side of the inlet at Yamba and visit the Scottish village of Maclean which I have been longing to visit for so long. The heat at the moment is exhausting (ok, so February is known to be the worst month of the year in Australia but does it have to be this hot?).

For my English relatives who received a calendar from me this year, Maclean is marked on the map of Australia inside it - about ¾ of an inch below 'Gold Coast'. At this rate, how far do you reckon we'll travel in nine months! Next week Grafton and we'll have travelled one inch.

Our days follow a similar pattern to our days at home because you still have to have breakfast, walk and feed the dogs and do housework (although our home has shrunk) and washing, interrupted by lunch, dinner, walk dogs again and feed them and bed. The main difference has been the lack of TV and therefore more reading a+nd the fact that we now buy the Weekend Australian newspaper although the Brisbane Courier Mail is still available everywhere. We tend to listen to the news on the radio - how very old-fashioned. We've had no choice as the TV wasn't working and now that it is, we are in areas where the only channel we can get is the one that we watch the least! It will be nice to get to Grafton and have a choice again.

We have been so impressed with our change of weekend newspaper that I reckon we'll stick to it when we get home. It appears we were even stuck in a rut with the papers! The Australian reminds us that there is a world beyond Australia and there is so much to read that it keeps us going for days and that's a good thing when you lead the kind of indolent lifestyle that we (and other rich and famous people) do. Of course, if you need to work, I suppose you don't have quite so much time……I'm trying to recall…..oh, it's too long ago. John reckons I shouldn't tempt fate by writing this - as if I could forget the stress of my last job!

INTERLUDE

Oh boy - it's hot - everywhere's hot. Poor Adelaide was 44C yesterday. If we hadn't got air conditioners we wouldn't be able to stay in this van. It's putting a damper on our sightseeing, literally, as the moisture drips off us. We spend most of the day making sure the dogs are cool enough and even Jack is starting to like being hosed down. The swimming pools in the parks are too warm, so the dogs and I have been enjoying sitting under the hosepipe!

One of the joys of a motor-home is emptying your 'black water' (from the toilet as opposed to grey which is not unpleasant as it originates from your sinks and shower). Our 'standard' black water waste hose hasn't fitted any drainage connection so far which means one has to hold it over the hole. Most of the 'dump' sites are also in the most awkward places. If you were one of the flies on the nearest post you would dance with laughter despite the blazing sun, watching John and I manage as its black humour at its best!

CARRINGTON FALLS

Well, **Maclean** was closed. Okay it was Sunday but how very boring of them to shut everything down. **Yamba** is bigger, busier and more geared to tourists than Iluka. It looked like a lovely place to have a holiday +break. You cannot take the dogs onto the main beach but we had a glorious time wandering over the flat rocks overlooking that beach and marvelling at the views, the colours in the rocks and their wondrous formations.

On our way to Grafton we stopped at the 'Historic River Port of **Ulmarra'** and it is well worth a visit as it's quaint and old-fashioned. There are some beautiful heritage buildings and it is beside the Clarence River. If you visit, have a coffee break at the Mulberry Court café as we did - a beautiful old home that has been tastefully renovated and their lemon & lime cheesecake is delicious. Dogs are welcome and ours were offered a huge bowl of water without us asking for it. They sat outside under an umbrella whilst we sat inside enjoyed the air-conditioning.

The river is majestic - John cannot get over how wide it is and likened it to the Mississippi and you get a wonderful view as you cross the bridge in **Grafton**. You can join a river cruise from $10 per head. As early as 1873 the council adopted a policy of planting and preserving trees in the streets and parks and there are now thousands of them and over 20 parks. During the 1870's a local seed merchant planted hundreds of Jacaranda trees and they are magnificently gnarled and aged and huge. On some roads their old branches have met overhead. We should have arrived here around October to November to see their beautiful purple floral display. They were my mother's favourite Australian tree (yeah okay they're native to Brazil but she'd never been there). Forget the town centre, tour around the perimeters and the roads are lined with a stunning array of original Queenslanders - we only saw one brick and tile home.

Tomorrow Woolgoolga and to a park I've stayed at four times before which holds many memories. It's only 25ks to Coffs Harbour from there and we'll be visiting to collect our mail which my daughter will forward to the Post Office. John, being an ex-accountant, will be beside himself with joyous anticipation of a huge amount of paperwork to sort out!

CHAPTER EIGHT

Wow, it's great to be here at **Woolgoolga** and as we have big rig we have a superb site. We are discovering that one bonus of having such a big vehicle is that we're always given so much space instead of a small grassed site, beside a cement slab packed between other vans. We're behind the tennis courts with a mini farm behind (run by the local High School students) and the river is beside us. It's at least 10 degrees cooler here than at Grafton and there is a beautiful breeze, plus we're under two enormous trees for shade. The park has been upgraded and is even better than I remember it and we can walk into the small town which has the major banks etc. John and the dogs have promptly fallen asleep and it's only two o'clock in the afternoon. I'm sure it's the relief at being so much cooler and all we can hear is the rustle of leaves and the birds and we immediately made the decision to book in for a week. I've just found out that we can walk to the beach and to the Bowls Club for cheap meals.

Well the dogs have met horses and cows for the first time and last night it was sheep but this time they couldn't get near them as they are behind a wire fence behind us. Callie got up onto a barbecue table near us to have a better look - both dogs seem to be completely bewildered by them. We awoke to the sound of cockerels this morning which I love and the quacking of the ducks (along with all the other birds chirping and twittering). At night the sea sounds quite loud. It is so-o-o relaxing.

I was in the pool last night and actually got cold and it was quite exciting to feel cold. I was chatting to an older woman who used to sell real estate and who is now studying philosophy and current affairs. She was probably my age come to think of it but I don't look in the mirror if I can help it so I don't know that I'm middle aged. Many people live at this park in a variety of pretty homes and apparently seventeen people from this park have enrolled at the University to study philosophy. I find that quite amazing. Perhaps it is because they have sold their homes and have downgraded in size to these small units. They now do not have to work to live and have the luxury of pursuing other interests. A philosophical question indeed! The upshot was that I was so interested in what she had to tell me that I stayed in too long and my fingers shrivelled. As I wasn't moving around I felt cold - a wondrous moment. I must remember to read this again in the winter as we have no heater in this van.

We spent the day after our arrival doing some local shopping at Woolgooga, and found the beaches and headland - beautiful. The next day we backtracked north to look at **Arrawarra** because we'd stayed there years ago with the children and Mum in 'Chuckles', our previous campervan and then we went to Mylestom Beach for a swim, we enjoyed watching the dogs go mad with excitement and loved having the whole beach to ourselves.

On Friday we went to **Coffs Harbour** and were surprised at how much it's changed over the years. It's a lovely town now but we didn't stop there long as we were supposed to be heading inland to drive along part of The Waterfall Way. This is a tourist route starting 25ks south of Coffs Harbour heading west for approximately 191 kilometres all the way to Armidale. So we travelled from the beaches, to tropical rain forests and up the Great Eastern Escarpment to the Northern Tablelands. We went as far as **Dorrigo**. The Dorrigo National Park is World Heritage listed. A leaflet tells us that the rainforests contain over 80% of the world's flora and fauna and we wanted to see some of the waterfalls. The scenery was stunning and I had forgotten my camera!

Our first stop on the way to the Tablelands was **Bellingen**, such a beautiful quaint village where we had a picnic by the river. (We returned later in the day as I could not get enough of the place.) To quote our leaflet - 'From Bellingen continue west through Bellinger River State Forest and Dorrigo National Park. This is a spectacular section of the scenic drive, passing the Newell and Sherrard Falls as you climb steeply up the escarpment.' At the top we stopped at the Griffiths Lookout where we had another coffee/dog-break and were totally alone. Apparently the Ebor volcano erupted 18 million years ago and the Dorrigo Plateau was born. The Tablelands were created much earlier. I am very grateful.

Just before Dorrigo we turned off to visit the Rainforest Visitors Centre and to walk The Skywalk over the rainforest canopy. At Dorrigo we went to the **Dangar Falls** picnic area and then to a park where we chatted with two young women who had arrived in Brisbane from England four weeks ago. They bought a kombi van the first day, stayed in Brisbane longer than expected as they liked it so much and have got as far as us in their three weeks of travelling and they are also touring for ten months. When they told us they were going to travel from Adelaide to Alice Springs and to Darwin I told them they'd better speed up a bit! They will naturally stop at Sydney, Canberra, Melbourne and Adelaide. We will be bypassing Sydney - that is if we get that far in the nine months that we now have left.

On Saturday it was too hot to do anything but today was cooler for us (not for Brisbane with 42 degrees). So today we went back to Coffs Harbour and turned off just before town to head down to the boat harbour. We backtracked to a park by the river/sea inlet for lunch - a beautiful area with many Aboriginal families and children playing and swimming. I joined the kids for a quick swim whilst their parents prepared lunch. I was having such fun with the kids that I didn't want to leave and the water was perfect. Feeling wonderfully refreshed, we then drove on to Sawtell and I have to admit the sea views surpassed any I've seen before. It's hard to admit that it is more beautiful than even the Currumbin inlet where we live! I had stood with John at the latter before leaving home and had turned to him perplexed and asked him 'Why would anyone want to leave this?' Now I knew why! There are two headlands and whichever way you look it is glorious. I went crazy with the camera. **Sawtell**'s small main street is very pretty with huge old trees down the middle and coffee shops galore.

Tomorrow, Monday, is washing day and time to clean up our leaf-covered van and outdoor furniture as we leave the following day. We're thinking of stopping at Nambucca Heads before heading down to Port Macquarie which is a very pretty town with many beaches and bays to visit.

CHAPTER NINE

I could write a book about all the peculiar conversations that I have had with complete strangers! For example, a lady was standing by our Ute talking to our dogs today. Her husband was in the car looking at the views. In a conversation lasting about seven minutes I heard a potted version of her life over the last eight years. This included her emigration from England, leaving her husband to return to England and her subsequent return after being beaten up by her female neighbour on their Council estate just outside Peterborough. I know all about this neighbours love of gin and tonic and who else she (the neighbour) beat up. I also know that her husband has lost a lot of weight since she arrived back in Australia but tests show he hasn't got cancer. However, I don't even know her name!

Likewise, in the pool last night in a conversation not lasting more than five minutes, I heard all about this guy's holiday with his wife and daughter, the kilometres they have travelled each day, his job as a fire chief in Sydney, his wife's work as head of a team of volunteer fire-fighters etc. Is it because they are never likely to see you again? Or is it because they are on holiday and have forgotten to be reserved? People sit on buses and trains and even if they travel the same route daily they don't even look at each other and if they happen to catch each others eyes they immediately look away as if it's a prohibited action and they fear being accused of harassment! Perhaps I look middle-aged and motherly and seem safe but I do hope not as I don't feel it! I wore my sunglasses tonight so no-one could make eye contact with me and had a very quick dip in the pool!

It is wonderful to return 'home' after our day trips. We both love our R.V. (recreational vehicle). It is so comfortable. Thank goodness we have plastic glasses though because everything moves when we travel and we have one cupboard which we open very gingerly when we stop - the one with the glasses - I now know why they are called 'tumblers'. Whilst I was typing this tonight, John was trying to put away two plastic wine glasses and as he did so a couple of other glasses fell out. When he tried again, more fell out. When I was able to stop laughing and speak, I suggested he leave it for me but he insisted that they were not going to beat him as another hit the floor!

However, we have been glad that we did bring so much and there is nothing that we have missed and we have a place for everything with so much outside storage. We have got our packing-up and setting-up on arrival down pat now and even putting the awning up is now easy! If we stay a week I do a big clean-up when we leave so the other days are free. If we only stay one night I just tidy up and wait until we stop for a week again! Same with the washing so I'm glad we brought so many clothes, towels and sheets etc. We use the commercial machines and I do the hand washing at the same time and spin it out in my machine and so far haven't needed it plumbed in. It is firmly jammed in the wardrobe by the laundry basket and I just put the outlet hose into a bucket in front (in the wardrobe) and switch on. We have our own rotary washing line which we erect whenever we stop as we use it to hang our swimming towels and togs on. It's a mini version but it holds so much and I have never yet run out of room which has amazed me. All mod cons! I could live in this full-time.

What I don't like is changing parks. I feel like Jack as he doesn't like it when our home moves. He would like to go 'walkies' all day long but would prefer that the R.V didn't come with us. I just get settled down and get to know my area and then we move. Callie takes it all in her stride and sleeps during long journeys whereas Jack is constantly alert with his head out of the window, frightened that he might miss out on something that preferably moves and smells good. When we arrive, I wait for the kettle to boil whilst I adjust to the different environment and Callie waits for her bucket of water to appear and then we both relax. Callie lies on her back with her legs in the air waiting for a tummy rub. I've tried doing that but John ignores me so I've given up and now sit on a chair.

Jack, being a German Shepherd has to guard his patch and seems frustrated and bewildered every time we move the R.V as he has to learn our new site perimeters, check out all the strange smells, is unsure how to react at the new strangers that may suddenly approach us and looks to me for guidance about them and generally wonders where on earth he is! I now walk him around our new site perimeter and he seems to be getting the hang of realising that there are boundaries and I'm showing him them. Once that's over, like John, he immediately wants to go and explore further.

However, they are both alert to our movements and both prefer to sleep in the utility. I believe they think that if they are in it we won't forget them and leave them behind. That I can totally understand - it is a very valid worry when travelling with John.

p.s It's RAINING tonight! Our air conditioner is off! It's COOLER!

CHAPTER TEN

NAMBUCCA HEADS

THE TAYLOR'S ARMS

O.K - I admit it - it's painful to admit it - one doesn't like to think one is a wimp. It is even more embarrassing to admit it to one's relatives in England and friends in Canada. I've fallen apart, quite dramatically to boot. Life is miserable. I don't like travelling and living in a motor home. I want to go home! Why the dramatic change? To put it nicely, it's the precipitation. To put it bluntly - 2 days of pouring rain is ENOUGH! One shower full of wet clothes hung on hangers, mud everywhere, miserable looking dogs and us stuck inside the van. Then getting changed into wet clothes to go out because there's no more room left to hang any more wet clothes so we daren't get any more clothes wet. Got up this morning and put on PVC coat (bought originally for when I went to England) over nude body - cold but no point in getting any more clothes wet. Put on my thongs and then realised my bum was showing. Put on heavy wet trousers and took dogs for walk. We're right by a sea wall and there's all these happy fishermen grinning at me - happy as larry saying 'hi' as I pulled my hood closer to my face and growled back at them. Stupid men - how can they choose to sit there getting soaked - I'm going to Woolworths to buy my fish.

SAWTELL

Suddenly the idea of shopping isn't so bad. It will be dry and warm in the Plaza. That will be my 'treat' today -a warm, dry supermarket. Instead of playing my usual game of timing how quickly I can get in and out of the damned place, I am going to wallow in it and probably buy bars of chocolate and cartons of cream and all sorts of comfort goodies.

Isn't our weather ridiculous - it dropped from 37C down to 21C overnight and people who come from cooler climates cannot understand why I'm wearing a jumper when it's 21C - it's the sudden change! My ideal temperature is 24C so when it's over 30C I feel like I'm in a sauna and anything below and out comes a jumper. I don't ever remember a drop like that over-night although my daughter tells me it does this most days in Melbourne. My friend in Canada is telling me how cold it is and there have been floods in Wales and ice in Europe and America and I've had enough at 21C!

John was my hero yesterday when we left Woolgoolga. We both put on our togs to get the mud off everything lying around outside and to pack it all away but he did the lot and I kept dry, organising operations through the windows! Two outdoor, large ground covers had to be washed, 4 chairs, table, dogs bowls & bucket, rotary washing line, dogs swivel chains and spike, awning had to be hosed off because of leaves and rolled up and he even did that alone (it's big).

He then came in and dried off and got changed into more togs and had a coffee. It was then time to lift the ramps, put electric lead and water hoses away and drive the van to the dump point to drain our black water.

ANOTHER BEAUTIFUL VIEW

At Woolgoolga we were surrounded by Rainbow Lorikeets twice a day (for U.K. friends - small brightly coloured parrots) but they were different to those at the Gold Coast - they had beautiful blue tail feathers instead of green. Here at Nambucca we are again surrounded by trees but this time there are hundreds of Galahs (much bigger, rose-breasted, grey-backed cockatoos).

VIEW FROM ROAD ABOVE

We'll stay here long enough to see the place (the rain is easing) but not for a week. We'll visit the Taylors Arms (The Pub With No Beer at Macksville immortalised by Slim Dusty and the late Gordon Parsons) before driving to Telegraph Point, 18ks this side of Port Macquarie where there is a new water-sports caravan and camping park. From there we can start touring Port Macquarie.

p.s. It's stopped raining - touring is wonderful!

CHAPTER ELEVEN

I LOVED THIS PHOTO

It's confusing at times for John and me when we're sight-seeing. Our journey to **Macksville** followed winding, narrow country lanes, up hill and down dale with cows in the meadows etc and we could have sworn we were back in England. It amazes me how alike the countryside is.

Now we are at **Telegraph Point** and today we went to **Port Macquarie** and what a wonderful town it is. We saw most of the different beaches and bays and lookouts but decided not to go camel riding on the beach as I have been told too often how uncomfortable camel riding is (are we in Egypt?). We then checked out another van park but it was surrounded by koala habitat so no dogs allowed (we're back in Australia).

The town centre is lovely. We went past the marina to look for an area called Settler's Cove and the whole area is being redeveloped into canal estates so I thought that the park had been swallowed up for development. The area is like the endless canal estates on the southern end of the Gold Coast - huge ugly rendered homes, soul-less! Lo and behold we found this tiny caravan park with about 10 cabins and room for 3 big rigs such as ours, right at the end beside the river and next to a beautiful park. Anyway, we felt that we were back on the Gold Coast and were definitely in Australia because I took photos of Pelicans and a large Iguana.

When we left Port Macquarie to return to Telegraph Point we were back to dairy farms and rolling hills and I saw a sign stating 'Deer crossing road for next 3 kilometres' - surely we were back in the U.K in the New Forest or Devon? I didn't even know that we have wild deer here! I've told John that I'm punch drunk with sightseeing and am beginning to take the scenery for granted 'Oh no, not another headland to look at' kind of attitude.

It's Sunday tomorrow and I want a day off - John wants to rush along and I want to slow down and enjoy the journey! There are free bikes available to ride around here and we have both enjoyed racing the dogs around this vast park and lakes. We can never beat them but it is fun trying especially now that I've found out how to use the brakes.

There's a covered barbecue here at the park with a surf board as the table and near one of the pergola posts sits a very handsome model of a crocodile. Jack hesitated when he saw it, then crept forward and eventually sniffed it. When he realised that it didn't smell of any living creature, he stuck his head in the crocodile's mouth. Obviously he was quite disgusted with this inanimate creature for he then turned around, cocked his leg and peed all over it. I was so glad nobody was around! Well, no people anyway but our two dogs have made friends with the park owners' two dogs and the four of them run around together and have a grand old time. We have also been trying to outride the dogs on our bikes but they beat us every time so they are getting heaps of exercise and so are we. You need the exercise when you have been sitting in a vehicle as much as we have over the last few weeks.

'Be careful what you wish for' - a fine statement which I keep forgetting. Instead of saying 'I want to slow down' I should have said 'I want a break from sight-seeing and everything right in our world'. Last year I kept saying I didn't want to leave before Christmas and John was itching to go and we got hit by the hail storm! Last night we were relaxing after dinner in our van and had just finished watching a documentary on Australia when the winds hit. It was instant chaos - blinds blowing everywhere, me rushing around trying to shut nine windows, dogs disappeared and John outside battling with the awning. He was too late, one bar of the awning lifted him off the ground and ended up on the roof and the awning was ripped apart. Found dogs; shut them in the Ute and in the pitch black, John managed to secure the rest of the awning by crawling over the roof. It turned out that we were the only ones who experienced it! The wind circled our van only. If that was a taste of a whirly-gig I'd hate to be in a cyclone because last night was bad enough. Today we have spent most of our time making phone calls. No-one in Port Macquarie can help us for a month so we're off to Taree. We have arranged for two companies to work in tandem with one repairing the framework and the other supplying new fabric. We'll miss a lot of sightseeing but we'll have to do the areas we miss on the way back home at the end of the year. Today is 24C - purr-fect!

CHAPTER TWELVE

IGUANA NEAR BEACH

TAREE

We have a site so close to the river we could almost dive in from the top of our van. John and I had confidently agreed that the repairs would not be covered by insurance as it was the original awning made in 1988 (thus 16 years old). We also didn't have the guts to phone and ask them because they have only just paid for the hailstorm damage but the repairer said 'Call your Insurance Company'.

'Hi' (insurance company) 'It's Mrs Timms'

'Hello Lisa, how are you?' They know me so well!

'Fine, fine. Um, can I have Claims?'

Haven't you finished with them?

'Uh, sort of'

'Hello, Claims Department.'

'Hi, it's Mrs Timms'

Hell, how are you Lisa?'

'Embarrassed'

'Oh dear, what's happened now'

I started gabbling at high speed without taking a breath. 'Well this wind hit our van and John grabbed the awning support and it picked him up and the arm was on the roof and our awning is ripped and the support is all bent but I didn't want to ring you yesterday because I was too embarrassed'

'You daft thing, is John alright?'

'Oh yes - he didn't end up on the roof, the support did'. I could almost hear the relief in her voice because it wasn't a personal injury claim!
'It was made in 1988 so I thought you wouldn't cover for wear and tear?'
'We'll sort it out. Get your repairer to send us the quote and we'll authorise it this afternoon'.

This is our second claim and we've only been on the road a month! With clients like us they'll go out of business! We have to pay the excess plus a contribution for wear and tear but we are getting a brand new awning plus the repair to the side of the van where it pulled out. Having just received a new roof, new hatches, new aerial and now a new awning it's getting quite ridiculous! Both claims have been for repairs for damage done when the van was stationary. The irony is that we were lucky not to have had an accident on the way here because the awning bars that weren't broken flew out horizontally just as we were going past road works and John only stopped because someone flashed him. I was screaming down the two-way phone but he apparently had it turned down! As he stopped, I leapt out of the Ute and pulled them back just before a line of huge trucks came whizzing past! As he said when we arrived here, we are certainly having some adventures. I honestly thought the word 'adventure' meant something quite different.

MANNING POINT.

We've shifted again! Did not feel comfortable where we were - we have no idea why but we both agreed. We decided to go and look at parks on one side of a very long sea inlet. This meant returning to **Coopernook** where the van will be repaired and then heading east to the coast, to a place called **Harrington**. We looked at 3 parks and were not satisfied - either cramped or too far away from the beach. We then went all the way back through Taree and out the other side and then down the other side of the inlet to Manning Point and found the most wonderful park. Relaxed, spacious, plenty of trees for shade, pool, friendly and on 40 acres of natural bushland with the Manning River on one side and the Pacific Ocean on the other. And the whole area is so dog friendly. One of the tourist leaflets we have states that the Manning Valley is pet friendly and 'Your dog can enjoy our beaches as well'. As we have to wait a week for the awning to be repaired, we needed to feel really comfortable. Taree has some pretty river walks but I prefer it here. So having run around in our Ute, we have now moved the R.V to this site.

IGUANA FALLS

This whole area is called 'The Manning Valley River and Rainforest Coast' and the Manning River is rare because it's Australia's only river delta system featuring two river entrances, at Harrington and Old Bar. It is a recreational fishing area with 150km of saltwater estuary and 1500km of fresh water in the Manning River and its tributaries -all accessible for anglers.

The airstrip was used by Charles Kingsford Smith and Nancy Walton for some of their early flights and is now heritage listed. There are a lot of places to visit around the coast including Mitchell's Island with over 40,000 orchids and there is the hinterland with Ellenborough Falls, Rawson Falls at Boorganna Nature Reserve with 6 different types of rainforest, Crowdy Bay National Park, Wingham Reserve, Coopernook Forest Park etc - 26 different reserves, parks and falls. We can picnic at the base of the 'Big Nellie Volcanic Plug' (I've never heard of a volcanic plug!). On second thoughts, perhaps not because apparently it's quite a climb! There's so much to see!

So what do I want to do tomorrow - absolutely nothing! I might walk to the beach, which is right behind where we've set up camp and I might go as far as a dip in the pool! John says that there are miles and miles of beach and that the dogs had a wonderful time there before dinner. I do so miss the free bikes and the cycling though.

CHAPTER THIRTEEN

WALLIS LAKE-FIG TREE ROOT

Did I tell you Jack has shrunk? Not from the exercise but because we cut all his long hair off to cool him down. He has long black hair with a white bib and white paws and he's normally very handsome. He looks weird but he thinks he now looks very handsome and he's been parading around greeting anyone who cares to look at him and making his odd, short howling noises which he makes when he's a pleased as punch, so who are we to argue.

John and I had a conversation about what constitutes 'bush'. We all know what we mean by the 'outback' – where, in my opinion sensible people should never go but when you go inland where does the 'bush' start? Anyway, on T.V the other night we discovered that the bush hugs the Coast - I never knew that. How could I when houses hug the coastline. So, if the bush is the coast, what's between it and the outback? I realise we have The Great Dividing Range in this part of Australia that's not that far from the coastline and I suppose you would call the other side 'the downs' but at what point does it become the outback. In the U.K. it's simple - it's either town or countryside.

Did you know that in Australia we have 98% of the worlds known species of flora and fauna? I'm quite willing to give a few of them away. Just think, we could get rid of termites, all snakes, all spiders, all biting insects, sharks and crocodiles. Send them all to America for example and whilst we're at it we can give them all their red ants back too. Not that the red ants are all over Australia but they are thought to have stowed away aboard a ship that landed in Brisbane and we are presently trying to eradicate them in the surrounding areas.

Did I tell you that I look as though I'm getting over the measles - I am pock-marked! Everything that can bite found me as soon as we left home. I've tried five repellents but they still come and visit me. Now that I've told them to feel free and just eat me, I find that I'm actually healing up! Luckily they didn't like my face, or my nether regions but everywhere else was fair game. I also had really bad hay-fever but that's gone now - perhaps it was just the time of year, hot weather and lack of rain.

We're still having problems with our 2-way UHF radios. John doesn't wait before he speaks so before I get the chance to turn the music down and pick it up my radio, he's finished and I haven't heard a word. 'What did you say?'

....'Fallen down and need to stop'

'What's fallen down?'

....'For the second time and have to stop' By this time I try not to worry about what's fallen down! I start to pull over.

...'Here, somewhere else' I'm in front but I guess that he means 'Not here' so I carry on, worrying about what's fallen down. I look in the mirror and he's nowhere to be seen so I pull over. 'Where are you?'

...'Up and leaving now'. He reckons that he didn't have to wait for a response when he drove taxis so doesn't see why he has to on these phones. Then it happens in reverse. I say 'Are we going the right way?'

...'You say?'

'Are we going the right way?'

...'You say something?' John's hearing in his right ear is very poor. I'm not to know but he switches the phone to his other ear as I scream down my phone 'ARE WE GOING THE RIGHT WAY?'

'Don't shout, I can't hear you when you shout, what did you say?' I have been known to be screaming down the phone as he draws up beside me with his window open and he can hear me without it! However, they have been useful, like when I'm in front and say 'Watch the speed bump, it's a nasty one' because he usually hears 'bump' and 'nasty'.

4th March

Got up late and managed to stay awake until 11am and went back to bed for an hour! I stayed up too late last night. At 7.30pm I did some email replies, followed by this diary and then wrote a poem to my niece who is getting married later this month in England. I bought her a koala because it is so cute with its Akubra hat with cork tassels. Sarah stayed with us when we were living in Brisbane. I wrote a poem for him (the Koala) to take with him. Did you know that the Akubra originated in Kempsey. Unfortunately the factory is not open to visitors.

KOALAGRAM

Yeah, I'm a little Aussie
And I've come to bring you luck
I'm here instead of family
'Cause they're travelling in a truck

It's rotten being over there
When wanting to be with you
But they've been over here before
And I wanted to come too.

They phoned the airlines 'What's the cost?'
For them or just for me
It really wasn't hard in the end
'Cause John's an Accountant see.

They wrapped me up in paper
And stuffed me in a bag
Then threw me in a big red bin
I felt like a wet rag.

It took a while to get here
But I made it and feel great
I see you've got some Champers
And I'm partial to some cake.

I'm hoping you'll adopt me
And keep me safe from harm
'Cause I'm a little lost here
But I'll be your lucky charm.

They filled me up with lots of love
And hugs and kisses too
There's hope and faith and peace and fun
To last your whole life through.

Okay, I know it's banal but 'bear' with me because I did not realise when I bought him that he is quite capable of making his own conversation and doesn't need me to write such rubbish for him as you will find out by the emails I received from by brother upon his arrival in Wales. I started getting quite worried about the poor chap – the koala that is - although judging by the letters, perhaps it is my brother who I should be worried about if he reckons the koala can talk. If it's read out in Coventry Cathedral where they are going to be, the walls will tremble with shock. I hope not because my Mum and I own one of those bricks in the walls because when it was rebuilt they asked people to buy them.

Anyway the koala brings back memories of my niece's brother when we were over there for his Wedding. He was born deaf but learnt to speak as a young child with hours of tutoring from his wonderful Mother.

At the reception he gave a speech which was, in part, incredibly funny. The point of it was that he had slept with his koala bear since receiving it in Australia when he was a young boy but his new wife did not want to share his bed with a bear. He had to make a choice between the pair of them and he told us how incredibly hard it had been for him to choose who to share his bed with after his marriage. As he now has two children I guess he made the right choice.

Anyway, by the time I had finished on the computer it was midnight and then I couldn't sleep! I had been racing around that same day at 7.30am packing up the van, then a fortnight's food shopping (I've done an advance menu now so that we eat properly again) in yet another new supermarket. Well, not new but new to me so that I can't find anything. I can no longer buy my No Fat Milk, or my organic eggs for example - I have to find new products. Then there was all that travelling, watching out for John and constantly wondering if the dogs need to stop for a pee etc. It took an hour to find places to store the shopping when we finally arrived here and then put the van back to 'normal' mode instead of travel mode. Then it was time to prepare dinner before I did the emails, diary and poem. So you see, I do work!

ANOTHER OF TIDAL MOVEMENT

CHAPTER FOURTEEN

We saw the weather forecast for Brisbane and the Gold Coast on television tonight and they are expecting heavy gales, winds up to 160kph and torrential rain. We had rain this morning and once sunny again went exploring along the coast. Found **Old Bar** which turned out to be a town, unlike here where we have one shop and a handful of houses. Shops shut Saturday lunchtime in NSW except for corner stores, unless you're in a major metropolitan area.

From Old Bar we went to Wallabi Point (where the road ends) and clambered over rocks because I wanted to collect shells. The Scouts had made a path through the bush over the headland - it was quite an adventure as it kept twisting back and forth and even the dogs had to stop and sniff on our return so that we didn't get lost. There were paths going off paths in all different directions but we found the Obelisk that we were supposed to be looking for. John said 'Kids would love this' and I replied 'Yes I do'. It was great fun. Both these areas are being overrun with huge, brick and tile monstrosities and land is for sale in both areas. It seems that only Manning Point has not changed for the last 100 years except they now have oyster farms there.

March 8th

A busy day. Washing then a necessary trip to Taree to collect post, get bread and milk (local shop here charges $3.80 for a sliced loaf!) and some good stuff like posting wedding present to England and buying baby clothes. On 3rd day of the 3rd month at 3.33am a beautiful girl whom I once fostered, had a baby daughter. She lives in England and this is her second daughter. I also had to buy the elder girl a belated Birthday present, not because I actually forgot her special day but because she is growing up so fast I'm never sure what to buy for her! Anyway, I enjoyed the shopping and got it all posted. By this time it was 4pm. John had read the following: 'Take the Bulga Forest Drive, on Tourist Drive 8 northwest of Wingham, past the spectacular Ellenborough Falls' etc. We didn't have time for a long tour as I had planned to prepare dinner as soon as we got home with the shopping and he decided this was just the job.

8ks he told me so we got to **Wingham** (which is about 8ks) and started looking for the falls. It's still pretty flat round there and I looked to the range in the distance.

'Well let's just drive and follow the brown tourist signs' I suggested 'at least we're in the countryside'.

John kept looking for the falls and after an hour I asked him if he thought we'd get there before nightfall. Then we hit the dirt road 'Ooh, aah, ohh!' It went on and on and on as John did his best to avoid the potholes caused by the recent heavy rain. I was hanging onto the door with one hand and the back of the seat with the other. Eventually we saw a sign 'Ellenborough Falls 7ks'. Have you any idea how long it takes to cover 7ks in those conditions. At one point there was one of those old 'No speed limit' signs - come on, the Government is having us on. The dirt road twists and turns around blind bends with a sheer drop on one side in some areas - yeah, yeah we'll go at 110kph! We rarely got up to

40kph. I'm not sure what time we got there but nobody else was there! It was worth the trip though. It is a gorge with a waterfall that drops 200m. It is one of the longest single drop falls in the southern hemisphere. There was a viewing platform at the top and 641 steps down to the bottom. No, not for me but I did manage the 80 steps down and back to see the head of the waterfall but you couldn't actually see over the edge from there. There was a lot of very interesting information about the two Aboriginal tribes who used to live in the area - around the Manning, the Hasting and the Macleay rivers. They were decimated in the 1840's and 1850's by the European settlers who had moved into the area. Man's fear creates havoc in the world doesn't it and unfortunately we haven't changed much.

On the way back I decided to give John a break from driving. Ha, ha - I could see the potholes as we were now going downhill and I had a ball. I've decided I'd like to do rally driving - it was so much fun! John casually reminded me about the sheer drop on his side which he said he hadn't noticed on the way up! Anyway, by the time we got back to Taree it was dark so instead of the pork chops, cauliflower in white sauce, buttered potatoes and carrots, we took the dogs to MacDonald's and doled them out two piles of biscuits on the veranda and a bowl of water. I enjoyed a cheese and tomato toasted sandwich! We still had to find our way back to our site, which is a fair way down long country roads with no street lights, unpack all our shopping and get the washing in. Then we went through our post and didn't get to bed until 1am!

CHAPTER FIFTEEN

TUNCURRY.

Well we are presently at Tuncurry and I have just worked out that we are in the Great Lakes region but not yet on the Myall Coast - well I don't think so anyway! The Myall Coast is part of the Great Lakes region though. I find it totally confusing. The Great Lakes region stretches from Forster and Tuncurry south to Tea Gardens and Hawks Nest on Port Stephens - 145 kilometres (by which time we'll be getting very close to Newcastle). There's a bridge over the Myall River's mouth called the Singing Bridge joining Tea Gardens and Hawks Nest. Further North, Bulahdelah marks the entrance to the Myall Lakes. Between the two lies the Myall Coast. We haven't got as far as Bulahdelah yet. There are four National Parks. So what, you might well ask? I'm here and I'm confused so you must be bored out of your minds but remember, this is my diary and as I cannot recall where I was two weeks ago I have to keep a record.

Suffice to say that there is water everywhere! Huge lakes, wide rivers and endless beaches greeted us, such as Nine Mile Beach. **Forster** is very pretty and is the second largest fishing region in New South Wales - boats everywhere. Tuncurry and Forster are also linked by a bridge across Wallis Lake. Tuncurry is not so pretty and there is rivalry afoot! Those that live in Tuncurry feel it is by far the best place to live and visa versa. We are in a lovely park in Tuncurry with the river on one side and lake to the other but I think that Forster is much prettier whatever the locals here think. There's only the bridge between the two and shops spill either side.

When we arrived yesterday it was late in the day as it took six hours at the repair shop to attach the new awning as neither model fitted! The bars which fix to the van were either too long or too short so they had to cut down the long ones. We were offered electricity for the night as it was 5pm by the time it was finished but I wanted to get away from there so we headed down the highway in the rain. We reached the park we'd chosen as it was getting dark, 10ks short of Tuncurry - another water ski park and we had the most stunning site and the park was absolutely beautiful. We had rain forest outside our door with covered picnic table and benches, wishing well and a drop to a grotto and water and we had it to ourselves. The park was empty - no visitors and all these empty cabins, not a light on anywhere! Unfortunately it was also a paradise for the biggest mosquitoes that we have ever seen and neither of us wanted to go outside the door and Jack had scratched off lumps of fur this morning, despite sleeping in the back of the Ute. It was horrendous - I know it has been raining but perhaps it is always like that - who knows - we left this morning. We have mossies at the Gold Coast but not nearly so many and certainly not the same size! We visited a chemist today and now have new mozzie sprays to try out.

I've done it again! I told John today that I wanted to lose him for a while because he said he was tired about five times just because we passed a few shops and I went into two! He hates shopping. We went to the beach for a coffee and spent at least an hour chatting to some locals at a café and the dogs got bored stiff so when we got on the beach Jack knocked John off his feet with excitement. I shouldn't have laughed so hard - John has hurt his ankle! He can't walk far now so he can't go out with me! He reminded me what I'd wished for and asked me to stop doing it!

I'm busy looking through tourist leaflets again. On the edge of Wallis Lake there is a canopy formed by cabbage tree palms called **The Green Cathedral** and it is a consecrated church! **Nabiac**, a town in the Great Lakes Hinterland has Australia's only Hamish family and apparently the families offer hospitality at their Country Barn. So much to see - do we want to go boating or swimming, on heritage walks or horse riding through the forests, to National Parks or coastal lookouts, rainforest and waterfalls or wetland area or just sit and watch for dolphins? Decisions, decisions. And that's without looking to see what's on the areas calendar of events. Some of their events sound very attractive such as Stroud International Brick and Rolling Pin Throwing Contest, Riverwood Downs Classic Billy Cart Derby, Golden Oldies Rugby Union Gala Day, Pacific Palms Battle of the Boats, Stroud Picnic Races and the Stoney Mountain Run. There are Dog shows, Cattle dog trials, Stroud Rodeo and Australian Rough Riding Championships and every other kind of sports imaginable. There's orchid shows, art festivals, motor shows, oyster festivals, Bulahdelah Bass Bash - how long do you reckon we ought to stay? Will a year be enough! I'm hoping John's ankle will be well enough for him to play in the Golden Oldies Rugby Day and chucking rolling pins sounds delightful.

CHAPTER SIXTEEN

Well so much for sightseeing today - John wanted to move again. It was a little crowded but a lovely park. He said he was sick of the mossies at this park too and I couldn't argue with that! However, he said he felt guilty because he knew that I did not want to pack everything up once again and by the time he had finished packing everything away outside, he could be heard mumbling 'I must have been mad to suggest it'.

Just as we were ready to go I remembered the ramps. Our motor home has four hydraulic levelling ramps which you can use individually. They are easy to operate and there are warning lights in case you raise them too high because it is possible, if you are really stupid and don't stop raising them they could flip right over and could break. If you were silly enough to do such a thing you would need deep pockets to replace them. You would think that with three wheels raised off the ground that it would be difficult to drive off with them still in place. Well we managed it quite easily, the van lurched backwards and 3 had flipped! We had purchased a special jack but even by trying to raise the jack by placing wood beneath it, we could not raise the van enough, so we had to call in help. One hour and $60 cash-in-hand later the ramps were in their correct position and were undamaged and off we went. I had stayed wonderfully calm throughout but one can only take so much!

John had found another lovely park over the other side of the river in **Forster** with much more space - 10 acres for camping, plus 60 acres of natural bushland overlooking Wallis Lake. This one offers canoeing and quite a large island to camp on. We are positioned right opposite the pool and we are alone except for a couple of tents a fair way away. However, before we managed to book in I backed into a boat trailer and damaged the right wing of my Ute. Simply everyone appeared from nowhere to see what the stupid woman driver had done - they simply materialised. Once we parked I told John I felt numb - I didn't know what to think, feel or say so he suggested I sat and did nothing - which I did.

I decided I needed a whiskey but forgot I had stored a new bottle of Extra Virgin Olive Oil in same cupboard until after I'd poured a glass! There are just as many mossies here and tonight, I was brushing my hair ready for an early night when a cockroach fell out! John said 'That's camping for you'. I won't repeat what I said but I'm obviously still up, waiting for my hair to dry having spent 45 minutes in the shower and having scrubbed my hairbrush so hard there are few bristles left! Not a good day.

I've just been blown away by an article about mind-altering drugs which included cannabis. I had no idea how lethal hydroponically grown cannabis is. I had a friend (now dead) who grew it and sold it and I just thought she had a neat way to earn a bit extra as she was unable to work due to ill-health. In 2002 nearly 40,000 youngsters hospitalised (in Australia) with mental disorders from drugs, 70% of which were 15-29 year olds with severe mental disturbance and all using cannabis and its use is growing in Australia. I know so many recreational users plus some that are regular users but they naturally all tell me that it is safer than alcohol etc. I thought the hydroponic stuff was safer/cleaner. I've never tried it because I'm too afraid of getting hooked on it! I learnt that lesson at 15 years old when I found that after one week of smoking I couldn't concentrate without cigarettes. I had taught myself to smoke to be cool - choked in private for two days until I'd mastered it! I also dropped 2½ stone in weight. I very quickly became slim, cool and attractive to boys! I got free gifts from the cigarette company too. However, I already knew that I relied on them and it stopped me from drinking much alcohol or taking LSD which was so freely available when I was a teenager. I've been told so often that I'd be better off smoking cannabis because it's safer!

It's wet today but we've been touring around the **Booti Booti** National Park which includes Wallis Lake, with our first stop **The Green Cathedral** - absolutely stunning. You approach under a canopy of trees and sight the lake beyond. I cannot imagine anywhere in the world more beautiful to be married! John remarked that even the dogs were silent as they walked slowly beside us instead of Jack's usual romping through the bush and yelping and barking. It was odd - they sensed something. Sunday morning services are held twice a month according to the weather and always at Easter, Christmas and other important religious days. The lectern is an upright log - everything is natural. The lake was grey today and the clouds were so low that they merged with the lake in places so virtually everything was grey, contrasting with the green of the trees. It was beautiful. I cannot imagine it being any more beautiful even if the sky and lake had been blue.

We continued on to **Pacific Palms** which has the most incredible examples of modern housing architecture I have seen. Mainly because it is a small area and every house is so different. There was one brick and tile lowset and one log cabin but the rest were constructed out of every kind of alternative material available today and in various colours. Most of the designs were excellent. A high majority are holiday rental homes as they have been built by people from Sydney for weekenders. It is a very pretty area. As you drive from Forster to Pacific Palms there is just one road width with the ocean on one side and the lake on the other. We continued round the bay to the Frothy Coffee Boat House overlooking Smiths Lake, a beautiful spot with a tiny park and a few chalet homes overlooking the water. We then returned 'home' and we still haven't travelled past Myall Lake, the biggest of them all. However, when we leave this area to continue south, we have to cover the same route to reach the Pacific Highway again as it is the only way out! Everyone in Australia should visit this area - I wonder why it isn't as well known as the Gold Coast or Barrier Reef because it is simply stunning.

We'll leave here on Tuesday - where to next - hang on, I'll just look at the map. Oh heck - just realised that we've missed Nabiac by turning off the Pacific Highway to come down to Forster - won't be supping with the Hamish families then - damn, I wanted to do that. So we'll be passing through **Buladelah** and going on down to **Tea Gardens** and **Hawks Nest** which are on the northern part of Port Stephens bay, at the other end of the Myall Lakes (what a huge area this Myall Lakes area is). So, as I said at the beginning of this, that will be about 145ks from here. After one or two nights there we'll be back on the highway and all the way around the port to Nelson Bay which is the hub of the area (for my U.K family, Port Stephens is approximately 200ks north of Sydney and around an hour from Newcastle).

CHAPTER SEVENTEEN

Today Oh, I've just seen a beautiful grey wild rabbit - wow - haven't seen one for years as they are banned in Queensland. Hopefully it is a sign of good luck! Well we left the last site about 11am as it takes a while to pack up and we had to dump our waste which is always a headache because every site has palm trees right on each corner to stop people cutting corners! Makes for some very interesting manoeuvrers with our big rig!

Then we had to get petrol which is just as amusing. This time we had 3 elderly men stopping to admire the rig and walking all around it whilst John was trying to get it into position. One man was so old and frail I had to hold the door open for him to get into the office to pay for his petrol. It takes ages to fill up the rig because of the amount the tank holds and we block everyone off in the process. I needed a toilet and there wasn't one there and I was standing with my legs crossed when I suddenly remembered that we have one with us! How handy to carry your loo with you and I've been using public loos on the road!

We eventually set off at 11.40am. We travelled the Myall Lakes Road in order to reach the Pacific Highway again and having gone through a 60kph zone it changed to 100kph so I sped up but John didn't. I thought that he hadn't seen the 100kph sign and tried using my UHF radio but it had run out of batteries! I turned the Ute around and drove back along the road until I saw the rig and called to John out of my window. He'd seen the sign but the rig didn't want to go any further - the engine kept dying on him. I'd turned around in a lay-by and thank goodness I had got that far before turning back because there was no way that the rig could be left where it was. I told John that he HAD to get it to the lay-by. He'd go a few yards and stop, over and over again until we eventually got off the road just before the road took a steep climb.

The road had continual warning signs as it is a 'black spot accident stretch'. There were many upside-down/back-to-front L's and they were correct and most of the time you were either climbing or dropping and the road edges had caved away at some points. I had to drive 17ks the next morning to find anywhere safe to walk the dogs - a 34k round trip - and that was in National Park with 'No dog' signs. I told Jack to keep quiet and he immediately went dotty barking. I became very nervous about two very rough looking guys who turned up in a Ute but luckily I was near my own Ute and I have never moved so fast.

Where we were, neither of our phones could get a signal as we were at the bottom of two steep hills surrounded by thick forest. We got in the Ute and drove to Buladelah which turned out to be only about 15ks away and I stopped at an NRMA recommended workshop (read RAC OR RACQ). A very helpful guy followed us back, having prepaid him $110! We are only covered by the RACQ for the Ute as they don't cover big rigs. He told us that he didn't think it was the fuel filter because although it needed changing there was not much dirt on it 'Do you know what I mean. So it must be the fuel pump, if you know what I mean. In fact I'm absolutely sure you need a new pump, if you know what I mean'. Half an hour of this and he suggests we drive to the highway and turn north - 'a fifteen minute drive to Coolongolook if you know what I mean'.

30 minutes later we arrive at 'State-wide Towing' and no they had not received the promised phone call from Mr You Know What I Mean. I phoned the caravan park we were heading to and no, they had also not received a call as promised. The lesson here is not to trust anyone who says 'You know what I mean'. No, they couldn't tow us out but would do what they could to help. In all we travelled well over 100ks to get help. They arrived at 6pm with a new multi-fit fuel pump but it was too small. This guy did not leave until well after dark (about 8.40pm) having found out that there was nothing wrong with the pump nor the filter but we did have an electrical fault. By this time his boss had turned up too. They promised to find a solution and to return the next day at 11am. Two guys turned up, (neither of them electricians) and they managed to isolate the one wire amongst hundreds of Australian and American wires and bypass them to get us out of there. They then followed John all the way to **Buladelah** (the wrong direction for them) to make sure John got up and down the hills without incident and then we paid them on the side of the road. $300 later we were off to Tea Gardens/Hawks Nest and straight to an auto electrician as recommended by those great guys.

So we arrived at **Hawks Nest** yesterday afternoon, got the awning/table/chairs out and settled in. We walked down a wooded trail to the surf beach where dogs are allowed to romp free and relaxed. This morning I did some hand washing and John had just put up our rotary clothes hoist when a storm hit. We got the awning in first! We packed everything away and shut the dogs in the Ute in the nick of time. The park owner told us that he's been here 17 years and 'that storm has got to be up there with 'em' Translation - one of the worst storms he's experienced. He looked perplexed when I said 'Yeah, it's because we've arrived'. He was walking around to see what damage had been done by fallen trees and there was an electrical blackout in the area.

I have to admit that it was all too much for me as I am now terrified of storms since the one we had at Currumbin before we left (that reminds me, I wonder if our house roof has been done yet). I ended up in tears saying that I am sick of being frightened and we may have only been on the road for seven weeks but I feel I must still be very English as I don't seem to be as tough as Aussie women or as tough as John wants me to be! I said to John that most people just go on a lovely tour for a couple of months and the sun shines and they come back all relaxed and smiling and doesn't he think we've been initiated enough! He agrees.

Tomorrow we pack up as we have to leave the rig at the auto electricians to be repaired. As we will have all day to look around this small area, I am staying here this afternoon to catch up on some typing and John's gone off for a round of golf. Just put the kettle on - both the electric kettle and our new gas kettle have lost their whistles - I know how they feel!

CHAPTER EIGHTEEN

Whilst we've been on the road we have also been keeping up with the T.V. news and sometimes when writing this I feel a sickly guilt when I waffle on about our ups and downs. Some things stick in your mind though like the 10 year old African boy who saw his parents being bludgeoned to death. I was reading how Prince Harry met a baby who had been raped because of the mistaken belief that a man can somehow heal himself of Aids by raping a virgin. Anyway, I do think deeply and care heaps but this diary is supposed to be fairly light hearted so I leave world events out of it and will do in future. My daughter, is actually going to do something (unlike me) as she is going to start walking next Friday at 11am until the same time on Sunday and has to cover 100ks to raise money for Oxfam.

Dear friend in Canada - a Ute is a vehicle, yes; a van or a utility. Some have two doors and some have four. Some with open trays on the back and some hard covered such as ours with windows all around. We have the four door version so that we can chuck our 'stuff' in the back such as maps, shopping, picnic stuff and swimming gear. Every so often we find that there's so much junk in the back that we have to have a mass clear out! It means our tray is shorter than the two- door but there is plenty of room for the dogs and they love it. They can get as wet, muddy or as sandy as they wish and we don't nag them! I call it our dogmobile. I sold a beautiful car for them, so I told them before we left that they'd better enjoy themselves because they've cost us a fortune.

I love your letters, they make me laugh. I can remember hanging shirts out in Wales and bringing them in the house as stiff as cardboard and standing them up and watching them wilt! It was great to offer a visitor a fresh towel and get a frozen one for them off the line. How can the Eskimos possibly have twenty different words for snow? No, we will not be going to the Australian ski fields in winter; we'll stay on the coast. I've told John to remind me when I am cold that I was longing for it! I usually hate the cold but I'm fed up with being hot! It is cooler now because we are further south and because we are now in our autumn. We are actually travelling the opposite way to most of the grey nomads (retirees with grey hair who travel) who are setting off in droves now, mainly from Victoria and South Australia to travel north for the winter and we seem to have bumped into them. Today we couldn't get into a caravan park because all the big-rig sites had been taken.

We had our van repaired today and apparently four wires had been rubbing over a 'pulley' and could have caught on fire! We spent a lovely morning on the banks of the river in Tea Gardens and had a fish and chip lunch. We are now at **Shoal Bay**, part of Nelson Bay which is Port Stephens! Yeah confusing - Port Stephens is the whole area, the town of Nelson being the hub and there are a lot of beautiful areas such as Shoal Bay within a few kilometres. John walked the dogs on arrival and said it's beautiful and has lots of cafes and pavement dining and the bay is stunning. We were offered two sites for the price of one so have lots of room and a tree for shade for the dogs. In most of the parks we have visited we have been offered very good sites, mainly because we have a big rig. Instead of cramming us in with everyone else on concrete slabs, we get offered grassed sites with plenty of space and trees. Here we actually have two concrete slabs but we have space all around us too. We cannot get TV reception here though and I have to admit that irritates me. I like to see the news and I am addicted to Home and Away as most adults hate it and I know that I will have the lounge to myself for that half hour! I totally switch off from everything and everyone around me. Almost like meditation! I also wanted to see the Michael Parkinson interview with Meg Ryan which is on tomorrow night! Well, we're booked in for three nights so here's to a few days of relaxation.

John was right and I too was stunned by how beautiful the bay is - the sand is so white and soft and the ocean so blue and calm - almost like a lagoon. Contrast that with the deep green of the trees and it is like paradise. Until we went in for a swim that is because the shadows which I thought were caused by the water's depth was actually seaweed. We sat in the few feet of clear water and the weather and scenery were perfect and to add to our good mood, no a mozzies in sight here! We are in a lovely caravan park and in a lovely area.

We will leave here on Monday, by-passing **Newcastle** (as there is nowhere to stay with dogs) and stop at the Lake Macquarie region. We are hoping to get into the one park that will allow dogs and seems to have the room. Then it is going to get mighty difficult because of Easter approaching and in most parks pets are not allowed in peak holiday seasons near the coast and I cannot find a place to stop in Sydney. Even if we do a big hike and get to the other side of Sydney we will again be in a very popular tourist area. We can stay off road for a few days but not for over two weeks unless we spend a fortune running the generator. Also we have to empty the black water once a week!

We went to the games room to watch their television and saw the Michael Parkinson interviewing Meg Ryan. It was an awfully tense interview but I don't think it was Meg Ryan's fault! I would have throttled him instead of continuing to smile as she did! I noted that he was the one with his legs crossed and arms almost wrapped around himself, then almost as though he had been given instructions through his ear-piece he unravelled himself, leaned towards her and accused her of not being comfortable when interviewed! She's an actress just playing a role in a film so why all the recriminations? If he'd spoken to certain other male stars (perhaps Russell Crowe for example) the way he spoke to her, he might well have been flattened!

Sunday - absolutely pouring down - stuck in van - hasn't stopped all day so may have to stay another day to look around the area. Apparently in northern Queensland Cairns is flooded and Port Douglas cut off - I'll have to try and see the news over in the games room tonight - the Sydney papers do not tell us the local Queensland news! We are lucky where we live at home because being so near the border, we get both the Queensland television channels and the New South Wales channels and when daylight saving is on in New South Wales, which we don't have in Queensland, we get the choice of what time we want to watch major television shows.

Did I tell you that it is only about 650ks from the Gold Coast to Newcastle via the main highway and at last count we had travelled 1300ks in the motor home and 2500ks in the Ute! There is just too much to see and to be quite honest, we've seen very little. We've 'touched' each area but rarely do we get inland as this trip is mainly our coastal trip. John's impressed with NSW - I think it is a beautiful State but feel more 'comfortable' in Queensland - they are different in so many ways. We love the traffic warnings here such as 'Speed limit will drop to 60kph soon' which gives you enough time to slow down - very decent of them. I'm just getting used to 90kph signs just prior to a T-junction. The first one I saw I said to John 'You wouldn't want to be driving at night down this country lane and see that sign and speed up because you'd end up in that huge tree opposite within the next couple of seconds'. I thought it was a mistake until I kept seeing them - then it dawned on me that they are letting you know the speed limit on the road you are entering. Fine - unless you're driving down a road you don't know at night with no street lights! You'd have to slow down at every sign just in case! Perhaps they don't have them at periodic intervals here - haven't worked that out yet. For overseas tourists it must be confusing with different road signs in each State.

We have found that the service in the shops etc is excellent - staff always so helpful and happy. They don't look worn out and tense as in Brisbane and the Gold Coast, even in really busy tourist areas such as Forster. Note to our friend in Tasmania - if you think Launceston has a lot of traffic don't go to Forster! Incidentally, how will you cope with Sydney when you come over for the first time! I am absolutely dreading the approach into Sydney and the Harbour Bridge bit because I can remember it being quite frightening with everyone else knowing where they are going and so many lanes and having to try to change lanes in an instant with everyone going so fast. I want to go inland to avoid it but John wants to go straight through - I really am dreading it! He'll have to lead the way because I'm not! Luckily you can bypass Brisbane - just take care not to miss the turn off to the Sunshine Coast - we live there and have ended up at Redcliffe twice whilst on our way North!

CHAPTER NINETEEN

FISHING POINT

We haven't seen my daughter for a year now - too long and she tells me that if she waits until we return next Christmas we will have been apart for longer than when we left her in Europe. I reminded her that I can talk to her any time here which is rather different to when she was in the Youth Hostel in London. She shared a room with three friends on the top floor so when I phoned and asked for her, I would hear a relay of shouts and then someone would run up five flights of stairs to tell her and I'd pray she wasn't in the bath! By the time we connected she would be hard pushed to gasp out a hello! Anyway, last night I suggested that when her lease is up she join us for a while, wherever we happen to be.

'What would we do with your food?' I asked her 'You'd have to keep it in the car as I don't have a spare cupboard!' Doesn't this sound crazy? My daughter and I eat a totally different diet, even though she's my daughter! She told me she'd baked for a friend last night - to me that means a roast dinner - and then described the vegetarian pizza (I recognised 'broccoli') and by the time she got to the capers I interrupted her and said 'Well we're having diced chicken breast, garlic, onions, capsicum, celery, avocado and mushrooms in cream on rice tomorrow with broccoli.'

'You lost me when you got to the cream' she answered and then added 'I can't eat rice'.

She did well to get past the word 'chicken'! At home it's fine, she clears a rack in my big fridge (we also have a small spare one) and there is so much cupboard space, but there's not room for an extra cup in here! Hopefully we'll get to see her in Melbourne before she leaves.

Do you remember my posting the koala - well this is the message I received tonight from my brother Paul:

'Koala arrived safely, a little jet-lagged, didn't like the food and said the in-flight film was rubbish. Otherwise he is well…'

Oh dear, a koala bear with attitude - I do hope he behaves himself at Coventry Cathedral. It's a worry. It's the Poms that whinge isn't it, not the Aussies. He'll give us a bad name if he goes on like that as soon as he arrives. He's a typical Aussie being so forthright though isn't he? I mean, if you are in the U.K. and you get taken on a trip which bored you silly but everyone else thought was wonderful, when you are asked if you enjoyed it you must say 'Oh yes, it was a wonderful day, thank you so much'. Aussies are just as likely to bluntly say 'Not bad but I've seen better but I can assure you that your host will react like a stunned mullet at your rudeness if you do. I recall wanting to dematerialise when someone with me from Australia responded in a typically Aussie fashion to such a query! And whatever you do, do not go to sleep when visiting someone. That is the ultimate insult to your host, however tired you are. My companion did that too! In true British stiff-upper-lip fashion everyone pretended not to notice which was really difficult after two hours!

Every time we walk around a caravan park here people smile and say 'Gooday'. Don't do it in English cities, especially if you are a man because you are likely to get a fist in your face. This was the reaction my son got when in England anyway but it could have been because he had long hair! Anyway, it might be o.k. if you add 'Gooday mate' because they'll then know you are from another planet but don't smile at strangers, which is all he did and always does being such a friendly guy and he has no problems in Oz. If you explain that you are from Australia they are likely to ask you where Australia is and can they get a cheap 'package trip there for a couple of days'. However, complete strangers can be very polite even though they don't look at each other. Queuing is a good example - people willingly do it in England, everywhere without getting irritated - so if there are three bank machines you form one queue and the one in front uses the next available machine, not like here where people form three separate ones and hope their queue is the quickest! We compete at every turn, that's why we're good at sports. What started this? Oh yes, the koala.

Dear Paul

I apologise for Koala's grumpiness on arrival, I did tell him that he had to be polite. If it continues, you have a few days to knock him into shape before the Wedding. If all else fails knock him out with some champagne - nobody will notice anything odd because Koalas sleep over eighteen hours a day to conserve energy because of their diet. Hopefully it's just jet-lag and he'll soon cheer up.

CHAPTER TWENTY

SWANSEA SUNSET

Well I managed to keep John here an extra day which gave us the time to go shopping in **Nelson Bay**, to the banks and to the Tourist Information Centre. Big mistake as my folder of leaflets had to be cleared out to make room for the new and I now feel totally overwhelmed at all there is to see. I picked up some brochures about the highland areas and now want to visit many more towns!

We went up to the harbour and purchased some fresh rainbow trout and then up the hill to the Inner Lighthouse which allowed us a wonderful view of the area and superb home-baked cakes with our coffee! That reminds me, you can get a ferry from here to Tea Gardens (where we stayed before here) and if you go there be sure to stop at the village bakery called The Pie Man because they have over 35 varieties of pies including an Oyster Kilpatrick Pie, Beef Burgundy, Satay Chicken and old-fashioned Steak and Kidney - buy these four, share them with your partner and you won't need to eat for the rest of the day!

We then headed off to the **Tilligerry Peninsula** but when the rain became so heavy that we couldn't see the road we had to give up and turn back. We did get to **Boat Harbour** yesterday which is one of the small settlements on the Tomaree Peninsula but despite it's attractive name it only had a boat ramp and a motley collection of homes, some which looked like they should have demolition orders taken out on them and then there were the new! There were a whole heap of ugly monstrosities, which you find close to major cities in Australia. The huge two-storey homes covered in granosite. Boat Harbour is almost surrounded by National Park. These homes looked like they'd been dropped down from space in the wrong place and it is someone's idea of a joke. It saddens me to see such poor planning in such a unique area and a pity for the few home-owners who had houses that did suit the area and which are presented so beautifully.

I think that, quite by chance, we actually picked the prettiest place to stay here in Port Stephens, that being **Shoal Bay**. I understand that Lemon Tree Passage is also very pretty - that was where we were heading to today, before being stopped by the rain and it certainly seems to be the place to spot some Koalas in the wild. Tomorrow we leave.

LAKE MACQUARRIE REGION.

We are happily booked into a caravan park on the edge of a lake at **Swansea** and can watch the vivid orange sunsets over the water at night and it is magic. I'm typing this with Nirvana playing in the background but my legs are itching like mad with some new bites I attracted today - difficult to concentrate.

My friend in Tasmania suddenly asked me on the phone last night 'Are you enjoying it?' with reference to our

travels. With most people I'd say 'It's wonderful' but this was my friend and I knew there was more to the question such as 'What is it really like travelling constantly?' or 'What is it like living with your husband 24 hours a day when you are not used to it? I found that I couldn't answer and after rather too long a silence I said 'I don't know!' Real friends are so important aren't they? They ask the pertinent questions, the obvious questions that perhaps you haven't asked yourself. The first thing I decided was that it didn't matter much because it is an experience that I will always remember and I'm seeing some wonderful places and towns that meant nothing when I heard them mentioned on the news and now they are suddenly very real to me with individual characteristics. A wonderful way to learn geography and children should have a 'gap year' when they finish junior school rather than when they finish high school and get taken around Australia on a trip like this!

Anyway, I began to wonder how many times you really know you are enjoying a new experience. How often do you realise it at the time or is it mainly when you look back on them that you realize just how great some moments were. For example, if you are at a pop concert listening to one of your favourite artists or watching a film that you really enjoy, you are totally absorbed with the experience and I guess that's how we are - we are absorbed. We still feel hungry, tired, too hot or annoyed that we can't put off that trip to the supermarket any longer and when we do find one, we won't know where anything is and can't find the products we want and are used to. We have 'irritants' that we didn't have before like worrying about how long can we can stay in one place before having to find somewhere to empty the black-water, where to stay next and how to find it, the insects, worried about our awning every time the wind gets strong, having to keep packing everything away and then unpacking it at the end of the day.

There's lack of space in the kitchen and bathroom, muddy sites when it rains, no routine, having to take the dogs everywhere with us and therefore not being able to go out to eat at night, ironing on a mini-board and neighbours changing constantly! So we are 'living' the life but I'm sure that when this trip is over we will forget the biting insects and the mud and the lack of space and they will fade into insignificance (and they probably seem to be insignificant to you) and we will want everyone to look at hundreds of our 'wonderful' holiday snaps and we'll probably make it sound like nirvana! That's why I'm writing this diary, so that I can remember all the good, the bad and everything in between!

John Timms

Thank you to our friends that write to us. I know that when I finish this tonight there will be emails waiting for us to collect and we look forward to your emails. We have no friends with us and we have found that is one of the downfalls of this type of life. We cannot pop around for a coffee and have a chat with people who already know us. On the road you have to go through all the preliminaries such as names and where you come from and where you are heading to, what you used to do for a living or if this is a short holiday or a permanent way of life etc. Either that or you just nod, smile and move on. So we rely on your letters although we are hoping to catch up with one of our friends soon.

CHAPTER TWENTY-ONE

CABBAGE TREE-NORA HEAD

Today we started out sightseeing at Swansea Heads near us and there was a road called Beach Road with huge two-story near new homes and I thought 'Yes, yes - this is what new suburbs should end up looking like.' I'm not advocating huge, two storey homes but these homes were all beautifully designed and although every one was of a different design they all complimented each other so that the overall effect was superb. We then went back on the Pacific Highway heading south and turned off to Catherine Hill Bay, a very quiet area with a lovely beach and a collection of beach houses and a Historic Mining Village. As we had decided to look at the coast on the way down and the lakeside villages on the way back we continued on until we reached the turn-off for The Entrance. If we hadn't we would have ended up in Gosford.

We were also checking out caravan sites. Again we had the lake on one side and the beach on the other and we turned left to **Noraville** and Norah Head. At **Nora Head** we stopped at Cabbage Tree Harbour and it is really quaint. In fact we liked the area as a whole. We particularly liked the six foot high granny in long dress, pinafore, grey hair in a bun and glasses on the end of her nose, who was holding a tray outside the Lighthouse Café. It's a good job she's so big because I'm sure that there must be countless people like me who wanted to pinch her and take her home. I'd love to have her in my hallway so that when I come in I'm greeted by a smiling granny who's longing to make me a cup of tea!

I can hear her say 'Sit down dear and put your feet up, you've had a long day. Dinner won't be too long and I've made your favourite apple pie to have with that fresh cream for desert.' See - I'm living one dream and imagining another - that's human nature for you. By the way, if you want to go and live there, I saw a small block of land for sale on the beach side but facing the main road for $435,000, which at this time is very dear although in a couple of years I will probably think it was cheap.

Next came **The Entrance** and just further on **Toowoon Bay** where we found a site we liked and pre-booked for next week. It is a lovely area by the sea and the manager was wonderfully relaxed and helpful. We returned to The Entrance and stopped in the main street. It is a very modern and very pretty town and I am really looking forward to exploring it next week. No doubt the name reflects the access between the sea and Tuggerah Lake. On our return we travelled with the lakes to our left and sea to the right. First Lake Tuggerah, then Budgewoi Lake, Lake Munmorah and then Chain Valley Bay which is part of Lake Macquarie. I am attempting to explain the fact that we travelled only down one side and we haven't explored north of where we are staying, nor the other side of all these lakes.

ROCKY FORESHORE

Last night, when we arrived, we were hanging around down by the lake and an elderly man told us that his move to this area was the best thing he had done since he was born. I asked him how long we would need to see the area and he rubbed his chin and said 'About five years or thereabouts'. He's probably right. The reason we have booked our next stop already is because we still have the Brisbane Water area and the Hawkesbury River region to explore further down, plus these other lakes. At the moment we are really only concentrating on the Lake Macquarie area. There is so much to see that you have to stop yourself from feeling stressed by the thought! We feel overwhelmed and rather like ants trying to explore a large town. We've started sectioning off the local maps so that we don't do too much in one day. Tomorrow we'll have a rest day for the dogs sake because they too get tired - they have no idea what is going to happen next and Jack has started an annoying habit of whining with excitement every time he sees water or a field of any size - even a long strip of grass sets him off. Everywhere is 'walkies' according to him and a new place to sniff out.

Callie has also started to 'talk' for the first time. If you've ever watched a film on crocodiles hatching out you will recall that distinctive rather sweet 'squeaking' sound they make. Well Callie must have heard them because we've discovered that it is Callie, not baby crocs that we hear outside our motor home. We heard it just now because Jack pinched her bed and we never get his out any more because he refuses to get on it. John's just gone to get Jacks out to stop them squabbling!

PLENTY OF ROOM

We were surprised by the town of **Toukley** as it was just a dot on the map and it turned out to be quite a large town and as it is on the lake on the other side of the road to **Noraville** (which is on the beach) it makes the settlement of Nora Head even more attractive - no wonder the land costs so much. What a perfect place to live. A quiet area on a beautiful beach so close to a large town and about an hour from Sydney, with lakes and beaches at every turn. Newcastle is just up the road too and that is an interesting city. Then there are all the National Parks, Reserves and State Forests (too many for me to be bothered counting) - so much - too much for us to take in - five years would be about right. I wanted to go back to Newcastle but have had to give up the idea for now. John wants us to leap past Sydney before Easter.

More news on the Koala's arrival in England....

Dear Lisa

Ok so he sleeps 18 hours a day but the six he is awake is still Australian time and so he keeps us awake all night with this strange Australian sound, is it the mating season down under? Any suggestions what we can do to keep him quiet, the neighbours are even complaining. One good thing, we have a Eucalyptus tree in the garden so he is getting plenty of fresh food.

John Timms

Dear Paul

Are the days cold there? Usually koalas sleep through most of the heat of the day! He should be awake during our night - which is your day!!! He likes having stories read to him and loves nursery rhymes. Not keen on singing but loves watching dancing. I therefore suggest that you read and recite for him and spend at least an hour dancing - you'll enjoy it and it'll keep you fit. The more vigorously you dance, the quicker he'll fall asleep.

Dear Paul

Suddenly realised that like most people you think that Koalas don't drink water - they do! He was able to talk when he first arrived and now you say he's squeaking - he's probably dying of thirst! (p.s unless there is a female koala in your garden, which I very much doubt, he's unlikely to get frisky). Please give him a drink urgently!

CHAPTER TWENTY-TWO

I'm great in an emergency - I become very practical and clear-thinking. I appear cool to the point of coldness - truth is I'm frozen inside and I am on automatic pilot. It's like I'm two people and the person that I am might be scared out of her wits but this other person takes over and I watch! I know it sounds weird and it is probably why I was so convinced from childhood on, that I was a twin. I actually thought I was adopted and at around eleven or twelve years of age and insisted on seeing my Birth Certificate. Well I watched my 'other person' in action today! I suggested a swim in the lake but John said he felt tired so I went on the computer to download my photos. He then started fixing cupboard latches so I guess he just didn't want a swim and I'm trying to work out where the photos were taken when he shouts 'Get a wet cloth, I'm bleeding everywhere'. I grabbed some paper towelling, wet it and went out thinking he had cut his finger or something. He's standing but bent double and there is blood pouring out of his head from a deep gash from where he'd hit it on the awning support. I ran back inside and stood stock still not knowing what to do. My 'sensible' self took over. I found a suitable pad in the medical box and when I got back outside I see that he has blood all down his face and all over his hands. I suggest that if he stands up and hold the cloth on the cut the blood might stop flowing so fast and he's saying 'Hose the grass, there's blood everywhere'.

I'll cut the next ten minutes out of this diary. With street map in one hand and glasses on the end of my nose so I could read it and look over the top of them to drive - both at the same time - we arrived at the medical centre to find it bursting with patients waiting non too patiently and he joined them at the receptionists request and sat down to wait. When I asked the receptionist for more tissues or they would probably find blood all over their nice grey carpet, a doctor materialized. 'Needs stitches' he tells us (I'd already worked that out which is why we were there) 'Look' he says to me, ignoring John and told John to bend his head and we discussed the length and depth of the cut. He ended up with five stitches in his 8½cm gash, plus a tetanus booster at my suggestion as John cannot recall when he last had one and awning bars don't stay that clean when travelling. John was concerned that he might not be able to wash his hair but the doctor looked him over and suggested that he definitely have a shower and washes his hair as soon as he gets home. He cleaned John's face which amused John who thought he was being very kind and considerate and the doctor answered 'Well you won't look like something out of a horror movie when you go back through reception'. I think he was concerned that some of his patients might leave or pass out. We were told on arrival that they did not bulk-bill so there would be a charge and my response was that I was past caring by that point. Anyway, the doctor told the receptionist not to charge us and I think that is because John was such a congenial patient (very brave too).

On the way back John insisted we pick up the gas cylinder that had been filled at a local shop and some poor customer walked in to buy sweets only to find that he had to carry it back to the car for me. Then John wanted to know if I was going to stop to give the dogs a run. I told John that I needed a cup of tea even if he didn't! He's quite enjoyed being waited on with tea and biscuits on return, shower whilst I got dinner ready, cigar outside whilst I washed up and a sit down whilst I walked the dogs in the dark! The anaesthetic is now wearing off - John will have a sore head. We have to find another doctor in 10 days to get the stitches taken out.

Friday

Today was relaxing - for us anyway but not for my daughter who started walking at 11am and I've just phoned her (it's now 7.30pm) and they are about to climb 1000 steps (yes three noughts). I climbed down and up eighty the other week and that was enough, let alone after walking for 8½ hours.

Today is our 21st Wedding Anniversary. John didn't have a headache but I awoke with a chronic one! Having one for him is taking sympathy a bit too far isn't it!

We set off around the Lake going north to **Belmont** first which we hadn't thought much of when passing through on the way down before when we had been looking for a caravan park to move to. It turned out to be lovely and I took three photographs of Belmont Harbour from the beautiful lakeside park. We completed the loop of Lake Macquarie and went to nearly every lakeside scenic view. Belmont certainly had the largest park but some of the tiniest public parks had the most stunning views. We spent time at **Croudace Bay, Woodrising**, had a picnic at Fishing Point along with quite a few Pelicans and also stopped at **Buttaba**. At **Morisset** we found Aunty Molly's Olde Bakehouse Restaurant and stopped with the dogs for coffee and John enjoyed the biggest slab of lemon meringue pie that I have ever seen, surrounded by single cream with raspberry drizzled through it! I only sampled it three times, just to check that it had been baked properly. The building is an original bakehouse and the fireplaces and ovens are original and there are some fine antiques - brass and copper mainly and it was like being in an old English restaurant - very charming and quaint.

We then explored all the small settlements along the Bonnells Bay peninsular. We drove around **Shingle Splitters Point** which had water on both sides and was very pretty (a lovely place for a picnic) but we stayed a while at a tiny park called Casuarina Point where there was only room for a couple of cars and it was magical. By the time we got back the sun was setting - a huge round red ball reflecting across the lake. A wonderful day - and yes I was aware that I was enjoying myself!

CHAPTER TWENTY-THREE

Last Wednesday we thought our new neighbours were leaving - their four wheel drive was being washed and polished and the boat disappeared! The next day the exterior of their caravan was thoroughly cleaned and the car buffed up again. Friday the annexe attached to the caravan was washed and dried and the car checked again and rubbed over. Saturday, apparently washing day and the annexe mat had been packed away. Oh I forgot - the car was checked again too. They were a constant source of wonder to us and we had just begun to get to know this lovely couple when they finally left today! Turns out they only live half an hour away and pop back home to collect their post and cut the lawn. They'd been here two months! Mind you they have been right around Australia and after two weeks at home will set off north to Cairns for the winter months. Once they had gone we moved our car onto their site and today we cleaned it - not they way we usually do it - the way he did it next door and it looks so good!

I realized as soon as we started why he cleaned his $49,000 new car every day - because of the bats. You learn a lot when you travel. I said to him the other day 'A bat has pooped on your car door on our side'. (Thought he might like to clean his car again.) 'Bats don't poo' he answered 'They regurgitate their waste'. I asked him if it was the Wattle tree blossoms giving me hay fever 'They're not Wattle. They are a type of oak tree'. Interesting to know how wrong I can be so don't believe everything I write! Anyway, bats eat fruit and they regurgitate what appears to be a yellow acidic substance - wasn't he sensible to check his car every day - I'll be doing the same from now on. I still can't get some stains off the bonnet! Anyway, we were offered two free nights here so we'll have been here one whole week when we leave on Tuesday and yesterday and today we've stayed 'at home' and we've even been swimming in the pool here. I've managed to book a site on the other side of Sydney for the whole of the Easter period, in the Southern Highlands - more about that area when we get there. On Tuesday we're off to the Lakes Entrance area.

I wonder how Koala got on at the Wedding yesterday - I do hope he behaved himself.

THE ENTRANCE (Toowoon Bay)

We're at a fairly large park and in the village there are a few odd shops including an antique shop and art gallery. It is only a few minutes drive to The Entrance shops one way and to the Lakeside shopping precinct the other and if you want 'the lot' then Erina, about fifteen minutes drive away, provides David Jones, both Coles and Woolworths, K Mart and Target and too many other shops! It is a huge, ultra modern shopping mall. John has just discovered that we can walk, directly from our caravan park, to the beach and that the dogs are allowed to run free. Prior to this he was walking out of the front gate and around the roadway. This is a huge bonus for us. It's very comfortable here. It's also cooler at last! Well, it's not cool but it's about 23-25C during the day and cool at night. It's so much better for sightseeing but today I suddenly felt very weary and we stopped for a coffee and I ordered a slice of banana bread - it was a big thick slice. 'Would you like it toasted with butter on?' I was asked and John piped up 'Yes please, me too'. I can recommend it - scrumptious. Full of carbohydrate and sugar - I felt much better!

John Timms

We went to **Wyong** today to collect our post and drove down to the lake whenever possible on the way back. Wyong is a much smaller town than I had imagined and the railway line runs right through it. We had to buy a local map in the end because it is a complicated area and now John feels overwhelmed too because there is too much to see. We booked in for a week and it was he who suggested we could extend if we want!

We also looked around the town of The Entrance which is so pretty and sat in the park by the river inlet waiting for an appointment we'd made to get my flue vaccine. Doctor told me off because of all my bites - 'Spray yourself and cover yourself up all the time' he told me. In this heat! When it gets to 4c I'll do as I'm told! One bonus, I've lost two kilos which I believed only after getting on a second set of scales. I needed to lose a bit. Seems all you need to do is to eat freshly baked white bread instead of wholemeal and go out for lots of coffees and cakes. I'd have done that a long time ago if I'd realized.

CHAPTER TWENTY-FOUR

We have two toilets. Most people are grateful for one in a van but we have two. We have a problem finding dump points so if the tank becomes full and we've nowhere to empty it we're stuck. We decided to purchase a portable toilet for night emergency use. If we take it out of storage, we can put it in the shower cubicle and I'll use the park showers like John. So we're discussing toilets in the camping shop and John can't seem to understand that they come in different heights so I got him to sit on the smallest! He looked hilarious as his knees were up around his ears. He decided the higher the better. Have you ever been in a toilet where the toilet is lower than expected? I did, at one of the caravan parks we stayed at. They must have bought them in bulk from a primary school. It's quite a shock because it's not where you thought it would be and you think you've missed it and then all of a sudden you hit it when you sit. I sat there thinking of some friends who have legs that go on forever and wondering what they'd look like and now I'd found out. Anyway, a lady is standing beside me with this plastic, shaped object with a bag attached. 'Can you get replaceable bags?' she asked the young salesman beside me.

'No, sorry' he responded.

'What is it?' I asked.

'For night-time wees' she responded.

'Isn't it for a man?'

'No, look, this is shaped exactly like women' she answered.

'It might be like yours but how do you know that my vagina is that shape? Have you ever discussed the shape of women's vaginas?' I asked her 'it could be an interesting topic for today.' The salesman went red. Like me, he obviously hasn't been to the theatre to see 'The Vagina Monologues'.

We were enjoying ourselves until the salesman said 'I'm glad I was witness to this conversation' and we stopped mucking about and looked at a bucket with a snap-on toilet seat. 'I haven't got room for it in my van' she told me.

'Well buy that original one and instead of using bags, put it over a jar and you can wash them both out' I suggested.

'How will I get a jar to fit?' she asked me.

'Just go into Coles or Woolworths and ask them to find you one. Just throw the contents away if you don't like the food' but she seemed to think that was too embarrassing.

'Buy a child's potty' was my next suggestion but she said she would miss it in the dark, land on the floor and wet herself with the shock.

'Put it on a chair' but at that suggestion she screwed up her face.

'For goodness sake, use a bucket' I called out and we left her with her problem and decided to buy our toilet. Dogs don't have this problem. Don't humans make life complicated? All this over a pee for goodness sake!

'It's the last one' said the salesman 'You'll have to have the one from the shop floor'.

'Where are the instructions?' asked John.

'Inside the bottom section, I'll get them out' says the salesman who promptly got his hand stuck. In the meantime my imagination is racing. 'In that case I want a reduction on the price because I don't know who's sat on it'. He wasn't in a position to think about refusing as he was still trying to get his hand back out and we were still waiting. He stopped for breath and said 'I'll look after you' which was very professional considering how ridiculous he looked. I was just about to call an ambulance when his hand flew out clutching the instructions. We got a $9 discount.

We got pulled up on a roundabout today whilst out in the Ute. John thought he had done something wrong and I thought the rear door of the Ute might be open and a dog had fallen out. 'What kind of dog is that?' called the man 'he's beautiful'. How crazy is that on a roundabout! We are always getting stopped by people. John reckons that Jack's getting too vain but today it was also Callie's turn! I was outside the post office and a guy approached me to ask me if she has Kelpie in her and I said she could have, I have no idea. 'She's beautiful' he told me and totally ignored Jack. Callie drooled with pleasure. I'm thinking of changing what I come back as – "in the next life", I had thought I would like to be a bird, but now I'm thinking Belgium Shepherd, If you are a single woman get one if you want to find a guy. If you would like to learn to fly, without having to think about it, buy two dogs – one with Jack's personality and one as determined as Callie. I was taking the dogs for their midnight pee before bed when suddenly three rabbits approached us. It is interesting to see how dogs react when they see a rabbit for the first time - I would have liked to have seen their reaction too but missed it as I was flying through the air on the other end of their leads. I found my glasses with the aid of a torch about half an hour later. There are so many rabbits running around this park at night but they are very timid which is probably a good thing because if they were tame I'd end up picking one up and then I'd want to keep it and the dogs would want to eat it and John would go berserk that I'd adopted yet another pet. I still miss my chooks though. Everyone should have chooks. Not cockerels though - ours woke us up earlier and earlier. It had no sense of timing and had not learnt to wait until dawn. By the time it started crowing at 2am John was so sleep-deprived that it drove him to running around the garden in the middle of the night, stark naked, with a hose pipe on full blast. Cockie did not like showers and would shut up until he had dried off, which gave us two to three hours of uninterrupted sleep. It was a toss up whether it was the cockerel or John who was becoming the most unstable but when it attacked my little girl when her back was turned we found a home for it at a domestic bird sanctuary and the last we saw of it was of it being chased up into a tree by two geese. We were assured it would settle in. John could be heard mumbling 'Serves you right, now you're not the boss any more'.

CHAPTER TWENTY-FIVE

John likes his peace. He can never hear a word I say but he wakes up at the slightest sound. I've often thought I should talk to him whilst he's asleep because he'd wake up immediately and ask me if I'd said something and he'd be so surprised that he'd actually listen. I used to write him letters but he didn't like that. He takes things in when he reads, particularly spread sheets! Now if I could learn to speak in a code made up of numbers he'd always understand instantly. So if A=1, of=2, you=5, cup=36 and tea=57, do=6, want=7, I could say 657136257 which would mean 'Do you want a cup of tea?' and he'd say 'Yes' straight away. Trouble is, I'm not that good with numbers. I've just bought a new calculator, not because we needed it but because it was only $9 and on the back is the answer to all those awful mathematical problems that I've forgotten since leaving school but sometimes need and I won't let him open the packet because I'm afraid the instructions will be thrown away by mistake. It also explains how to use those symbols on a calculator that I've never known what to do with like MC or M- or MR. It's sat in the cupboard for three weeks but I will get around to learning how to use it properly - one day - probably in a panic when John needs it as the other one has broken. Naturally, as seasoned campers, I bought a solar-powered one!

Sunday April 4th

Our current caravan park manager tells us that dogs behave better and bark less often in parks than at home. We pondered this statement and then a comment by another lady that 'My dogs demands 25 hour constant care and attention' gave us the answer - we are with them constantly. They know that if they bark we will come hurtling out of the van because we do not want to get into trouble and if they whine we will rush out to try to work out if they are hungry or need to pee! Our two dogs also get a lot of attention from children and Callie spent a full hour being cuddled this morning - she just lay on her back and grinned. Jack looked pleadingly at me because he wanted rescuing as he's not that bothered about getting affection from others, only from us.

We went touring again yesterday and John mentioned that he admires the New South Wales government for having expanded their 'green belts' with so many National Parks, State Forests and Reserves. It has certainly stopped developers from creating more urban sprawl. Thus the south eastern outskirts of Gosford are pretty, with mature trees in the gardens and plenty of winding, hilly roads. We travelled south again and headed for Terrigal. We had called in on our way back from Wyong the other day and I have fallen in love with the place, probably because of its headland called **Broken Head.** It is a large hill area adjacent to a large sports field with plenty of car-parking at the bottom, a café on the sea front and the whole area overlooks the pretty town and a beautiful bay. The hill is easy to walk up (there is another called The Skillion which we didn't climb) and from the top there are several viewing areas which provide many different sea views and the rock formations are so weird and beautiful they look as though they've been painted. How can rocks be so beautiful? Whilst we were there we watched a wedding which was taking place in a large grassy area in one of the viewing areas with the sea as the backdrop. The shops are three minutes walk away so everything is compact and most of the homes in the area are built on the hill and all, of course, with magnificent views. We drove down the hill one way to get there and back in a loop to get out and I don't think I saw a home without a view - they tumble down the hill. I'm not talking 'Amalfi' or like those in Greece but there are similarities to where I lived in Campione, opposite Lugano in Switzerland. It's the gardens here and the size of the house blocks and the much larger homes that makes the difference. The area is north-east of Gosford and you could drive to work in Sydney.

Anyway, we then went on to **North Avoca** beach and then had to go inland and all the way around the Bulbararing Lagoon and across the bridge over Avoca Lake to get to Avoca Beach but didn't stop there. We went on the beach at Copacabana, John had a swim and we bought a fish and chip lunch. John wanted to go to Tumbi Umbi and Kincumber just because of their names (he kept calling the latter 'cucumber' by mistake) but Callie hadn't been well and by the time she had romped in the sea with Jack and two other dogs who were chasing a big plastic ball, she had a job to get back in the Ute, so we headed back. She's as fit as a fiddle today so I can recommend sea therapy - you just have to find a young guy who will continually kick a ball into the waves for an hour for your dog's amusement. We will have hardly touched the area by the time we leave but I'd love to come back here again to explore the area more thoroughly. We want to get past Sydney before the Easter traffic starts and as the school holidays start on Good Friday this year we need to leave on Tuesday as planned or at the very latest on Wednesday.

John wants to know how I ended up talking about his having chased a cockerel whilst naked when I'm supposed to be writing about our tour! I don't know but I'll blame a friend who I used to work for! We have worked together twice for two different real estate companies over the years and she is always in such a hurry that we could have conversations in a language that only she and I understood. She would have mentioned five different subjects such as a house she'd listed, did I want a coffee, had she told me about her son or daughters latest adventures, she had bought a new pet and her garden pavers had to all be relayed because the work the tiler had done was so bad and I'd call out 'Wait! Now backtrack - have you got a key yet for that house, yes to coffee, tell me about the adventures later, why on earth have you got yet another dog and the tiler subject can wait until we've got the coffee - we'll start with the key for the house so that I can have a look at it'.

In time I learnt to store everything up as a list in my head and told her I would check my computer (meaning head) and catch up with the subjects she wanted to talk about later. If I hadn't I would never have got anything done because she would fly in the door, interrupt whatever I was doing and drop all these subjects and fly back out again. Sometimes it would be days before I crossed items off this list in my 'computer head' as I too was overworked. Luckily we didn't work together from Thursday (my day off) to Monday as she had Friday and Saturday off and I had Sunday off. If subjects were not covered between Monday and Wednesday, they got held over until the following week. Thus we evolved our own language. On Monday she would start to tell me something else and I would interrupt her with 'Saw the house, not bad, might have a buyer' and we'd continue the original conversation but anyone within hearing distance would look puzzled. All our conversations included many odd comments and were therefore totally disjointed but we knew what each other meant every time. Very often I would appear to totally ignore her but I heard every word and she knew I'd stored the information and would get back to her. Trouble is though that I now do it at home! I'm absorbed on the computer and John will say something and accuse me of not listening but although I have slipped up on occasion, I nearly always get back to him later. So my colleague and I could cover a multitude of subjects at one time and I got used to one subject leading to another very quickly, so now I ramble on in letters too. I've told John I have no idea how I got onto the subject of cockerels, my head just took me there. It's normal for me and would be for anyone who had worked so closely with her.

CHAPTER TWENTY-SIX

8th April-MITTAGONG, BOWRAL, MOSSVALE.

John passed another Birthday quietly and gratefully (as he said) on the 5th and it made us both think of our Dad's and reflect on how young they were when they passed away, both with cancer and I thought of my brother who also died too young. John celebrated by having his stitches out! We set off yesterday and our trip via Sydney was a nightmare and we'll never do it again! Next time we'll go as far as it takes inland to avoid the traffic, particularly the trucks which each seemed to be the length of half a football field. We were constantly surrounded by them and there were some very scary moments with trucks overtaking John and cutting in front of him and then he'd have to overtake them when we got to hills. Then back they'd come again, thundering past and we were travelling on the speed limit! We came out the other side stiff from the tension and welcomed the sight of the rolling green fields.

We are now 675m above sea level, it was 8c at 5.30 this morning, the dogs wonder what's hit them and can't wait to get into the Ute as soon as the sun goes down and I love it! Had to go out to buy John some warm slippers and a heater today (he has it on now, directed at his feet). I was so excited at the cool weather that I had walked the dogs twice before John got out of bed this morning. We arrived via Mittagong, Bowral and then on here to Moss Vale. We were so impressed with Mittagong that we returned today and had a look around and coffee and Danish pastries of course! We then stopped at Bowral (slippers and bank) and after lunch Moss Vale (heater and Post Office). To sum up, I'm ready to sell up and move here! This area is magical for me with a plethora of book shops, galleries, antiques, shops that delight like the 'Needles & Yarns' store, 'Tobacco Emporium' 'Old Farm Kitchen', fabulous clothes and accessory shops and art and craft shops with fine linen tea towels and hand-made cushions etc. Add to this pretty towns, some stunning homes including a number of sandstone homes (I love sandstone), timber cottages, mock Tudor, and the usual mix of huge acreage versus golf club villas and you have the variety that delights the eye. There were a few up-market brick and tile areas with not a leaf out of place and all surrounded by the green hills and vales.

We drove up Mount Gibraltar via Mittagong, to the lookout and admired the beautiful homes on the way up and down but it was at Moss Vale that I picked up the Real Estate paper when I saw a cottage for sale in town. Couldn't help myself - had to find out the price - not bad either!

To my delight the trees are dropping their leaves and I stomped back and forth on them tonight, listening to them crunch. It was such fun. I now know its autumn - it is so good to be in a part of the world again where there are recognisable signs of the seasonal changes as we do not get that in Brisbane. Brisbane is hot or wet or cool and different plants flower at different times of the year of course but that's it! Here, they usually have snow in winter but didn't last year. Houses advertised have central heating (what's that?) and fireplaces are mentioned in house advertisements! I had to change into something cooler at lunchtime as it was very warm today but the jumper is back on now and my Ugg boots have been unpacked! I had such a wonderful nights sleep last night that I'm actually looking forward to going to bed tonight, which is rare for me as I tend to look on sleep as a necessary evil (such a waste of time) and something that is only necessary for health reasons such as keep-fit regimes.

Tomorrow is Good Friday and a friend of ours is arriving and this is one Easter that I'm sure I will always remember. I feel very excited about all the villages we are going to discover, the books I shall be browsing through and many other scenic attractions that I will tell you about in due course. The rural scenery reminds me of Wales and I feel like I'm sinking into a bath of green serenity, being gently enfolded in its beauty. How I have missed this environment - it's so hard too explain, it goes deep into my soul.

Saturday was wonderful day. I wanted to go to the Easter Street Fair at Burrawang but we got lost and found the Fitzroy Falls instead! It is on the 'must see' list of local attractions and was swarming with Japanese tourists! It's in the Morton National Park, 640 metres above sea level and the falls drop 81metres - not very high but the scenery was wonderful - rugged and wild with sandstone cliffs and what appeared to be impenetrable forest. We had a bird's eye view of the valley below. From there we eventually found **Burrawang**, not because there were any signposts but because we knew the name of the road we had to take. Perhaps the locals like it that way – not having any signage - as there is very little about the village in the tourist books, but I think it is a shame as so many of the buildings are heritage listed. We saw a cottage for sale and spoke to a man in the garden to ask how much it was on the market for. Turns out his great-grandfather built the house and died there, his grandfather was born there and he was only there as a visitor as they were having a big reunion party with relatives this weekend and he is staying there because it is now a guest house. Apparently the property was sold outside the family years ago. 'Wouldn't you want to buy it, to get it back in the family?' I asked him. 'Not for the million dollars it will sell for' he replied. He said it was sold by his family for about $34,000 (I think that's the figure he told me) when the village was the back of beyond and no-one was interested in it. That was not that long ago. Come to think of it, his great-grandfather must have been one of the original settlers because the first people settled there in 1862.

We had a wonderful time there and it wasn't because of the markets which were fascinating but because of the atmosphere of the place and the original buildings. There was the original bank, the original post office etc but some of the buildings had been purchased to be occupied as private homes. I had no idea where to buy a newspaper for example and it turned out that the building I thought was the newsagent was a home and the papers were purchased in the greengrocer's store. Whilst buying the paper I saw some giant field mushrooms and bought two for dinner tonight - they are as big as our plates so I'll top them with eggs and some slices of tomatoes. Apparently the shop itself is often photographed as the ceiling is covered with hanging dried garlic and chilli. The original old hotel was there and was doing a roaring trade with two dining rooms full of patrons, the bar full of people and the garden full of customers. We were accosted by two Grimm's Fairy Tale characters who were about to put on a free play in the hotel garden but we were trying to choose which village stall to go to for lunch. We watched as a huge joint of meat was being carved for hot beef rolls, smelt the freshly baked meat pies and then saw someone with a plate of mouth-watering food and asked what it was. We followed suit and bought 'jacket potatoes with the lot' which meant cheese, bacon, mushrooms, cream and cole slaw with shallot rings on top and I left nothing for John, which is unusual for me! We sat on the grass and watched the action, revelled in the atmosphere . Whilst there, we got talking to a stallholder who was selling hand-made jumpers at ridiculously cheap prices and I bought a beautiful pink wool jumper for my 'foster granddaughter' which I will send to England next Christmas and pink is her favourite colour. I also found some beautiful towels for my kitchen and discovered the gourmet food counter in the local hall where I taste-tested every sample of their pate's. I ended up purchasing the Pate Forestiere with mushrooms and thyme for our lunch tomorrow.

We stopped at a park on the way back for the dogs to have a run and Jack wouldn't run. We then noticed he was holding his leg off the ground. He has developed the dreaded hip problem inherent in many Shepherds. Now we have a problem. We are back at the van and he is lying down and we are going to have to stop all exercise for a couple of days and if he doesn't improve we'll have to find a vet open at Easter somewhere! They do operate on hips but it is going to be very difficult with our present lifestyle because of the rehabilitation afterwards. If he was small it wouldn't be so bad. Poor Jack. We won't be going anywhere either for a couple of days - if Jack is grounded, so are we.

CHAPTER TWENTY-SEVEN

Our friend arrived from Sydney yesterday but returned the same day because he didn't want to bring his dog. However, he must have enjoyed himself as he's coming back to visit again. He's never seen me in winter clothes and was rather amused - asked me if I was going riding with the hunt, cheeky bugger. I had beige cord jeans on, a beige thick jumper and my Ugg boots (which are knee high) and he kept looking at me and laughing!

He wanted to know where Picton is. It's off the Hume Highway, on the way here from Sydney and it's apparently an historic town which used to be called Stonequarry. Its fifteen minutes from Camden and you can join murder and ghost hunts there on weekends! John says that as it is back towards Sydney there's no way he's going there.

We have apparently missed the annual gathering at the Scottish town of Bundanoon which was held on 3rd April. I was disappointed until I was told that we wouldn't have been able to book in here anyway as the place is booked out a year in advance for this memorable event which was started 25 years ago. There is a steam train from Sydney and they have a parade with horses and vintage cars. They have pipers, highland games and the 'Tartan Warriors' show off their skills. Some years ago they had a competition to find the strongest men from around the world and the Australians won! The competition is now held each year and the idea is to lift sandstone balls and place them on a row of barrels. Some of the stones weigh up to 140 kilos. Bundanoon has its own registered tartan. I would have loved to have watched and listened to the massed bands performing. Not sure about the caber and the egg tossing though! Anyway, as soon as Jack is mobile we'll be off to visit Brigadoon because I have had a yen for many a year for a kilt.

So far, I'm glad we chose to park ourselves at **Moss Vale** because it's centrally located as well as being pretty. It was once a contender for Australia's capital city until it was discovered that it was just under 100 kilometres away from Sydney and it had to be 100ks or more. What a blessing for this area. For my non-Aussie friends - Melbourne and Sydney both thought they should be the capital of Australia and following much debate it was decided that a city would be built somewhere between the two - thus Canberra was born on the road to nowhere! Most Europeans still don't realize that and have never heard of it. Ask people you know and they will say 'Isn't it Melbourne, or perhaps Sydney?' They also have no idea how different the three cities are in design and character and the same argument rages today with Sydney and Melbourne citizens still claiming that their city is much nicer than the other.

Easter Monday (**BUNDANOON**).

Today we went to Bundanoon and found a bakery which offered free cups of coffee, so John bought a Danish pastry! We did not find the Bundanoon tartan though. The village is pleasant but has a railway track running through it and at least two loud hoots from trains were a bit disconcerting. We could not go into the Morton National Park because of the dogs, which is a pity because they have some wonderful walks, both easy and hard, to some very interesting places. From there we headed towards

Goulburn, passing through **Penrose** and **Wingello** to **Tallong** where we found a sign to Badgery's Lookout and that was spectacular. The view looks over the Shoalhaven River Gorge, surrounded by forest.

On the other side of Tallong we found the sign to **Long Point Lookout** (with no warning that we'd end up on a dirt road) and I had to take a second short video on my camera as a still shot would not have done it justice. We sat on a stone bench looking at the view. There was one other young couple there and as we sat in silence he started playing his guitar and sang Amazing Grace, in his strong Aussie accent. As I told him when he'd finished, he made a beautiful moment very special. I will never forget it. We returned to Bundanoon for freshly baked meat pies and more free coffees and on our way back called into a shop called 'Little Piece of Scotland' (where I could have bought a hat for $110 or some Yorkshire Tea in a caddy for about $54!) and I asked to see the Bundanoon tartan. A lovely shop but today I did not have the wallet to match their goods! On our drive around this part of the Southern Highlands we expected to see many herds of cows, because it is dairy farming country, and horses but did not expect to see a huge gaggle of geese in one field, another field with miniature horses, many fields with goats or the three Alpacas - well I think that's what they were! First I said 'Llamas' and then thought 'Surely not, must be Alpacas' but Alpacas have long coats don't they and these had short woolly coats - unless they'd just been shorn. I suddenly feel quite ignorant.

On our return I noticed Jack licking his back and on investigation I have found hundreds of small wounds - from the dog wash he had the other day. Now I am beginning to wonder about his hip - did he hurt Jack? I knew he gave Jack a good brush before his bath but I did not realise how heavy-handed he was being and Jack didn't appear to complain. Jack is still bleeding in spots. I'm so angry, poor Jack.

Ha, ha! Further investigation has revealed that they were indeed Alpacas and there are 50,000 odd farmed in the southern states - and I got excited about seeing three! Apparently they have their own personalities and are friendly but can get aggressive and can kill a dog! They look so cute and cuddly though! There is a place called Coolaroo Alpaca Stud near Berrima and they have the largest herd outside South America. Apparently with their breeding program, their wool is akin to cashmere. There is a factory outlet shop in Berrima - guess where we'll be going to next! All these towns and villages beginning with 'B' - it's so confusing! Berrima, **Bowral, Braemar, Burradoo, Bundanoon, Burrawang** and then there is the **Berkelouw Book Barn** which I want to go to and the **Belgenny Farm** Sunday Tour and the **Boot Hill** Markets or **the Bungonia** State Recreation Area etc. I keep asking John 'Have we been to Braemar?' We probably have but I cannot individualise them all yet and need prompts to remind me which place was where. John just changes the name and calls Bundanoon 'Dundanoon'. Actually, **Berrima** should be interesting as it was first settled in 1831 and is an Australian Georgian colonial town - I wonder what my architect Grandfather would have made of that - he built English Georgian homes! Are they different styles I wonder?

Well, John still has five major golf courses to investigate; there are over sixty vineyards here, numerous parks, reserves and state forests, a lavender farm, the Don Bradman museum (if we feel like a bit of cricket history), lots more villages and all those antique stores, art galleries and of course - books, books and more books! Utter bliss.

CHAPTER TWENTY-EIGHT

I went out with my Ug boots on by mistake today - I normally only use them as my slippers! So we're in the car and I say to John 'When I get back, the first thing I'm going to do is take my slippers off and put my shoes on. That's daft isn't it?'

The answer I got was 'What sheep needs shearing?'

John's left ear isn't working. I'd first thought this a couple of years ago when he surprised me on Valentine's night by booking a boutique theatre night out, plus dinner and it was all very romantic. We turned up to find a courtyard where we were offered champagne and chocolates by one of the cast - a very jolly, plump lady. John asked her, in a very British, theatrical voice, who she represented.

'The Queen of Hearts' she answered smiling.

'Oh, the Queen of Tarts, excellent, excellent' he said. I wanted the ground to swallow me up because of the look on her face and without hesitation she stormed off. So, he eventually booked a hearing test just before we left and they told him he was 'border-line' for a hearing aid. That delighted him because that was what he wanted to hear. Come to think of it, perhaps they didn't say that! Perhaps he didn't hear them properly! Whatever, it is now getting comical because I get so frustrated and he asks me to be patient but sometimes it is just impossible and we end up laughing, as today. Sometimes I burst out laughing and he doesn't know why but he starts laughing too and his laugh is infectious. I asked him three times in the car today about Alpacas and he just couldn't get the word and we ended up hysterical again with him trying to guess what I was saying and me hitting the dashboard with frustration shouting 'No. Alpacas!' I think I'll drive next time because then I'll be speaking into his right ear!

It's a bugger getting older. We hear about what we should tell our children about their development and in our twenties we think we know it all but we don't. It should be mandatory for parents who have forty-year-old children to sit them down and tell them what happens next! Not that we have children of that age yet but I wish my mother had warned me. I recall running into the legal centre where I worked shouting 'I have a white pubic hair - is that normal?' I was horrified. I didn't mind them on my head - I felt I'd earned them. Luckily there were some older volunteers who tried to calm me down but I was upset for days. It's when you realise that even though you use your eyes flirtatiously the thirty-year-old good-looking guy hasn't noticed you and is looking over your right shoulder at your daughter and that happened when she was only about eleven! Or when you say something which you think is profoundly deep and meaningful to your son and getting an answer like 'Yes, well you have to think that way because you are a parent. I can understand that'.

'Hello, hello - here I am - I'm me, not just Mum. I thought that was a pertinent comment. Obviously not - why not - what's going on?' I heard on T.V a while ago that children will always know more than their parents because each generation learns at a faster pace. The thought of grandchildren is suddenly rather frightening!

Thursday

Thanks for all you enquiries about Jack - his hips are fine! Saturday and Sunday he was hardly moving and we kept him quiet to rest his hip. Then he started constantly licking a couple of sores. I got him to the vet and they said he has a Staff infection. He had a very large and painful injection immediately, he may be on his antibiotics twice a day for many, many weeks, has to have a special bath every two days and the lather has to be left on for 15 minutes, plus a spray for those areas he licks as he got the infection on his gum and he was spreading the infection by licking. I find it hard to write this because I am still so, so angry. The Staff infection set into the wounds caused by the dog-wash man. Jack had been unable to walk because he was in so much pain with scratched skin which had tightened as it tried to heal. Yes I've complained, yes I've spoken to the franchise manager and the dog washer and yes we're getting the vet bill paid but what horrifies me is that the vet also spoke to the dog washer and he said that he disinfects his bath once a day with strong chemicals - he washed up to ten dogs without washing out the bath! We had to fight to get the bill paid but I cannot get through to anyone in the company that this guy should never brush another dog unless they retrain him and their policy on cleanliness is atrocious. The vet has told me never to use them again (meaning mobile dog baths) and that they never use them and hand-wash all the dogs because of the infection possibilities. We've used different ones for years without any problems but I'll now do them myself until we get home and can call the franchise that I trust. I am so amazed that Jack did not turn on the man and so grieved by the pain he went through and it was so, so unnecessary. I have been bathing them but they usually feel so good after their massage bath that I thought it would be a treat for them and really clean up all the sand and salt which tends to stick to their skin. I'm still finding it hard to come to terms with this - can you imagine someone raking you all over your back and hips until you bleed - he brushed Jack for at least half an hour. To be so bruised that for the next two days that you cannot move because of the pain and then getting an itchy infection in all those same places. He's now bouncing about and John does not have to lift him up any more to put him into the Ute - it's good to see his spirit returning. We took them out today to explore Berrima and we all romped around that beautiful village with excitement.

BERRIMA - an historical village with the oldest continuously licensed Inn in Australia which we felt upon inspection was not worth the visit. However, the White Horse Inn was fabulous and had outdoor dining as well as indoor and the original old, intimate dining room and the lounge were set up for private dining which would be lovely for family groups. There are so many original old sandstone homes and original shops that it was tea-time before we left and we still hadn't seen everything. We spent quite a long time at the old Court House which was completed in 1841. The first trial by jury 'in the colony' took place here. We watched a film, looked at all the old things and personal writings (they even had old copies of a speech of Abraham Lincolns and the Magna Carta) and old newspaper articles. There was a set of instructions for the employment of school teachers and what they had to do when they arrived at work, like light the fires and wash the floors and the fact that they had to save so much of their annual earnings and instructions on their moral behaviour and the fact that they could have two hours off one afternoon a week and male school teachers could have one night off for courting purposes but if a churchgoer, they could have another night off for church. There was a similar set of rules for nurses. To think that we moan about working conditions today - we haven't a clue how lucky we are! Then there was a section on different types of whips and another on entombing people alive which I stayed well away from - quite macabre! The original courtroom was set up with models and we listened to the words of the trial of the first man and woman who were sentenced to hang there. The models were so realistic that it looked like they were all frozen in time - it was quite weird - like they'd all died right there and had stayed in those poses! Not the sort of entertainment I usually go in for!

I naturally went to the Alpaca shop and very nearly purchased a jumper which I fell in love with but the medium size swamped me on the shoulders and they did not have another in the same thickness and style in the small size. I was then informed that it was a 'seconds' shop which I hadn't realised as that jumper was over $100 but we did look at the main shop albeit with a little less enthusiasm! Next stop was the bakers where I bought a loaf of bread which they had to hand slice as they do not have modern slicing machines, which I thought was fabulous! We also marvelled at a large shop full of jams, mustards, pickles and sauces. There were varieties I'd never heard of but I dreamt of my cottage in Wales and purchased bramble jelly (which I made every year there) and gooseberry (as they grew over my front gate). Then it was the Teddy Bear shop where I finally found what I wanted for my foster-daughter's new baby. I enjoyed long conversations with the owners of these shops and John kept tying the dogs up and coming in to find out what was keeping me! We finished our trip with coffee in the garden of the White Horse Inn. The village is quite large, mainly because everything is spaced out with lovely lawns everywhere and four of five shops would be grouped together with another village green between it and another row of shops going off at an angle to the street. At one point we could not make out where we had been and what we had missed as we wound our way around the village. We did not find the Alpaca Farm, or the Book Barn, which is where we were originally heading! We'll get there soon hopefully as I still haven't set foot in one book store! Incidentally, the gaol there is still operational and has fifty odd inhabitants at the moment. What a place to have a gaol, in the middle of a beautiful village and a top tourist spot to boot! If you escaped you wouldn't want to venture far because they'd be too much to look at! We didn't have time to go into the antique shops, art gallery, patchwork shop, and all the other craft shops nor the churches.

CHAPTER TWENTY-NINE

We are getting some jobs done whilst here though. We had new wiring put in for our aerial this week - that took hours as access is so hard in insulated walls! Result - wonderful T.V reception at last. We've also managed to purchase some marine T.V grips, to hopefully keep the television in the overhead compartment provided, but we're still a bit edgy having had it fly out before, so are going to add some straps too. We've had a 'three monthly spring clean' today to get into all those nooks we usually ignore. We have quite a list of jobs so have one day domestic duties and the next day sightseeing. An experienced tourer was saying to John the other day that there are always things that need doing just like at home - you may leave behind the lawn-mowing and gardening but new kinds of chores take their place. We are now having trouble finding someone to service our gas hot water system which is getting temperamental. When you travel you never know who to call, unlike at home. Finding a doctor or vet or electrician for example, can consume a lot of your spare time and shopping takes longer for the same reason. Also, the floors get dirty quickly and cleaning in very confined spaces can be quite difficult as is storing purchases. We shop more often as we don't have room for a bag of oranges for example or too many vegetables. Just finding the milk I like can cause excitement! It's very different to being at home! What would appear to be a minor repair at home becomes a major issue on the road because once the repair is completed it can make the world of difference to our comfort. John's bed frame needed repair for example and we could not say 'Swap the beds around and we'll get that one repaired sometime'. We are so happy with this van though because it is so very comfortable for long-term travelling.

A lady the other day was boasting that they'd 'done the Northern Territory in a tent with their only concession to comfort being a blow-up mattress'. I'm not sure if we were supposed to congratulate her because we were both staring at her in disbelief! Her husband said that they'd only bought their caravan as they were now getting older and preferred a bit more comfort. I nodded madly in agreement and said 'I can understand that' and was able to avoid answering his wife. They've been around Australia a couple of times. I'm way past that kind of lifestyle - a week or two in a tent is fun but trying to keep a tent clean of grit and sand and avoiding falling over bags, quilts and pillows along with the other bits and pieces stored under cover can get quite irritating after that and if you've got to put it up and down and pack everything away every night or couple of days - well I wouldn't last the distance! I'd rather sleep in a car if I was travelling like that and store my cooking things in the boot. We see a lot of kombi vans with rear opening doors with kitchens in and they seem very convenient and can accommodate a comfy mattress - but we feel very lucky to have found this. We also get advice from people that we can save money by using a field outside some town or other or where the free barbecues are to save using our gas. They probably spend as much on petrol finding free sites to move to all the time and free barbecues as we do just going from A to B and paying for a caravan park. We are averaging $18 per night and can use our air conditioner whenever we want (or the electric heater), leave lights on, have endless hot showers and leave the van for as long as we like knowing that it is safe and so are the things we use outside, like tables and chairs and dog beds etc. We would not be able to do that if parked at a truck stop, a field or as one person suggested 'You can camp free at the back of that car yard for a couple of weeks'. We will spend some night's off-sight and will probably bring our average costs down but only on long boring stretches of road and we have not reached roads like that yet. It feels like home when we get settled into a park. Like chameleons, we adjust to our ever-changing surroundings.

At this very moment John is at the dentist, Jack needs his special bath, I must sew some tags back on the front screen curtains, just finished hand-washing jumpers which will dry quickly as it is such a beautiful day again today (about 24C, sunny and breezy), have organised for a new pergola roof at our rental property at Cabarita as they had a storm which blew part of it off and this again is an insurance job! The gas water-heater is playing up again and we're going to have to find someone to service it albeit we've failed to find anyone in this area so far who is willing to take on the job. We also need to clean and polish both vehicles before they ban hosepipe use in the Illawarra area and the water restrictions are imminent unless it rains soon. Got a cheque off the dog-washer this morning and he's still standing as I stayed inside the van so I couldn't strangle him. Do I need to get any meat out of the freezer for dinner? What shopping do I need today? Still haven't finished the weekend newspapers. I must clean the fly screens..........

When I started this diary I named it 'Should I Tour Australia' and I'll read it next Christmas when we are back in our house because it is at that time that we have to review this trip and decide whether to go right around this gigantic continent or not. I have to be realistic and include all the things that go wrong as well as remind myself about the wonderful days that we spend sightseeing. Nearly everyone who travels like this loses an awning at some time or another so that's pretty normal everyday stuff. Pets get sick, people get sick, things break down - all the same things that happen at home. I had no illusions prior to leaving home. I did not really think it was going to be some long, lazy holiday and that we would drive off into continual sunshine and spend our days lying on beaches. In fact I was actually a little wary about the venture as some of you may remember. The biggest complaint that we've heard is from women who cannot get used to having their husbands around twenty-four hours a day. That's not a problem that I have because we had both become used to not working and being at home together all the time. We have guaranteed time alone to dream when we travel from place to place as we drive individual vehicles - we both enjoy that space. On the whole, it has probably been easier than I imagined and John has certainly not had the time to get bored yet, which he feared. I rarely have the time to read a book, let alone do the puzzles I expected to do, nor have I had time to have another look at the desktop publishing manual! I enjoy life in the van and I enjoy it when we settle down for a while. John has also slowed down so it is now far more relaxing. Could I go on doing this forever? Too soon to tell yet. I always said that we would need more than six months because I think that at the six month point I may have had enough and I will need to get over that and come out the other side before I can make any judgements. At the moment it still feels like we have only been on the road about three weeks and by this time next week it will have been three months and I'll have aged another year to boot! Doesn't time fly!

Sunday

Our van park had filled up not only with vans but also with vintage cars! Today was the parade in **Robertson** and we'd not yet been there. We set off on an indirect route as we wanted to see some more waterfalls on the way. First stop was the Hindmarsh Lookout which looks over the Kangaroo Valley and then on to Belmore Falls. This time we met a dirt road and a ford, but our Ute handled the water depth even if John's shoes didn't - yes he decided to get out and explore! The waterfall drops into Kangaroo Valley and on into the Kangaroo River so John had another bird's eye view of that area and is now satisfied that he's seen it. The journey to these lookouts was so beautiful. We rolled up and down hills with views of green pastures, the shimmer of the water in the Fitzroy Falls Reservoir, over creeks that shone like diamonds in the sun and the colours were so varied because of the autumnal colours of the trees. The deciduous trees clothed in gold, glistening in the sun - their final tribute before winter hibernation - others in a tartan of green and red, the deep green of the evergreen pines and the lighter green of the weeping willows. It was one of those journeys that you wish you'd captured on a video. We came back down to earth in Robertson which is a fairly ordinary town with some quite attractive old buildings and we spent a while inspecting the vintage cars. We found the Robertson Pie Shop as mentioned in our guide and bought a couple for lunch but my steak and mushroom pie had so much pepper in it that John ended up eating it for me! We then turned towards the coast in our hunt for the Carrington Falls. That was quite crowded with people having picnics and enjoying the various walking paths. In summer it would be a good place to go for a swim in the water holes there. We returned along the Illawarra Highway to Moss Vale which is the road we will be taking to Kiama when we return to the coast to continue our journey.

CHAPTER THIRTY

KANGAROO VALLEY

To some of you who find the details of the routes we travel boring, I must tell you that this letter goes out to many people and several are keeping every letter as they intend to travel this way. It's not meant to be a 'tourist book' but more of what it's really like living on the road. However, I have friends in Tasmania who want to know the names of every caravan park and as much detail as possible. Another friend is also keeping a copy of every letter. There's a friend in Canada who apparently has had the same misconceptions as I had about Australia before I left England and who has found through my letters and the internet sites that I have recommended that this country is actually quite beautiful. There are friends who have toured but not yet in this area and others who hope to one day like my daughter's friend who cannot even tour around her own home without difficulty at the moment because she is nine months pregnant. There are also friends who just want me to keep in touch and they have no intentions whatsoever of even considering this type of travel.

I have to write this anyway as nearly everyone who tours like this gets muddled up with names. We were chatting to a couple the other night and the lady has an in-depth knowledge of history including all the names of the kings and queens of England and who married whom and who was related to who or who had affairs with whoever and then she asked her husband 'That place where we saw (whatever), was that (wherever)?' and most times her husband said that she had the wrong name for whichever town or village she was referring to. I felt much better about having to get the map back out after some trips so that I can record this for future reference. They also find it necessary to keep records. In a year's time, if we want to come back this way (and I'm sure we will) I will be able to refer back to my list of caravan parks that I am keeping, our photos and the areas that we've visited. Already John and I refer to parks that we've stayed at in the following manner 'What area was that park where they had a weekend party under a marque and we had a lot of space next to a lake?' or 'What town was that where we stayed at a park and met that lovely couple who had just started travelling and who had to return to Sydney for the birth of a new grandchild?'.

MONDAY

Today was my day as it is my Birthday. I chose to go to **Bowral** with a list of book shops that I wanted to go to and a shop that sells cashmere! The bookshops varied from the ABC shop to one with newspapers dating back to the 1800's. One of them had a coffee bar attached so we stopped a little longer. We could not resist one antique store as all we could see from the road was an archway and were totally amazed to find a Tudor street inside, with doorways off to Tudor rooms where all manner of things were displayed including old uniforms. I rather fancied one of the male models in a red soldier's uniform - thought he would go well with that granny model I wanted for my front hallway at home. When we left Bowral we headed over the bridge and found a golf club which John checked out for future reference and then we just drove - it didn't matter where as the scenery is all so beautiful. So, it was by accident that we found the Berkelouw Book Barn and Café and realised that we were just outside of Berrima again (the village that we liked so much with the Court House). By this time it was 3pm and we were so hungry for lunch that we headed straight for the café. After a fabulous spinach quiche with salad and a berry muffin I was ready to tackle a few of the thousands of books inside the barn. John had quiche too but then returned for a meat pie and salad plus a coffee! We returned home tired and content - another lovely day.

WEDNESDAY

This **Illawarra region** has got into my blood and I think it has captured John's heart too, because of his exclamations today when we travelled home via **Kangaroo Valley**. We cannot get into a caravan park at the coast for another week because of the dogs and school holidays - the two do not mix according to the park owners. As we have to wait, I suggested that we start exploring the coast now, using Moss Vale as our home base. We set off for Shellharbour this morning but only stopped there when taking photos, mainly because we couldn't take the dogs onto the beaches there. We headed for **Kiama**, stopping at Bombo Beach on the way. We did a fair bit of trekking around there, up and around a headland and thought we'd found the blowhole we'd heard about. We hadn't, we found the right blowhole at Kiama and that was obvious because of the amount of tourists. We actually think that the blowhole at Bombo Beach is better but it was a little difficult to find. Kiama is a lovely town and fascinating. We will definitely come back here another day as there is so much to explore.

The journey down from Moss Vale to the coast had been so precarious that we decided to try another route back. We were hoping for a road without 25k speed limits around blind bends, 360 degree tight corners (or so they seemed) a road where John would not have to back up the van to try and get around the bends in the way the semi-trailer did this morning whilst a queue of cars waited impatiently behind. The only route we could find was to continue south towards Nowra and turn inland at Berry and back via Kangaroo Valley. At every turn John said 'I can manage this' until eventually he said 'Well, we're up and it wasn't too bad at all'. I then reminded him that we had not yet reached Kangaroo Valley and it suddenly dawned on him that we'd probably drop again, which we did. The scenery was fabulous and **Kangaroo Valley** turned out to be a village which is so pretty that we want to go back to it. When we climbed back up towards Moss Vale we did face severe bends but we only saw one car all the way, so it will be our preferred route. We also noticed how much cooler it became. It has been so hot here, 'unceasingly hot for the last fourteen days' we are told on the News. That would be right, just about the same length of time that we've been here. I don't seem to escape the sun! This morning saw me up at 6.30am and outside in the heavy mist with the dogs - it was so cool and the peace was only disturbed only by the sound of the chattering birds. Oh yes, and me laughing at Callie because she suddenly howled like Jack does - it was a bit croaky but she's trying so hard to talk like him! She just sat down, looked at me and made this tremendous effort to do it; it was fabulous.

Anyway, we feel overwhelmed again tonight because we have realised how much there will be to see and explore along the next section of coastline. When will we reach Melbourne! The guide books don't mention a lot about the scenery and how the rolling hills continue right down to the sea - I thought I'd have to say farewell to them when we left for the coast. The only time that 'spectacular scenery' is mentioned is when referring to the mountains further inland. One of the tourist attractions inland is the Wombeyan Caves, about 1½-2hours inland from here. I have suggested to John that we drive at least part of the route through the mountains because I cannot imagine any scenery more beautiful than we have already seen. I do know that a good part of the road is unsealed, so how far we go may depend on the road. Not tomorrow though - we need these alternate days off as we feel almost drunk with beautiful scenery. I haven't been anywhere in Australia that compares to this area. Mind you, I've hardly seen anything really when I look at the map - oh my, Australia is so big.

CHAPTER THIRTY-ONE

Our friend from Sydney lobbed up again at 9am and I was still in my pyjamas and we were surrounded by tins of food, kitchen drawers, cutlery and all the other paraphernalia we keep in our kitchen cupboards. I had found what I had thought to be cockroach droppings in the cupboards on Thursday but by Friday that had turned into a hunt for a rat! It had chewed through the cap of a bottle of oil and through the lid of our bread bin. My friend in Tasmania told me about the trouble she had had with her car when a mouse chewed her wiring and we are surrounded by a maze of wiring in the walls, ceiling and floor of this van, let alone the engine! John started checking mouse traps and asked our visitor to look under his bed whilst he held it up. So he found the dead mouse for us and disposed of it for us. Having explained that we were flooding the caravan park and couldn't use the mains water power any longer, he also investigated and repaired the problem with a $7 part from the local hardware store and then he took us out for a roast lunch! We had paid over $700 for an 'expert' to find out where the leak was in our water pump and to stop our house tank from overflowing a couple of months ago and after two days nothing had been accomplished and now both are perfect. It is so good to have a friend like him.

I've just finished a long novel and all is well with the world until John shows me a newspaper article on the joys of camping. Thanks to an article in the Sydney Morning Herald, I am now in deep contemplation. To sum up, the writer talks of the joy of not feeling guilty when relaxing by a river in a tent having left behind her home office, dishwasher, cleaning projects and home maintenance and all of the other electrical appliances that consume so much of our time rather than saving it. She asks why we cannot relax in our own homes any more without feeling guilty because there is always something that needs doing. I can so understand what she is saying - I feel like I've found a friend! Our problem is that we've bought our home with us and yes we have the computer which needs attention in case it catches bugs (as she mentioned) and maintenance and cleaning projects (I've just cleaned the ceiling and the fly screens at long last and the carpet needs scrubbing) and we do tend to feel that if we have one day doing the washing, shopping and cleaning then we ought to be sightseeing the next day. We also watch T.V. Thank goodness I have just read a wonderful novel because that was relaxing and if I hadn't I would now be feeling guilty that we don't relax enough! Obviously we have the luxury of this motor home rather than a tent and a motor home is going to require more maintenance but are we doing this the right way? Would it be better to live in a small home which we lock up every three months or so and head off without computer and quite so many kitchen appliances and eat out more and relax more? No, that wouldn't work because I need to download my digital camera or it would fill up too quickly and I find hand-writing difficult and I'd want to keep some memories written down. So I'm a bit confused. Perhaps we should stay at home and buy a tent after all! Just go off for weekends or a couple of weeks at a time. Will we adjust to relaxing - what a question. It's three months now and yes, I think John is slowing down - hold that thought right there - John has just walked in and said 'I want to do something today. Come on, let's not hang around'!

We went to Kangaroo Valley. On the way there we stopped to investigate 'Grandpa's Shed' which amused us for an hour. There was so much there that reminded me of my childhood. The old wringer that Mum had for so many years - I used to turn the handle whilst she fed the sheets through and she refused to ever have a washing machine. There was a handbag with a long shoulder strap which I used to play with so often whilst pretending to be a bus-conductress and give tickets to all my dolls to ride on my bus. There was an old tin tea caddy, the wind-up gramophone player, even some old dried flower arrangements in baskets that surely must have been hers. There was even my potty that lived under my bed! In fact, there were so many items that seemed familiar that I realised that today's trash is definitely tomorrow's treasure. It's strange to see things used in my own lifetime now being labelled 'collectables'. I feel that I must stress that my mother had me very late in life and I am not ninety plus years of age! She also loved antiques, painted and taught flower arranging and anything that she could do with her hands, like knitting ceaselessly or planting out the most beautiful garden in the area was just bliss to her but offer her anything that was new and electrical and she hated the sight of it. We didn't even get a television until my brother got hold of one when a golf tournament was being televised and my father, being an excellent golfer himself, was instantly smitten and so it stayed. When I was a small child we lived in an enormous old house, the bedrooms were upstairs and the bathroom and toilet were down – about a mile away from the bottom of the stairs, or so it seemed to me on my little legs – thus the pot under the bed! Where were we?

At **Kangaroo Valley** we were surrounded by old stores selling every kind of craft imaginable, pottery, art gallery, antique stores and so many places to eat and drink. We chose the wrong place to have coffee as the outside table was swarming with flies, the chairs inside were stacked against the tables and obviously not to be used, service appalling and the young girl came outside at my request, flicked a tea towel over the long table to 'clean' it and collected dirty crockery only to go back inside and serve customers without washing her hands and without using tongs to pick up the cakes! They have all these awards for their bakery items, which is why we had gone there and there was me feeling sick because of the staff's appalling attitude. When I said that my coffee was not hot I was told it was because I had milk in it! There are so many lovely places to eat so be warned.

We took the dogs down to the river under the Hampden suspension bridge and Jack kept returning to drink the water whilst Callie danced about in it - it was so clear it was like glass and obviously tasted good too. Kangaroo Valley is well worth a visit and as we will be using this route to get to the coast next week, John was pleased to get another look at the bends he will have to negotiate. And yes, it was relaxing, unlike some of our other days sight-seeing which have been exhausting.

CHAPTER THIRTY-TWO

FITZROY FALLS

As today was a public holiday we cleaned up the van and did all the washing as though we were about to leave tomorrow. We're actually leaving on Wednesday morning but I want tomorrow free to walk around the shops in Moss Vale as I haven't yet done so! The last three weeks have flown by. I would also love to get the chance to get back to Bowral and buy some more hormone and chemical free meat! I cannot recall when I ever had meat like it - it equals the horse meat I ate in Brittany, France and the steak fondues I ate in Geneva (probably also horse). I had bought some lamb cutlets and veal steaks (we have yet to eat the chicken, chicken breasts and bacon) and they melted in our mouths. Both were cut about three times the thickness to those purchased in supermarkets and any butchers I've been to in the past. The veal steak was so thick and large I only ate half and John sliced the rest for sandwiches the following day! I will certainly be more selective as to where I buy my meat in future.

We left Moss Vale yesterday having stocked up on meat on Tuesday! We never did make it to the mountains but on our journey down to Nowra we stopped again at Kangaroo Valley - mainly to give the traffic a chance to pass us. John drove superbly but some of the hills are so steep that he was flat out getting up them at 20kph! We refreshed at the Blind Toucan Café (where did they get a name like that from?) and chose to share a huge slab of carrot cake and fresh cream with our coffees. If you pass by that way, stop and enjoy! We then had to climb out of the valley again and then drop down to Nowra. After a great deal of debate we had settled on basing ourselves at Nowra so that we can explore north to Kiama more thoroughly and also south, without having to move the van again. When we arrived here we were given a site right near the entrance, opposite the office and toilets - it was under trees but I wasn't overly enthusiastic. Anyway, we had to empty our waste first and when we returned the guy in charge called us and said that he'd forgotten that we are self-contained and would we like to park down by the river. We jumped into the Ute and went to explore. We found a beautiful stretch of grass and long river frontage with three barbecue areas under pergolas where we had been told we could plug into the electric socket and to the water tap there and it was so lovely we moved the van immediately. It's great for the dogs too and for fishing! John still uses the shower block as it's not very far away but I just love our own shower/bath.

BADGERY'S LOOKOUT

Today we first went to look at an Australian Winnebago centre and checked out the 36tft one to compare it with our American one. The lounge has the slide out so it is very large but the kitchen had less than I have now (which is minimal), the fridge and freezer were both smaller, there was only one sink, the tiny bathroom vanity was in the corner of the corridor with a cupboard immediately above it which we would both hit our heads on when cleaning our teeth and the shower was smaller. There were several things we did not like in it and it sells for around $498,000!

From there we headed along the coast to visit all the seaside villages and towns up to and including Kiama. There was little to see at Shoalhaven Heads unless you like very quiet areas, **Gerroa** was quite nice, **Gerringong** was lovely and we ended up stopping there for a beautiful meal, wine and coffee at the Bowls Club. It was really very pleasant there and a lady kindly explained the rules of bowls as we watched a ladies match. So I now know that someone chucks (sorry - 'bowls') a little ball out first and that is called a Jack. You try to bowl your ball as near to it as possible. We watched someone do that and then the next person knocked the Jack with their ball and it and the other balls went all over the place but apparently that is allowed. I came to the conclusion that it's best to be the last player because at least you know where the Jack is going to end up and no-one is left to knock yours out of the way! There must be more to it than I yet know.

We went on to **Kiama**, which is just up the road and spent some time looking at The Terrace which was a row of miners cottages which have been turned into speciality shops. It was 4pm by this time so we set off to return to Nowra via Berry. The road was closed because of an accident and we were diverted through Gerringong again but got back onto the highway just before Berry. What a lovely place that is with so many old buildings and they had such interesting shops. One was a children's toy shop and John and I loved it. In the window was one of those big, brightly coloured, metal spinning tops that both of us had had as children - the type you press and the faster they spin, the louder they hum. I haven't seen one for years. We saw heaps of art shops, antique stores, fine furnishing shops and all manner of crafts including an organic gift shop. As we returned to the Ute, the first of at least thirty giant semi-trailers came thundering by and we realised that the road must have been reopened. The cars had all been diverted but not the trucks as they would not have been able to go under a bridge. We didn't even know how to get across the road but eventually we got the dogs in the back of the Ute and ducked into a very old hotel which had three log fires blazing and settled down with drinks whilst we waited for the road to clear. We got on so well with another couple there who had also come in for sanctuary for the same reason, that they asked us to visit them in Manly! We explained about our 35ft vehicle and how we avoid big cities especially Sydney and they agreed that there would be nowhere to put it in Manly! She was saying that if they did not have to stay with friends that night she would have liked to have stayed on with us - 'ships that pass in the night' as the saying goes - you meet, you 'click' but you have to move on, even with a lifestyle like ours. Life is strange at times and we parted with regret when the friend they were to stay with phoned to find out where they were!

When we looked inland across the rolling fields to the hills today, John said that the fields look so green and soft you feel that you could wrap yourself up in them like a blanket. Moss Vale and its surrounding scenery affected him as deeply as it did me. However, today we could not see the tops of the hills as there was a huge blanket of black clouds completely engulfing them. We must have left within hours of the heavy rain that was forecast. Everywhere has had rain, right up to Brisbane but we've only seen a sprinkling of it and have been travelling around in sunshine all day! We were told on arrival here by one man that it can get down to -8C in winter in Moss Vale - he had a car mechanical business there for fifteen years. Another man told John that it is very cold and damp in winter. The town I'd like to live in was Bowral and it is central to all the villages and not far from the highway. In the winter we could get in our motor home and drive up to sunny Queensland! I kind of know it's not practical because I'd miss my kids too much but it's a lovely dream! Tomorrow we'll investigate Nowra and then we'll start exploring further south.

CHAPTER THIRTY-THREE

Nowra is an interesting town, sort of spread out with some fine old arcades as well as having a bridge over the main road to connect the original shopping area to the Woolworths, Target, K Mart and Coles complex on the other side. I like the town side as it's easy to park and it has a very good variety of individual shops and I do get so fed up with the same old shopping complexes with all the same fashion shops etc.

Nowra comes from an aboriginal name meaning 'black cockatoo' or 'camping place'. We went up to the Nowra Showground and found the Hanging Rock Lookout with wonderful views across the Shoalhaven River. The streets around the town are wide and attractive with heaps of trees lining the roads and some lovely old houses. After lunch we went south-east to explore. The area we travelled was so flat and contrasted with the scenery we have been experiencing over the last few weeks but when we reached Greenwell Point we found a quiet area with the most beautiful water views. It is a lovely area and would be a good place to stay, especially if you like fishing. We back-tracked to Pyree and then followed the road to Culburra, Orient Point and finally to Crookhaven Heads. These areas were even quieter - not a sign of commercialisation which was refreshing - unless you want to buy a cup of coffee that is, on a very cool and extremely windy day! The kind of day when you need two jumpers and there is no way you can keep a hat on but the choppy seas were a delight to look at. The dogs found it very exciting, in fact Jack was like a puppy and was totally exhilarated by the weather! I was a little concerned tonight when I was trying to cook dinner and the van was rocking but it has calmed down now thank goodness.

Sunday 2nd May

Another touring day - bright and sunny but with a very cold, gusty wind. How long we stayed in a place was determined by how sheltered the place was! Hats blowing off, eyes running and hair blowing over the camera lens! Nowra, **Huskisson** (a fabulous place), **Vincentia**, where we boiled the billy and then continued down the road and found **Blenheim Beach** which wasn't even on the local tourist map and standing at the lookout John said it only needed a couple of Hawaiian dancers to complete the scene! Next **Hyams Beach** (don't eat at the café there as the price of fish and chips goes up if you want to sit down to eat, the fish wasn't cooked and nor was the inner batter and it was horribly slimy). However, go past the village shop/café and when you get to a No Through Road sign you will see a car park to the left. This has to be one of the most beautiful beaches I have ever seen with the purest white soft sand. There's another beach the other side of the shop, where the boats go in but unless you need the loo, don't bother. When we got to **Jervis Bay** we found an entry fee of $10 ($5 for pensioners) and apparently there are fifteen houses in the village for the workers and that's it. That's fine unless you want lunch as we did so we didn't go in. By this time we had seen all the villages around Jervis Bay and headed for the **St Georges Basin** area - **Erowal Bay, St Georges Basin, Sanctuary Point, Basin View** and then around the other side to **Sussex Inlet**. We missed Swanhaven (on the lake) and ended up down the coast at **Cudmirrah** and **Berrara**. We came home with heads spinning again and the camera full of wonderful photographs and so glad we'd found that unadvertised, well hidden beach. So we're off again tomorrow and the next stop will be Kioloa.

CHAPTER THIRTY-FOUR

KIOLOA. We finally parked the R.V. put the awning up, got all the outdoor furniture set up, connected up the electrics and then realised there was no water tap! Our water tank was only a quarter full as John had been working on a leaking tap. Apparently we should have filled up on entry to the park but we weren't advised of that when we booked in! We washed up outside the laundry and had a bucket of water to flush the toilet and both agreed we might just as well of camped off-road for nothing. Apparently you can in the State Forest here. Our water heater wouldn't heat because the tank was near empty and we had to pay for showers, which were on a timer so you had to be quick. To cap it off, neither the Optus phone nor the Telstra phone could pick up any signal. With direct access to the beach, the dogs loved it and sulked when we arrived at our next stop. They watched us set up everything - they know the routine - and then refused to get out of the Ute! I tried to coax Jack with a dog treat but he wouldn't eat it. We got him moving by saying 'Walkies' but then he tried to get back in the Ute again! We are now at **Cullendulla**, about 12ks north of Batemans Bay and the park is on 45 acres surrounded on three sides by the Murramarang National Park. It is becoming very hard to find parks that will accept dogs and our R.V. If we had a caravan we'd have more options. After this park we will have to travel about 71ks to get to another park that will accept dogs and I do not know if they have room for our rig. No dogs, no problem as there are plenty of parks in and around Batemans Bay.

When we moved to Kioloa we jumped about 100ks and I didn't want to do that as I felt we'd miss too much. We stopped on the way at ~~Ulladulla~~ where you can park on the bridge overlooking the harbour and it was so lovely that I wanted to return so the next day we did. John wanted to see the two golf courses on the hills overlooking the ocean. We went to Mollymook first though, which is just north of the town and the whole area is lovely, hilly and with a beach advertised as the most beautiful of eastern Australia. It's not but it's worth a look. It's a big bay with a lovely natural rock pool up one end and apparently a lot of surf championships are held there. I would think that the homes around the area would fetch a high price. We went up to a headland overlooking Ulladulla, the harbour and other headlands - quite beautiful. We traced the golf clubs and visited the lighthouse at Ulladulla and then went to the RSL club for lunch. I had 'all you can eat from the salad bar' along with three huge sausages covered in thick mushroom sauce and chips - all for $6. By the time I had finished my wine I could have curled up in the sunshine and gone to sleep but we were on a mission to find the stingrays that we'd been told about by a young woman back at Mollymook. I wish I could find her to thank her.

We had to backtrack up the highway to the area that we'd missed on our journey to Kioloa, to find a beach at **Bendalong**, 13ks off the highway along the Bendalong Mountain Road. The journey back along the highway through **Milton** seems even more spectacular when driving from south to north than it does the other way around, so that was a bonus in itself! We turned to the coast past **Lake Conjola** and the Conjola National Park. There are so many small bays in this area, all stunning but we had to find a beach where metal tables are set up on the rocks for the fishermen to gut their fish. It actually turned out to be **Washerwomans Beach**! Apparently when the sea is rough the tides come in from both ends of the bay and the result is turbulence with high peaks of frothy water. We were lucky as it was the first beach we stopped at and I immediately saw a stingray in the water and leaving the dogs in the car I ran down to the beach.

JOHN FEEDING STINGRAY

We had been told that we would find some fish carcass on the rocks, left there daily by the fisherman when they gut their fish, but I immediately found two whole fish, tore off my socks and shoes and ran to the water. Apparently, if you paddle around they will come to visit but I wanted food ready. By the time John joined me there were two stingrays circling around and I gave him a fish. John, who hates the thought of handling fish, let alone gutting them, was as entranced as I was and went and found another with the entrails hanging out to attract them back once they had swum away. Unlike fish who swim away once fed, the stingrays hung around, squirted water at us and flapped their huge 'flippers' (for want of a better word) as if to say 'Thank you'. Then off they would go around the bay only to return for another stroke, another flap of thanks and off again. It was a magical experience. As John said, they are so trusting. They are also so graceful. Apparently, if angry, they can hit you with their tails and if they do the end comes off and is left attached to wherever they hit you. We did not take the dogs down because we were not sure how Jack would react, although there were other dogs on the beach. The stingrays were so huge that I think Jack would have been frightened. We stroked them and I felt a tail which was so hard - you wouldn't want to be hit with one. This experience has turned out to be one of the highlights out of all the scenery we saw and places we visited. (We have a printed photo of John feeding one of the stingrays on a coffee mat on the desk beside this laptop and we always look at it in awe and the memories flood back.) There is a caravan park there called Bendalong Bay Tourist Park but they do not allow dogs.

We went on to **Manyana** and then to **Red Head Point** and then on to **Cunjurong Point** where we looked down to an island we had been told about. You can walk out to it through the water but by this time it was getting too late. We did trek through the bush to the viewing platform though and raced back with the dogs - Callie could not catch on that if I shook her lead and said 'Gee up' she was supposed to run faster but Jack, who was behind knew it was a race and was determined to get past me! Back in the car, John took a wrong turning and we ended up at **Conjola Lake** and it was so very beautiful. With not a soul around it was also so peaceful. When we left, wild kangaroos ran across the road and Jack went absolutely wild in the back of the Ute and Callie was nearly exploding with excitement. I believe it is the first time Jack has ever seen them and two of the kangaroos were really huge. We saw some more but not at such close range. Anyway, it is an area that you mustn't miss if travelling this way - just as that young woman told us back at Mollymook. I have so many stunning photographs I could make a book out of them, including some of John with the stingrays. That night all had been quiet when suddenly I heard a sound I didn't recognise. 'What's that?' I asked John optimistically

'What's what' he responded - I should have known better.

'That weird noise' I said but of course it had stopped by then. Then it happened again. 'That' I said.

'Yeah, I heard it' he answered and carried on reading.

'Well aren't you going to investigate?'

'I don't know what it is' he answered.

'But it's a strange noise!' I exclaimed getting frustrated.

Have you ever watched ABC at 6pm on a Saturday when 'As Time Goes By' is on - sometimes I think we are so much like them it is quite embarrassing. John feels uncomfortable because he reckons the male role was based on him, when he's being grumpy!

'Well I'm going to investigate if you're not. What about the dogs?'

'It could be Callie' he said.

'No, what about the dogs being attacked by something and they are tied up and wouldn't be able to defend themselves' I said. With that he looked mildly interested. Feeling really irritated by this point I grabbed the torch and as I went out I said 'It could be a snake about to attack them and kill them.' (I had to find some way of getting the man up!)

He calmly followed me out and I waved the torch around the ground to emphasise the point that a death was obviously imminent and to ensure that he realised just how heroic I was being, totally ready and prepared to fight to save those I love – with a torch – but I couldn't see a thing! I started to check the trees for snakes and then it happened again. It was a bit like a cat when it hisses but different. John was now showing interest but I don't think it had anything to do with my theatrical display but that he'd probably just heard it for the first time! Or perhaps I'm being too magnanimous because at home we were both in bed about 1am and heard a noise downstairs once but he couldn't be bothered getting out of bed so I had to get up to investigate! Anyway we found 'it' and 'it' turned out to be a rather large possum in a tree beside our van. He was on the trunk about eight feet off the ground and it did not like the dogs. I pointed the torch at its eyes and after a few seconds of hissing and glaring at me it moved up the tree. I repeated the process and it went higher and so forth until it finally decided that here was not a good place to stay. Now I know some people say they are cute and make little possum houses for them in their gardens and leave them fruit to eat and all that but they can also leave a nasty smell if they decide to live in your roof, even if you can put up with the patter of tiny feet overhead at night but we are surrounded by National park here and they have plenty of places to live. They can kill a cat and I don't want a scuffle between it and my dogs but at least I will recognise that strange noise in future. It was so cute though with such beautiful big eyes.

CHAPTER THIRTY-FIVE

DURASS SOUTH

Saturday 8th May

I nipped into **Batemans Bay** this morning for a bit of female retail therapy – no that's not the truth - I'd broken my glasses and needed some 'time-out' so used the glasses as an excuse. It's a five minute drive down the Princes Highway so this is a very convenient park to stay at and having seen some other parks today, I'm glad we're staying here. My glasses were repaired for free and I enjoyed wandering around by myself.

I returned to collect John and to have a cup of coffee and then we drove to **Nelligen**, a beautiful old village on the river not far from here, along the Kings Highway (very Royal around here aren't they). It really is worth a look because the river winds all around it and if you stroll across the spare block of land by the old house which used to be the school, you will see the most glorious view of the river. A couple of doors away there is the old Court House which is now used for a church. At the bottom of the hill is parkland along another stretch of the river. After lunch we had a look at **Durras South** and then went to **Long Beach** where I nearly lost Callie out of the Ute window. She saw another kangaroo and I glanced in my side mirror to see her front legs protruding and then her stomach and managed to stop the car before she fell out! Now the window is nearly shut as we cannot take the risk. Either the kangaroo would run off, with her after it and she would get lost or it could attack her and she probably wouldn't survive. She and Jack bounce around like lambs sometimes when they are happy and because she's seen Jack doing it she thinks that the kangaroo wants to play with her.

Whilst shoving Callie's bum back through the Ute window I got talking to a young mother with four-month-old twin boys. She told me that if a woman has invitro-fertilisation she usually has girls but if a woman needs injections for polycystic ovaries (another form of IVF) she usually has boys. I don't need to know this of course but I found it an interesting fact! She was told she couldn't have children and had her first child quite naturally, a boy. To have another child she had the treatment and had twin boys and now she has a second set of twin boys. I suggested she stop trying to have children and she may find she has another one naturally and it might just be a girl and she agreed that is exactly what she is going to do. Apparently she will still need the injections every three months or so though or there is a chance she could get cancer in the ovaries. She added that she always wanted a big family anyway but that the cost of this medical assistance is so expensive - what a choice - pay for the treatment or chance getting cancer and she's only thirty now!

A little further on, at the end of the beach, we were about to get the dogs out to take them for a swim as it was a leash free area for dogs, when I saw about twenty kangaroos on the grass next to us! The nearest one had a joey protruding from its pouch and two of them were big males. John approached them and then stopped, with the dogs watching from the car window. Then he retreated again back to the car without getting too near to them and we are hoping the dogs are getting the message - don't go near! Who knows, we can but try!

TOMAKIN HEADLAND - LOOKING NORTH

Long Beach was a lovely residential area, very hilly and winding roads with a stunning variety of architecture - old and new and renovated all blending together and if you stay on the coast road you can get back to Batehaven although the road does not show up on our map. Batehaven town centre is attractive, modern and bustling and it's not easy to find a parking place on a Saturday morning! In the centre there are free half hour spots but everywhere else you pay fifty cents for two hours. They are building a multi-storey complex at the moment which has free parking beneath not far from the Tourist Information Centre. The town is right beside the harbour so you can walk to everything and you can suggest your man explore the harbour whilst you find where to spend his money! Tomorrow we explore the coastline south of Batehaven before moving off on Monday down to Narooma.

Mothers Day

My son was the first to wake me up! I'll amend that. I was not that coherent! I had just got back to sleep and then it was my daughter. I was up and dressed by the time my other son phoned. Bless you all my wonderful kids. I miss seeing you all so much. My foster-daughter in England wouldn't know it is Mother's Day here as the day is celebrated a different month in England and I have no idea when theirs is. She has too many mothers anyway as she has met her birth mother and has had a second long-term foster mother who, in my mind, is her real 'Mum' and as I've said, she's now a mother herself. Her 'parents' are great and keep in touch with me which is really lovely.

We set off about 10.30am. South of Batemans Bay we saw **Surf Beach, Lilli Pilli** and **Malua Bay** which was quite pretty. We were mainly looking at the beaches and bays rather than the actual places. We found a place called **Mackenzie Beach** which was not on our map and I grabbed my camera - a beautiful small beach fronting a wide bay. We then turned off to **Gorilla Bay**, which was also not on the map, which was stunning. We headed towards the beach and turned left at the T-junction and found a National Heritage Area. It seemed that the places not mentioned are the most spectacular. We went up to Burrewarra Point (which is mentioned) but dogs were not allowed and you needed to go down walking tracks to see anything and we decided that we'd move on. We found **Tomakin Headland** further on and that had fabulous views. We stopped at Tomakin Beach for a coffee (flask), toilets and found that dogs were allowed on the beach so we all enjoyed a half hour run around - yes I can still run! **Mossy Point** and **Broulee** were next (the latter suburban) but if you carry on until you see the caravan park sign and turn left up the hill there is a small parking spot on the right and a short, small path on the headland with wonderful beach and hinterland views of the mountain range. Continue to end of road (short distance) and there is more room to park and a path between the trees. Just a little way down you'll get a wonderful view of **Broulee Island**, which you can walk to from the beach below. We left the dogs in the car for these mini walks.

At **Moruya** we had a fish and chip lunch and drove around looking at some fine old buildings and as usual, the Court House was the grandest. This has been the case in most places we have visited. We returned to Batemans Bay along the Princes Highway (only 26ks instead of double that via the coast road) and stopped at the historical town of **Mogo**. There was a fine variety of craft, gift and art shops/galleries and we saw some lovely leather and wool products but the shops, although fascinating, tended to be spoilt as nearly all of them had a vast selection of imported Asian goods. It's a pity they did not stick to Aussie products. I have some bird ornaments at home which I bought from Crazy Clarkes for about $3.50 which are outside in an old fashioned bird cage and here they were priced at about $7.50 plus items of clothing that you can buy from any old import shop for about $10 being sold at very high prices. On the other hand they had some candles made by a local artist selling for $2 which were really good. It put me off buying anything from any of the shops though as I did not want to find out later that I had been fleeced!

CHAPTER THIRTY-SIX

In all it's been an interesting but emotional week! When we last moved we were driving along the highway when I started to feel weird. Stomach started rumbling and then my chest and I seriously wondered if I was becoming ill! Then I found my throat constricted and then my cat Tootsie flew into my mind from nowhere and I found I was starting to cry but I couldn't as I was driving! Well, my mind could not overrule my emotions and this time and I couldn't stop! It's taken me four months to really grieve and it was when I was quite relaxed on a good road with music playing and nothing much on my mind and I was taken completely off-guard. Even after I had stopped the car I started again. It took me ten years to grieve for my father so I guess it always comes out in the end but it's so weird.

Then yesterday one of my sons said to me on the phone 'I told a friend that you wouldn't last nine months on the road because your home has always been important to you' (or words to that effect). That set me thinking and I couldn't get to sleep and was still awake at 2am, which is why I was incoherent this morning when he phoned! It's so true - I need my nest and like a bird I can leave it but I need to know it's there and safe. I'm not worried about our house at the moment but he's right that I could not do this continually. The problem is John as he wants to, with just short breaks between. He reckons he's too young to do voluntary work and be tied down by it yet but may consider it in the future. Wanting to travel different roads (literally) caused a very disturbed night and a lot of talking this morning. He said that he had already considered getting a smaller van on our return and going on alone. We have a lot to think about. As I said to him, we only have one life each and he must fulfil his dreams and I don't want to limit him. I also need more time to try things that I want to do, like write, which is a very selfish occupation, as I can sit and write for nine hours and I do not want interruptions. I know this as I wrote a children's story once over two days when I was off work and could not believe that the hours had passed and was quite annoyed that I had to stop to cook him dinner. I didn't tell him what I had been doing all day when he got home as I felt sort of guilty as I'd got nothing else done but was exhausted! It's lucky we both understand each other so well though that we can talk like this without feeling hurt that the other wants to follow a dream alone. I simply couldn't keep this up and I miss my kids just too much. They are more important to me than new places. I want to be available even if they don't need me and I want them to be able to pop in when they want or stay the night. I still need my nest and I'm still a mother hen - it's who I am and what I was born for - to be a mother. And I'm still learning how to be one! It's mostly a rewarding learning curve and I get great joy from my son telling me the obvious - child telling parent. They continue to teach me so much and I love it.

I'm still bemused by the fact that I tried to justify the trip by saying to my son 'Well, we have seen a lot'. A silence and then he answered 'Well isn't that what the trips all about?' Why do we sometimes say the obvious? John went to collect an order for me the other day and as he paid in the shop he said 'It smells very fishy in here' - yeah, he was in the fish co-op! He says he felt so stupid!

Anyway, having pondered for two days on the fact that I am becoming so blasé, having been punch-drunk with beautiful scenery for so many weeks now that I'm not certain that I want to keep this up, I got another lesson. We were nearing Narooma. The road into town is steep and very winding and then quite suddenly when you come around a bend you are almost on a bridge over the river and wow! I cannot recall what I said out loud but the view could cause accidents. I'll tell you about it later.

CHAPTER THIRTY-SEVEN

NAROOMA.

Where are we - I can never remember! Oh yes, I have a leaflet here - Narooma Golf Club and Surfbeach Resort and it's a fabulous place. The golf course is on a headland with the most beautiful views and the caravan park is part of it. A few steps down and we're on the beach and the dogs are allowed to go on most if it. Behind us is a lake and the golf course has all these lakes and crevices in cliffs where your ball can disappear forever. To cap that off Narooma is lovely - wonderful scenery. Oh yes, that bridge - well, we found it yesterday by accident when we followed a board-walk along the inlet and there it was again - the most beautiful scene of the clearest light blue water that you have ever seen - an extraordinary colour - it doesn't look real. It is so clear that you can see everything beneath - absolutely stunning. The dogs couldn't make it out because as we walked along the timber pathway they could see the fish swimming beneath them and all the plants! The name Narooma is derived from the Aboriginal 'clear blue water' and it is so aptly named. So as you arrive you travel down around winding roads and then all of a sudden you see this beautiful river (the inlet from the sea) and the startling colour of the water - such a light blue (in the shade its green) and as clear as crystal and its very hard to keep your eye on the road. You have to approach Narooma from the North to get the impact.

We also drove to **Dalmeny** yesterday which is north of town. We did a big loop and ended up back on the highway and wondered how they could possibly call it a tourist route. There were some long beaches but the town of Dalmeny is a huge residential home area and quite boring. However, on the way back we detoured along the coast road and found a road called Ocean Parade and at the end there was parkland where you can stop and you get the most beautiful view back towards Narooma - well worth finding. It was as we were approaching Narooma but cutting off towards the water all the time, instead of following the tourist route, that we found the boardwalk. So in the end it was worth going!

Shopping and washing day today and not a bad day for John as he's only knocked his head twice on the overhead cupboards. He went to have a look at the cemetery on another headland we can see from here. He was surprised to find that the Catholics and Protestants have separate areas! He said there is a third unnamed area for the rest of the rabble - discrimination is alive and well in Australia, even when you die!

14th May

John wanted to go sightseeing again as he'd had a relaxing day yesterday whilst I did three loads of washing, did the grocery shopping, defrosted the fridge and worked on my new photo album until midnight! I got fed up having to look for photos on the laptop and prefer hard copy but by now I have so many photos that it's been a major job deciding which ones to print and then I had to label them. I also spent time last night resending my emails because I had received a call from a friend to say that my diary letter had not arrived but once they had gone, my inbox filled up and I found that you had received my emails after all! Before we could go sightseeing I had to empty my camera as I had forty-seven photos still on it! John approached me whilst I was downloading with his face screwed up. 'We've caught another mouse' he stated as his face contorted even more.

'Umm' I agreed concentrating on the computer screen 'Where?'

'Under my bed again'.

'Oh dear'

'I suppose I could leave it until we get back?'

'No, it might smell by then'.

'I think it's still alive'.

'Yuk!'

'I suppose I'll have to get rid of it?'

'Umm'. I kept my head down.

He comes back in the van later saying he'd had to kill it. 'That's very brave of you'.

'Brave?'

'Yes, brave. You don't like touching things like that. Couldn't you have let it loose?'

'No, its nose was trapped and I had to hit it with a stick to kill it'.

Ah, my hero. Well I think he's brave because I couldn't have done it.

It was an extremely cold night. The sort of biting cold that keeps you in bed although you are dying for a pee. I returned straight to bed at 7am so I wouldn't have to do the dogs and John would have the fire on before I got up. Yeah, I know I said I wanted the cold but that's all right in a nice warmly-heated house! Ok, that's an excuse. It's been warm today but yesterday the wind had a bite and I loved it. We've been south today. John reckons that 'This place knocks spots off many other places we've been to because of its topography'. I like that word so I said I'd use it in this diary.

CHAPTER THIRTY-EIGHT

CENTRAL TILBA

First stop was **Mystery Bay** but I haven't found out the story yet - I think there's supposed to be one. It is the most glorious spot - sublime - and you can camp there off season for $9.40pn for two people on the grass beside the sea, so long as you get a permit. There's toilets and water provided. We talked seriously about doing so for one night but I've decided that if we're going through all the hoop-la of packing up again, I don't want to do it for one night to a place that's only ten minutes drive away from here and I'd rather move down the coast to Tathra, which is about seventy kilometres. However, Mystery Bay is one of those 'must see' places if you are around this way. We then went to find Central Tilba, west of the highway and a National Trust classified village and **Tilba Tilba**. Do not turn off on the tourist route where it says Tilba Valley Wines like we did. We drove around Mount Dromedary for about three quarters of an hour, mainly on dirt roads and ended up back at Narooma! Go past that sign and Tilba Central is clearly signposted. It's a fabulous village with heaps to see with mainly 19th century weatherboard architecture. Allow yourselves a couple of hours.

Next stop **Wallaga Lake**. Do not take the first sign to the lake that you see. It is an Aboriginal settlement just before the 'Umbarra Cultural Centre' (Aboriginal). What we saw put me off visiting the cultural centre. First to come into view were piles of smashed cars at the side of the road and down ditches. Then a dog loose, then more dogs loose - it's hard to drive along the road because of dogs chasing your vehicle. You can't speed up as there are speed bumps, probably requested by the elders as there were skid marks where car drivers had done wheelies all over the road. Then we saw a modern, lowset brick home totally smashed up. We decided to get out of there. The position of this estate is right beside Wallaga Lake - a beautiful spot but they seem to have no pride in keeping their living area as pristine as their surroundings. There was rubbish everywhere. I saw a woman, who appeared to be very elderly, sweeping her front veranda and I thought that the mayhem we were seeing must make the older women despair. Is it yet another area where the introduction of drink and drugs has desecrated a once proud and dignified tribe? There are so many Aboriginals that have rejoiced in their various talents but why is it that some of the Aboriginals, who have so much of value to teach us about the care of the land, now have so little hope that they too now desecrate it? I find it sad as I have always admired the way they so honoured nature in the past.

Further on there is an open parking area with 360 degree lake views - wonderful and a great place to stop for a picnic. We then went on to **Bermagui,** a tourist town. It's largish but not because of shops but because of motels and units to stay in. A real holiday area with the river, the beaches, swimming pool and golf club all centrally located. A very nice place to stay I should imagine. We headed back to the Princes Highway via **Cobargo**, another old village but there is so much to see there that we decided that we will stop there for coffee tomorrow, en route to Tathra as it's on the main road. So I'm back here writing to you with a camera full of photos again! I must catch up with photos, update my virus scanner and I must answer emails tonight.

I have an emotional battle with computers. I hate them, yet I love the fact that I can use them to write, as my hand writing cannot keep up with my mind and I love the fact that it makes communication so much easier!

I also constantly battle with showers. The kind you use to wash yourself. Many of you will have used caravan park showers and I expect you all managed admirably. I don't as I always get everything wet. I thought I'd got it down pat by going there with nothing on but my thongs and dressing gown, with a pair of clean knickers stuffed into the pocket, plus a small bag with washing stuff. John uses the park showers all the time as he likes the extra room. I prefer to use our own as I can use the whole bathroom and bedroom. However, if I want to deep condition my hair as well as wash it, I use the park ones because our hot water would probably run out! So this last time I forgot the soap, used the shampoo to wash in and just as I was congratulating myself because the shower did not soak my towel or dressing gown, I dropped my clean knickers on the wet floor! Note to all parks - we have been in one where there was a shower curtain and it makes the world of difference as it almost guarantees that the shower water won't attack your towel and clothes hanging on the door!

I decided that I would stop using hair dye and find out what colour my hair really is - go 'au naturale'. So first I started growing it long and now every three weeks I trim it (it grows so quickly) and so far, over four months, I haven't seen a damned bit of difference! I had thought that it would be grey or white by now because I got the first white hair in my thirties (it's still there). All those years of colouring it for no reason!

CHAPTER THIRTY-NINE

EDEN 1

Tuesday 18th May

We're at Merimbula Holiday Park now although we did stop at **Tathra** for a couple of nights at a park which fronted the beach. It's very pretty but there's very little there, the Optus phone didn't work and T.V reception was very poor with no cables provided. We had lots of space down the end of the park and exclusive use of a toilet/shower/laundry block and the dogs could stay loose. We decided to come and have a look at Merimbula yesterday and as soon as we arrived and came across this park we returned to Tathra to move the R.V here. The park owner at Tathra queried our late departure from her park and I told her I had got up late after a couple of bad nights with my back, which was absolutely true but I didn't much like her attitude considering that the park was practically empty so it wasn't as though she had turned anyone away because of lack of available sites.

EDEN 2

Merimbula is a nice town with water everywhere again – lovely beaches and river, an esplanade and a great place to be if you like fishing. They do deep sea fishing tours from here, dolphin cruises and diving to wrecks and sea caves and lake cruises. There's also an airport with air tours. It's very cosmopolitan. The park is on a headland with sea views and with a choice of parking on flat, clean grassy sites or up amongst the trees which we chose, mainly because of the view and for the dogs as they have the whole area to themselves and don't need to be tied up. If you pre-book with a dog ask for site number forty-one as you'll get a flat site on the hill with nothing in front but grass with a barbecue and a lovely sea view. The dogs love it and have been romping around together today. We went into town this morning to have a look around and to have a coffee overlooking the estuary and it's very pleasant. From here we can visit Eden instead of staying there as we'd planned and then it will be over the border into Victoria.

I'm starting to get a big concerned now about the fact that we are heading the wrong way around Australia! We need to get to Melbourne to see my daughter but today they have gales and heavy rain there. We can cope with the cold but we cannot keep the dogs cooped up in the back of the Ute if it rains a lot and they have been miserable a couple of times when they have gone into the sea mid afternoon and have not dried out before the temperature plummeted at sundown. We've already had five degrees at night and Callie, in particular, finds it hard to keep warm. Now we ensure that they only go in water in the morning however sunny it is to give them chance to dry out. Gale force winds do worry me; in fact the thought frightens me. We had a look at a map today and if we got in the Ute and drove, we could get to Melbourne in six hours from Eden. I'm now wondering how much further we go before turning around because we had planned to return via a route further inland and Canberra is one degrees at night and this is still autumn! If we leave it much longer it could get pretty miserable and we don't have to put up with it – after all, that's why we have the R.V! It has so far been a huge bonus going the wrong way though as there is always so much room at the caravan parks. With all the sites that we could have chosen here, we parked right next to the only other van as it was the next best site available! Luckily, the couple who were parked next to us turned out to be a lovely couple, a couple of years younger than me, who are on holiday and live at Peregian Beach in a thirty square unit with three bedrooms and a study – sounds nice. They hired a van to see if they liked this kind of life and they do. Sandy has parents who need her time and attention at the moment but they will be visiting the motor home show and joining our club and will start on the learning curve that we went through prior to buying our van. They told us about a place where we can park for $6 per night at Kilcoy, a place where we can park free at Metung (near Lakes Entrance) in Victoria and suggested we visit Victor Harbour in South Australia. I have to write this down or I'll have forgotten it by tomorrow!

Apparently Koala has been having some adventures and is now stuffed in a box but my brother is not sure where! My brother has moved, his daughter is moving and between the two of them they've lost him! He's moving to south Wales as my niece has a new position (she's a wild life officer) and Koala will have to learn Welsh! Poor bugger, he must be so confused. Perhaps being left alone in a box to sleep (either in Newark in the middle of England or perhaps Coventry towards the south of England or maybe in Wales) is a blessing as he must be exhausted by all these comings and goings and how the heck he is going to master the Welsh language I have no idea. I lived there for several years, first in Mid Wales and then in South Wales and could never pronounce the names. Luckily the rate bills used to come in English and Welsh or I'd never have understood them. So there we are then - if you visit the U.K and hear a koala speaking with a Welsh accent, give him my love.

CHAPTER FORTY

Last night I couldn't sleep again so gave up at 2am and walked around a bit to loosen up my back, then went back to bed confident I'd be in Noddyland. Then I heard a noise on the roof, then a thump followed by pitter-patter all over it. It made me giggle as it reminded me of my cat Tootsie, not that I believe that she's come back to haunt me as it was obviously a Possum. In her last months Tootsie became my shadow. She'd be fast asleep in the lounge with us when I'd go to have a bath upstairs at the other end of the house and I'd no sooner get in and there would be Toots standing by the bath and she'd stay until I'd finished. Same if I went to the toilet etc. as she'd insist on coming in with me. When she hadn't been to the toilet for a while I'd tell her 'Toilet', open the back door and she'd go straight out and do the necessary but not if I went back in without her so I'd have to wait for her! Long before the dogs were aware, she would wake up and jump down to the floor and walk to the door if John was returning in the car so I'd know he was coming three to four minutes before he arrived. I could also take her for a walk as she'd follow me everywhere. Anyway, it got to the point that when I went to bed I'd hear pitter-patter along our timber floors, down the corridor and into our bedroom. She'd stop by my side of the bed and look at me and I'd keep quiet so that she wouldn't start 'talking' to me and then she'd pitter-patter around the foot of the bed and check out the other side and look at the sliding glass door to the balcony (presumably to check it was now shut) and then, content that I was safe, she would pitter-patter back downstairs and go straight to sleep for the night. She was so predictable, until the day the vet was due at lunchtime to put her down. She got on John's chair, curled up and wouldn't move or respond to us and as she knew she was never allowed on John's chair we were pretty spooked out by it. The Vet put us through hell by prolonging her death (I have only just come to terms with it and strongly suggest that if you have an animal put down you ensure that they do not give your animal a 'sedative' prior to the final injection as ours did because she wandered around vomiting and crying for 15 minutes until I said 'This is absolute sh…. - do something for God's sake' (because by this time both John and I were sobbing). A couple of days later John reckoned he 'saw' her in the study. I calmly said 'Oh, on the chair asleep' and he said 'No, standing looking at me with back arched and hairs raised and looking terrified'. So ensure you know 'exactly' what will happen down to the last detail and say that you want it to happen instantly. Tootsie is now immortalised on paper and hopefully your pets will never suffer the same fate - Tootsie's gift to other animals. She was so sweet and so loving that she would like me warn you.

John heard the possum last night on the roof and went out with a torch to investigate - gosh it was so pretty. It was golden brown with white patches and not very big. It was so cuddly looking that I wanted to take it home and put it on the mantelpiece. It wouldn't move and I came in and went to bed and next thing I know it's either playing marbles on the roof or pelting us with nuts! John couldn't sleep when he came to bed but I had stopped giggling and was asleep. Apparently in desperation he turned on the air conditioner and it ran away. What an easy solution.

CHAPTER FORTY-ONE

RED ROCKS AT EDEN

Today we went to **Eden**. Every time we think there can be nowhere prettier than where we are or have been we find another place that surpasses anything we've seen. This part of Australia is so different to Queensland and the coast between Sydney and Brisbane. This whole coastline is truly stunning. Although there are holiday towns they are not commercialised. We are lucky to find a Woolworths and haven't seen a Coles store for some time now. Everywhere in between the towns seems to be National parkland, rivers, lakes, forests and the hundreds of beach bays, all of which have been devoid of humans when we've been there. The majority of headlands do not have houses on them - a few do but many have graveyards and a couple have had golf clubs. Most are pristine and are probably exactly the same as when the explorers discovered Australia. Obviously there are walking tracks in them now but the overall view from across the bays is that they are untouched. However, where there are towns, they are pretty, have everything you need and many tourist activities but without the billboards and signs and traffic that you find the other side of Sydney and beyond. A man said today that he no longer ventures any further north than Kiama and I can understand that. He also added that it gets too hot any further north and I can understand that too. Today was a lovely warm day again and Eden was as beautiful as we'd been told. The red rocks contrasted with the clear blue water and colours of the sand and there were beautiful green, translucent shells on the beach which I wanted to gather up but they were so delicate that they would have broken by the time we finished touring. We also checked out a van park that we had planned to stay at and it is certainly in a wonderful position along the sea front. We went to the harbour and up to headlands and found the lighthouse - there is a fair bit to see there. Again, it's certainly worth a visit.

I realised today that adverts on T.V used to say 'interest free for six months', then the interest free period was increased to a year, then two and now three and if the momentum keeps going it will reach say nine or ten years and then people will be able to tell their kids that they can have whatever they like because they'll be old enough to pay for the things themselves by the time they become due for payment. 'Yeah, you can buy that DVD and 2 metre flat screen T.V. son. You're five years old now. You can put it on your account and I'll put your name down for a job in MacDonald's. You'll be old enough in ten years time and you can pay it off then.'

We are looking forward to the change in T.V. stations when we go over the border. We won't have to hear the traffic reports of Sydney every night during the news - why do people live there! They have this reporter in a helicopter and every night he says that someone has broken down on a main road out of Sydney or there's been an accident on a freeway and every night we see kilometres of cars stationary on nearly all the major routes out of town. Even when he says 'it's moving' he actually means that the traffic has managed to reach a speed of twenty kilometres an hour - that's what it looks like anyway. Wouldn't you think a train would be easier! Our friend in Sydney asked me when he came to see us how those reports on television could possible benefit the drivers. Easy if they have a partner, because the partner knows why they are late home for dinner and can call them on their mobile phone to tell them, just in case they hadn't noticed that they are stuck in the traffic!

Saturday 22ⁿᵈ May - LEFT EDEN & CROSSED BORDER - HELLO VICTORIA (EAST GIPPSLAND)

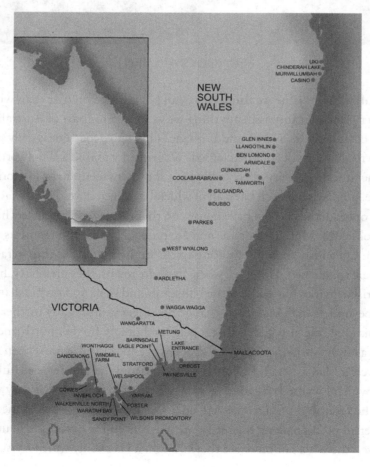

The journey was quite uneventful with just a sign saying you can't bring fruit over the border. I had already eaten our last tomato and zucchini and had chucked out the rest of the capsicum being very environmentally aware (what rubbish I write - it had gone all slimy in the container because I had forgotten about it) only to hear John say when we stopped for a coffee 'Where's that apple that you told me to eat yesterday? Oh yes, here it is'. I made him put the core in the rubbish bin instead of throwing it in the bushes! We stopped as soon as we could once we passed the Welcome to Victoria sign to celebrate. I have already told some of you in a letter prior to leaving, that my daughter left the Gold Coast early one Friday morning to head for Melbourne, stayed in a motel for a night and reached the outskirts of Melbourne early Saturday afternoon. It is has taken us four months!

Between Eden and Mallacoota, where we are now, there was little to see on the road except for trees, trees and more trees. However, if you are a hiker there are thousands of acres to explore. **Mallacoota** is a pretty fishing village with a vast shoreline along the Mallacoota Inlet and within a few minutes drive to the beach. Boats are moored along jetties and an enormous caravan park stretches all around the lake foreshore. A few shops, back-packers hostel and pub and a couple of cafes and Post Office complete the village with a small tourist information centre on the foreshore, manned by volunteers. If you are interested in hiking, walking trails, boating, swimming or fishing it is a great place to be. There is also a bowling club. It is protected from the winds here and therefore warmer and we were surprised to find mossies (mosquitos) again.

John is at the golf club at the moment but you have to be careful of the kangaroos. Two of them overtook our Ute when we were driving back from there yesterday and they then swerved straight in front of us to cross the road. There are warnings not to approach them. Apparently there is a particularly large male at the Golf Club and if your ball lands near him you may just as well forego two shots as he will not move. John asked if he could approach it and was told he'd get punched by the roo if he tried. This means that the dogs are tied up all the time because behind our R.V is a reserve and Mallacoota is surrounded by The **Croajingolong National Parkland**, a World Biosphere Reserve. There are roo droppings all around our R.V. and I'm glad the dogs like sleeping in the Ute so we can relax at night.

Tomorrow we are moving on to Lakes Entrance which is a 212ks move, twice our usual limit. We will be bypassing a lot of the coastline because it is mostly National Park with corrugated dirt tracks from the main road to the beach. There are so many places to camp with tents in the area but it would be preferable to have a four wheel drive vehicle and no dogs! We will probably stop for about a week at Lakes Entrance and may even be lucky enough to get our gas hot water system serviced as we were told at our last stop that we'd have to order a new 'master control box' from America. That will have to wait until we are home again. For the last four days we've had no hot water and then this afternoon it worked perfectly!

I have had to face a new shower block again! In the meantime we received an email from a friend who has just been touring and his letter concerning showers made us chuckle. This is an extract '....the majority are designed by people who are on a vendetta against Campers & place the rose pointing directly at the door. If somebody did a maths thesis in the UK on mathematical formulae to boil the perfect egg a few years ago, I think I could do a thesis on the perfect shower for a camping area.' We are now in a park where there is no path between the shower block and the dirt road. I wear thongs but by the time I get back to the R.V. my feet are filthy again!

CHAPTER FORTY-TWO

WELCOME TO OUR NEW HOME AT ORBOST

Monday 24ᵗʰ May

By the time we reached **Orbost** we were 'treed out'. That's all you see along the highway until you approach Orbost when farmland at last appears. We left the R.V at the side of the road and drove into Orbost in the Ute and found a park by the Snowy River where several caravans had parked whilst their owners had picnic lunches. By the time the dogs had stretched their legs we were well ready for our own lunch but stopped just past the park to look at the 'Slab Hut' which we'd seen in the tourist books. It was originally built in 1872 about 3ks upstream and moved to its present site in the 1980's and it was fascinating. No nails are used, it was all wired together and we spent a fair while there reading old newspapers, looking at the old bedding, furniture tools, kitchen utensils and the construction of the hut. There was a wonderful, long poem about a flood and the story of the priest who got drunk and got stuck trying to wade to safety. Two constables had to rescue him. I could not resist buying a recipe book with some really weird meals that were once normal family fare. I bought it for my daughter who is a vegetarian but it's a fascinating read despite the fact that most of the menus are meat based!

We stopped at the Orbost Snowy River Café and as we walked in three staff welcomed us. We ate outside and were amused by a stone planter box in the shape of a coffin with a plaque up one end with 'RIP Snowy River Man' etched on it, the tips of a pair of old boots sticking up out of the other end and along side them an ankle shackle! Flowers grew all over the 'body'. After eating we ordered a coffee and the owner came outside and thanked us for visiting their town and for eating in his café and a neighbouring customer left us with 'Have a good day' and a lovely smile. We were assured that this is a very friendly small town and we felt a little sad to leave it but we needed to get to Lakes Entrance before the threatening rain materialised and before it got too dark for us to set up camp in comfort. We had no sooner got organised and the dogs fed than a mobile home owner approached us with the gift of two stewing bones for our dogs. We had also received a lovely welcome from the parks owner. If this continues, we won't want to leave! Tomorrow we'll be off to explore as we're parked two kilometres out of town and haven't seen it yet.

We are parked on a large grassed area which we thought was reserved for Big Rigs. John has discovered that it is the area where everyone has to go if there is a fire in the vicinity or presumably some other natural disaster! 'Well if something happens I'll put the kettle on' I said and then realised that was quite true. A typical British response. The morning Princess Diane died, we were staying in England with my sister-in-law and her adult children and partners (lovely big family weekend) and I thought she was kidding until she said 'I'll put the kettle on'. I knew then that it was true and rushed to the television. When a neighbour was shot and killed in Browns Plains one Saturday afternoon as we were having a garage sale, I put the kettle on and offered the police a cup of tea! I don't even drink the stuff! They came in and had one, leaving the poor young teenagers sitting out on the lawn in 30C+ heat, without shade. After a couple of hours of watching them sit there I insisted the police allow me to give them drinks of water. I don't think the kids had seen anything anyway as they were inside the house and most of them had been asleep, but they were in shock. John ended up being one of the prime witnesses but at that moment he was still on the lookout for anyone who might like to pay us some money for the things that we think are rubbish. The police eventually stuffed us up and cordoned off the road.

One of the recipients of this diary had a brilliant suggestion. I had phoned to tell him that when he came to see us that night he'd have to park his vehicle some way away and walk down the road and that he couldn't come up the road from the other corner as that was the murder scene. 'Dial a Pizza because they guarantee that if they don't deliver it within fifteen minutes you can have it for free and the Police won't let them through'.

John has typically British responses too. We saw a small brick building at the side of the road with a large letter 'L' on the front the other day. 'Lavatory' he said as we passed. What Australian says 'lavatory'? We have lots of colourful terms for the 'loo' but I've not heard of that word here. It wasn't a toilet anyway. It was the Lions Club sign!

CHAPTER FORTY-THREE

I was putting maps into my photo album tonight to complete the New South Wales section. By the time I had reached the latest photos my head was spinning with the names of places that we'd visited and I muttered 'Where are we now?'

'Western Australia' John answered. I stared at him in shock

'Where?'

'Western Australia'

'We can't possibly be!'

'Not us, on the telly'.

'You frightened the heck out of me. I thought I had amnesia'. The house on Hot Auctions was being sold in W.A.

So what did we do today - watched the rain because we haven't seen any for so long and found out that the only large store in town is Safeway. 'Goodness, I haven't seen a Safeway sign since I was in England about five years ago' I told the caravan park owner. He looked at me as though I was from another planet but it's true. We also did a bit of sightseeing this morning. We went to Lake Tyers, a tiny coastal hamlet not far from this park. We went into a fabulous pub on the front and everyone was so friendly. One lady was telling me that she lives in Metung and we must call in there and certainly the tourist information makes it sound like nirvana, so we will. She was also telling me that she wished that there was a Woolworth's here in Lakes Entrance because that's her favourite food store. Safeway is Woolworth's! We also took a look at Ninety Mile Beach and as you'd expect, it's endless!

I also purchased a pair of black trousers and black, grey and red jumper - very smart. The reason for these purchases is that last Sunday I had wanted to go to church and couldn't think where my 'reasonably decent' clothes are! I had found the church, checked out the service time and found that this Sunday they would be holding Communion which was what I wanted. I set the alarm and we went to bed and then I couldn't sleep. 'I've got some summer black trousers but what will go with them? I'll freeze. Where are those shoes I never wear? Black socks - under this bed but I can't lift it - I'll have to wake John up in the morning. Where are my good tops? Probably outside in one of the side storage bins, in that huge suitcase inside that bag but I can't lift the suitcase out.' The alarm rang. I pulled myself upright, remembered the clothes problem and groaned, turned the alarm off and slept until 9am!

I decided that as I'd spent $200 on a pair of Kumfs flat shoes several months ago, that I never wear as I have nothing to go with them, it was time to remedy this oversight. It was during the period of physiotherapists and doctors and months of podiatrists appointments because my spine is crooked due to various sporting accidents and I had to find shoes that would take my 'inserts' which help me to walk as though I'm sober and 'lifts' which also go in my left shoe to make that leg the same distance from the ground as the other. I can get the inserts into my trainers and my Ugg boots but most shoes are hopeless as my heels would be above the shoes at the back! I also bought a pair of $200 sandals (I like to follow my podiatrist's orders) which are not much good for trekking about over beaches and rocks (I love clambering over rocks). So every single day I wear the same pair of trainers! I'm always complaining about falling over John's various pairs of shoes but really its envy. So, although I never did get to church, I've gained a new outfit to go with my old/new shoes! Now I need an excuse to put them on.

Lakes Entrance is quite attractive. The actual 'Entrance' is man-made because it used to be all beach. After construction started, a storm finished it off for them. The shops stretch along the road with the inlet opposite all the way along. I haven't taken any photos yet because of the weather, so I'm hoping that it brightens up a bit tomorrow. It will have to because I cannot keep buying knickers as I did today only to hear that John is down to his last pair too! As the washing basket is full, we are now filling up a garbage bag and the sheets need changing! Life's good.

Thursday 27th May

Current temperatures 7-15C and weather 'variable' so we know we are in Victoria! We sat around yesterday morning in beautiful sunshine saying that we must get the washing done. Two overfull machine loads were hung out to dry. Half an hour later black clouds, then sunshine, then black clouds - yes, we're getting close to Melbourne. It poured down with rain of course and I finished the day in the laundry, feeding money into the dryer slot and watching my knickers fighting with John's socks. Once finished the weather cleared! The ski resorts are getting snow again so we won't be going inland. However the dams are low here and it seems that in every state we go to, the news reports the drought and discusses water restrictions. As I speak, there is talk on T.V of the States meeting with the Federal Government next month to form a national drought policy plan.

We went out yesterday afternoon to look at the seaside village of **Metung**. The leaflet we picked up says 'Metung is Boats' and I was delighted to see boats everywhere from dinghies to fishing trawlers to ocean going yachts and cruisers. There are many lovely wooden boats too. Metung is on a strip of land in the heart of the Gippsland Lakes with Bancroft Bay on one side and Lake King Beach on the other so this is the place for all water sports and fishing. Stock up with food before you arrive though as the village mainly boasts cafes, craft centres and studios etc. This whole area of East Gippsland claims to be the boating capital of Australia and boasts 400 square kilometres of lakes, rivers and canals so we see boats all the time but it's great when you see them en masse. We have yet to visit Paynesville (which claims to be the boating capital of Victoria) where they have over 1000 boats moored. It is known to the Aboriginal people as Toonalook, meaning 'plenty of fish'. It's not far from Bairnsdale.

CHAPTER FORTY-FOUR

We moved to **Bairnsdale** today as we'd set up an appointment with a gas fitter/electrician. He tells us that our American heater is an Electrolux model and that we can get it replaced in Melbourne. It was worth the $25 call-out-fee to find out that we do not have to get one from America. The temperatures have now dropped to 5-15C. My daughter tells me it gets uncomfortable when it's minus one and I wonder how we'll defrost the dogs in the morning if we stay in Melbourne too long. I'm enjoying being in a good size town again and had a good look around the clothes shops and book shops this afternoon. I found a superb pure cotton jumper in a second-hand shop for which I paid $5. The label is new; it's very smart and beautifully made. I'll have to start looking in 'op shops' again, like I used to. When I worked in Brisbane I used to buy designer clothes for an average cost of $25 as there was one shop that kept a special rack and I'd check it out weekly. All the best stuff used to be sent to this one shop. My feet are 'bliss bombs' now - I treated them to a new pair of trainers - aaah, heaven. We are going to stay here another night and then we are on the road again. John likes the 'feel' of Victoria - gentler and more British he reckons. The news is certainly different on the telly being more business-like and interesting! The people are definitely friendlier. I can understand what he means though - somehow less 'abrasive' generally but having said that, whoever carved up the States knew what they were doing and must have come from New South Wales as they've pinched the most stunning coastline!

I've just checked my emails. I don't usually do it until I send this letter on Sunday or Monday nights. Something kept nagging me to do so and four arrived. I'm glad you're enjoying this diary because it all seems so pointless and silly when one of your friends tells you that their youngest granddaughter has leukaemia. How do you possibly explain to a five year old child that they have to put up with the pain of those tests and chemotherapy and their loss of hair? I'm so glad to hear tonight that she has a good chance of survival - but two years of treatment! And you are not even allowed to go into her room - how very hard because all you'd want to do is go in and gather her in your arms and cuddle her. I cannot imagine what her parents are going through.

Congratulations on your special Birthday brother Paul and your hot air balloon flight. You've got good kids - new golf clubs - what a great gift. I thought you told me that you played aqua-golf in Wales because of all the rain? Still, they'll look good propped up in the hallway of your new home. Another grandchild on the way! Would you mind doing a family tree of your Brady Bunch family? And as for another friend's suggestion that I write a guide for 'slightly older' campers - 'nearly mature' would have been better or 'adult teenagers' because after all we are doing what teenagers usually want to do. As for your mention of 'the older set' - I'll deal with you later!!! In future please remember that the media classifies us as SKINS (spend the kids inheritance now) which is exactly what we are doing.

We've also been asked about costs but I cannot recall who asked. The petrol was a bit of a shock to start with because we are used to Queensland being subsidised by 8c per litre but with the world shortage and higher prices we have become used to petrol being more expensive. In total it is costing us approximately $490 per month extra because we are travelling and that includes such things as Landlord's Insurance. We save on electricity bills of course and any water excess bills (as the tenants have to pay it) and usually the phone/internet calls are lower (however they weren't last month but we don't talk about that bill any more!) We have contents insurance to the value of $52,000 for this R.V. but they forgot to put the bankcard order through and because we reminded them and it was their fault they have decided that we don't have to pay it this year! I've already told you that they are a pretty special insurance company! The Insurance on the R.V. itself is about $600 more than the Jag per year. However, because we rent out our house we are actually gaining about $1000 per month. The question arises - can we afford to go home!!! Someone else is paying our mortgage whilst we trip around the country.

We've heard other campers say that they couldn't rent out their own homes and they leave them empty. I'd hate to leave mine empty as I'd worry too much about it. I suppose I ought to tell them that we like the $1000 extra income with all our costs of touring covered - perhaps they wouldn't look at us as though we're mad to do so! We are lucky to have the granny-flat to store all our furniture in of course but if we hadn't got it, I'd have a big shed built on the property and still store it for free. You never lose money on having a big double shed as it is always a selling point. As long as your belongings are dry and safe, why not store them? They are inanimate objects, not pets!!!

CHAPTER FORTY-FIVE

I'm a miserable specimen today as I awoke with a stinking cold and as this is a rare phenomenon for me I have not suffered in silence. I moaned and groaned my way between the bedroom and lounge until well in the afternoon, collapsing on the sofa with a box of tissues and with the fan heater on high, regularly emitting moans and sighs between sneezes. Bitterly cold winds rocked the van along with intermittent rain. By the afternoon John and Jack were like caged animals despite John and the dogs having scouted the town for new tyres and having walked home after dropping the Ute off and walking back again to pick it up. I agreed to go sightseeing and we set off to see Paynesville and then the Silt Jetties at Eagle Point. On the way we had a lake on one side of the road and a canal on the other. Just beyond the canal was the sea. **Paynesville** was pretty and I sat in the car having a discussion with a black swan. It spoke to me first and I was so surprised I talked back. I had wound down my window to take a photo of them and one walked up and made this funny, gentle cooing sound. I told it I had no bread but it continued making these sweet noises. Its mate completely ignored me. Further down the road a group of people were walking off the jetty and there were two irate swans swimming alongside following them and they were not so sweet. They seemed distinctly angry.

We loved **Eagle Point** which is beside a lake and at the start of the silt jetty. It looked as though it cannot have changed for the last fifty years with the old timber houses, farmland and not a shop in sight. The **Silt Jetties** are second only in length to those of the Mississippi. For those of you who have no idea what a silt jetty is (I didn't) it's where floods, over thousands of years, have deposited enough silt to build natural jetties eight kilometres in length. Naturally this changes the seascape and the views were stunning. There were a couple of caravan parks down there but the one in the best position does not allow dogs which is unfortunate for us. On our way back through Bairnsdale John took me to see the Court House - what an amazing old building that is and we continued driving around some of the back streets. It is a lovely town with wide roads, some very beautiful old homes (a lot of Queenslanders) and some of the best town planning I have ever seen. The schools and all sporting venues, which include every kind of playing field and a racecourse, are all in one area of town. All the way through the town and out the other side are gardens down the centre of the road. So to get from one side of the 'high street' to the other you walk through gardens - it's lovely. The gardens run for over 3ks, possibly 4ks. The hospital and all the medical centres are in another section, not far from the schools and sporting venues. The vehicle repair shops and new car yards are all together along the same long road but past the hospital. There are some lovely old buildings in town and a church that begs to be photographed with a hand-painted ceiling inside. We're very impressed and think that members of other town councils should visit! Development can be good when the old is preserved and enhanced and in this town there is a modern development just behind the main road with modern mall area but it is low-level and does not dominate, just provides expansion. On our return I 'allowed' John to buy a take-away meal (I usually cannot tolerate them but had no energy) and he bought a well known brand of chicken and chips. By the time I had removed the skin and fat and found the bones,

I had about two mouthfuls of meat left. Luckily I ordered a container of coleslaw for myself! I should have made scrambled eggs!

Saturday

We didn't move on today as I am still pretty crook but did go to see the inside of St Mary's Church in the morning. I also bought a very good parka-style coat for $5 in a second hand shop with a thick fur inner lining so now I'm warm again! John's been very aware that I have a very bad cold because of all my moaning and groaning and I was so proud of my frugality and as I proudly displayed it he asked 'What on earth do you need more clothes for. Haven't you got enough!' I had one of those 'marital moments' when you wish that divorce was instant.

St Mary's Catholic Church 'blew me away' as the Aussie expression goes. After dropping John off at the cinema complex in the afternoon I took the dogs for a walk along the river and then went to photograph the Court House and then went back to the Church. Just as I was taking a photo of the Church a bride was getting out of the bridal car. She was so excited she was waving to everyone around and had great difficulty keeping her veil behind her as the wind was so strong. The bridesmaid shivered and tried to collect metres of train as the bride continued to turn and wave to everyone. I wanted one of the information booklets about the Church and as the church was somewhat occupied, I went to the Tourist Information shop nearby and bought one there. Actually, I suppose one could say it is another example of thoughtful town planning because you can go into the Tourist Information office and collect lots of leaflets, walk next door into MacDonald's and have some lunch whilst you read them and then walk into Church and thank God for so many wonderful places to see!

Anyway, the booklet on the church says in part 'One of the most remarkable of the red brick Roman churches…combining Romanesque and Byzantine external features….but distinguished most of all by the remarkable decorative scheme over the whole barrel-vaulted interior…executed by the Italian Francesco Floreani…' The interior painting was organised by a Rev Father Cornelius Cremin who appears to have been a mighty fine and very enthusiastic kind of character. Francesco, the artist, was born near Venice in 1899 and studied there and at Turin before leaving Italy in 1928. He worked as a house painter in Melbourne until the depression when he was forced to get any work he could, including picking peas. He knocked on Father Cremin's door to ask for work in 1931. On hearing he was a painter, Father Cremin asked him to repaint some of the statues and then some murals and so he continued, covering the ceiling with flower garlands and over three hundred seraphim and cherubims, each with a different face. So you stand in this church and are shrouded by beautiful angels. But that is not all - everything is decorated. Father Cremin paid him three pounds a week out of his own pocket and over two stages (an extension to the church was added in 1937) he spent many years on the project. In one of the panels he included a self-portrait with Father Cronin beside him. In another he painted St Patrick in honour of the Irish. Apparently some of the Catholics did not like the interior painting and Father Cremin said 'Bad luck. I'm the one paying for it' or words to that effect. No-one went hungry in Bairnsdale during the depression apparently because if they could not afford to pay, the shopkeepers would 'charge it to Father Cremin'. He was also very kind to Italian immigrants and that was unusual in those days. This is not in the guide book that I bought but we heard this verbally when we visited. The locals believe that he inherited some money and that is how he could afford to be so generous. Whatever, he did a lot of good with it and left a lasting, heritage-listed church for us all to enjoy. The church contains some beautiful statues including two kneeling angels, sculptured in Belgium from marble, on either side of the high altar. Marble altar rails and wall panels depict various scripture stories and Saints. The stained glass windows are absolutely beautiful and at the back is a wheel window with the twelve apostles surrounding Christ. Outside are more statues.

On the way back I had a look in a second hand goods shop opposite this park. It contained every kind or ornament imaginable, furniture, glassware, bedding and memorabilia and I could not get over how cheap they were. Pewter tankers for $8 and a cut glass fruit bowl with three legs for $18. There were old irons (that you heated on the fire) and old biscuit tins and other kitchen stuff, decorative wall dishes which are collectables, even a rag doll and they would sell in antique stores for a considerable sum. I heard the lady behind the counter say to a customer that she had no idea how much the glassware was worth which was blatantly obvious. It is a very large shop and someone could buy most of the contents and start a shop in the highlands making a 500% profit on each item! I then returned to our park and had a second look at the art studio at the front where they sell some original glassware and it's very good indeed. I couldn't resist a beautiful hand made glass ornamental plate for a present.

What fun I've had whilst John has been in the cinema. The park owner said that our dogs are well behaved and I said that it's been more fun travelling with them than without them. If I hadn't had them with me today I could not have played hide-and-seek at the man-made hills for the BMX riders at the river front. Well I could have done if I had an imaginary friend to play with but I may well have been committed if anyone had seen me. The dogs and I had a ball, particularly Jack who cottoned on to the game immediately. Callie stood on top of the mounds and watched us most of the time as though we were nuts but had to join in when Jack chased her too. What with the beauty of the church, the romp with the dogs in a beautiful park and the sight of beautiful artwork my mind is at peace and it's good to be married again as I have so much to tell John when he returns. Of course, if I hadn't purchased my cheap and incredibly warm jacket I wouldn't have done any of the above as I would have been too cold - what a difference $5 can make!!

CHAPTER FORTY-SIX

STALKING WOMBAT

Sunday 30th May

Well we travelled from East Gippsland, through Gippsland and into South Gippsland today and ended up at Foster. It was a very easy drive along mainly straight, flat roads with very little traffic and it was a fine, although windy day. We stopped at various places along the way, leaving the R.V. parked whilst we nipped off to explore in the Ute. **Stratford** has a River Avon (which was down to a trickle of water), a theatre and not much else. As you drive into Sale you first notice a Catholic College - it's huge and quite magnificent. Sale is a large and very attractive town, with wide streets lined with many old homes and commercial buildings. One huge old Cobb and Co building now houses the markets. There is a clock tower in the centre with several benches for people to rest, meet or simply to 'people watch'. There is even a small train museum. There are two lakes (Lake Guyatt and Lake Guthridge which link to the Sale Common Wetlands) with a 7.2km track through the reserve or a boardwalk if you feel like stretching your legs. There is an outdoor swimming pool and sporting complexes (the netball courts were full as we passed by). The old swing bridge is one of the first of its type ever built. We stopped opposite Lake Guthridge to give the dogs a run. From Sale we could have adopted the direct route straight into Melbourne but no, not us, we're sticking to the coast.

We had a fish and chip lunch at **Yarram**, another attractive town and with buildings such as the Federal Coffee Palace and the 'Yarrum Club 1912 Hotel' and the old Post Office with the royal crown. Just outside town we left the R.V. and drove down to Port Albert (only 8ks) which has Victoria's oldest licensed hotel. It was first settled in 1841. The tide was out so the sea vista was not attractive as there were mud flats rather than sand. Then on to Wales - oh no, Welshpool but the sudden change of scenery from flat terrain to wonderful green rolling hills (very steep hills) reminded us so much of Wales. Virtually all we had seen, other than the towns and villages, were trees and fields. Since crossing the border we have noticed so many fields that are not being looked after and have weed growing all over. Not all farms of course but the majority. Some have had cattle and sheep on and the grass looked far from a good feed! Now we were seeing rich, green grass and the small, pretty village of **Welshpool**. We again left the R.V and went to look at Port Welshpool which boasts one of the longest piers in Victoria. Again we found mudflats and a rather uninteresting sad-looking seaside town but with some nice grassy parkland to the foreshore. Just before Foster is the Toora Wind Farm - i.e. they have windmills on the hills. (That set me off thinking of Devon, or was it Cornwall where we kept seeing these tall white structures with their arms spinning - it was the first time I'd seen windmills like that.) Off the highway between Welshpool and Toora are the Agnes Falls which has the largest single span drop in Victoria of 59 metres. And now Foster which John had thought was a good size town but it's not - it's not much more than a village.

Foster is the gateway to 'the Prom' as it is known locally. **Wilsons Promontory** is a National Park of 50,512 hectares - huge and it is surrounded on three sides by the ocean. It is also the southern most tip of the Australian mainland although was once joined to Tasmania. The climate warmed about 15,000 years ago, the sea rose and the granite mountains and low plains were covered. The Prom was an island, later rejoining with the mainland via a ridge of sand. There is an entry fee for this National Park and dogs are definitely not allowed so I am dog-sitting and writing to you all whilst John is cavorting around the Prom with the camera.

John's Diary

Travelling from Foster to 'The Prom' you cover a windswept 29ks of good fast road via the isthmus, which joins the mainland to this famous area, with great views of Corner Inlet on the way, passing Yanakie prior to the park entrance.

For about 10ks past this entrance there is not much to see as the road is lined with thick bush but then the true nature of this magnificent area starts to unfurl. The extensive plains and mountains are covered with thick growth and boulders of granite. As you wind your way down the Promontory the vistas are joined by distant views of the oceans on either side and sudden dramatic views of **Whisky Bay, Picnic Bay** and **Squeaky Beach** come into view from high parts of the road. There is a road to **Mt Oberon** Summit but upon reaching the end of the road it was disappointing to find that there was a track taking one hour to reach the real summit, amongst many other choices of track one taking seven hours - true hiking country.

Tidal River is the end of the sealed road and a hiker's paradise and a starting point for exploring the beautiful pristine country and beaches. I now understand why my friend travelled all the way from 'Brizzie' to spend time here. He is a true bush lover.

Squeaky Beach squeaks when walked upon, hence the peculiar name. I kept an eye out for wildlife whilst on the road, apart from plenty of bird life, but did not spot one kangaroo nor any emus, but was lucky to come across a wombat at the side of the road which was quite unconcerned when I took a close up mug-shot of him with the camera.

I also went to visit the **Windmill Farm** whilst Lisa willingly dog-sat! It was well worth visiting the observation area to view the twelve giant windmills. The sheer size is very impressive when standing close to them. From there the trip through the winding valleys and green hills to Agnes Falls was a wonderful short trip. The Falls were a picture of rugged, untouched beauty.

CHAPTER FORTY-SEVEN

ON WAY TO MELBOURNE

June 1st

Hi again, Lisa here. The following day we drove down to **Sandy Point, Waratah Bay and Walkerville North** (nothing but a few houses and beach) and we marvelled that these isolated sea villages still exist! We talked of the difference between the NSW coastline and Victorian coastline and for those in England and Canada I will explain it by saying the NSW is like Devon and Victorian more like Cornwall. NSW has a 'soft' coastline with Victoria more 'rugged'. Obviously this is a general perception as The Prom is different again. However, past Melbourne when you travel the Great Ocean Road it is interesting to note that it is also called the 'Shipwreck coast' so you get the picture. As we travel the coastline by car we also notice the difference in the terrain. The fields do not seem so green as they were back in Welshpool, the landscape more open and windy. I gave Foster town another 'go' as I did not feel I had done it justice but felt no different after a two minute walk and finding two shops that I might have gone into closed that day. The Information Centre only had information on the immediate area but nothing about where we were heading to. John's friend who loves to stay in the wilderness of the Prom stocks up in Foster prior to departure and tells me that I should have visited the bakers. As he has a completely different perception of the place than I, you must visit and decide for yourselves. When returning from the Prom it must seem like a big town.

We left the next day and travelled via **Inverloch** where we stopped at a lovely park offering several interesting walks to the beach and through the trees but needed to push on as we wanted to detour off the main road to travel to Cape Peterson. It was an easy drive for both vehicles with some lovely views. We rejoined the road at **Wonthaggi** and headed towards Melbourne, turning off to **Phillip Island**. That was an absolute delight and the little we saw, we loved.

We went to our chosen park at **Cowes** but before booking in we parked the R.V and walked around the delightful town and down to the seafront and bought ourselves a rather late lunch. The roads are lined with huge old trees and it is very, very picturesque. We had a wonderful site overlooking the ocean and the park is very dog-friendly. The dogs could go straight onto the beach for a run without our needing leads and they were like two frisky lambs. It was very windy and cold but we settled down to watch the news and the weather report warned of severe wind, very high seas, rain and hail, due the following day all along our stretch of coastline. We were parked a few steps from the beach and the weather was beginning to get worse. I started to become very concerned as I am no longer partial to the odd hail storm. 'Do you think we should get out of here?' I asked John.

'What on earth for, we've just arrived!'

'It's just said on the news that we could get hail here.'

'So what, a bit of hail won't hurt you.'

'But you were not around when that hail storm hit at home' I reminded him 'and to be honest I'm terrified of hail storms now.'

'Oh, you're just panicking over nothing.'

'How long did it take to get our van repaired? Was it two or maybe three months, I can't recall?' I asked him.

He didn't answer so I added. 'So if we did get hail damage you wouldn't mind getting stuck in Melbourne for the next three months or so?'

He started packing up and we moved the following morning!

CHAPTER FORTY-EIGHT

We decided to go straight to **Melbourne**. We stocked up with necessities in town and topped up both petrol tanks and by the time we left the area it was late morning. After an hour of travelling through driving rain we pulled up at the side of the road for a coffee and it was 1pm. We went via **Dandenong** as I envisaged a quiet road through a small town. How wrong can one be! I actually thought we were already in the heart of Melbourne but no, this was Dandenong. We reached our destination just before 5pm and for the last hour it was dark and teeming down with rain.

It was a horrendous four hours and I kept thinking about my friends in Tasmania who are not used to traffic. We ended up in the city and we were lost. Then John had to stop in a very awkward place as his left mirror broke. I had no idea why he had stopped as I had one of those usual messages '……. broken off. Got to stop'. I had no idea what was broken but we were both stopped in a 'no-stop' zone. I waited five minutes with hazard lights on as four lanes of traffic streamed past us in the rush hour. I was too far away to back up to him so ended up moving around into a side street. He was outside without his phone and I was frightened I'd lose him. A little further on and we managed to stop and ask for directions - sounded easy and it was but the road signs kept directing us onto yet another highway, including the tollway through the tunnel which we had been trying to avoid as we had no idea how to buy a ticket and we knew you could get fined if you went on the tollway without one. We went on about five major highways before finding the Hume Highway.

We headed straight out of town in the peak of the rush hour and we were both tense and exhausted by then. I phoned the park (whilst driving) to ask how much further to their place as all we had was a number on the highway and it goes on forever and we also knew that it was on the other side of the road. A lot of these roads are four lanes either side with a strip down the middle with bushes and trees. Her directions confused me even more as I was told to drive about 3ks and go through traffic lights and then drive 5ks and go through another set but we passed about sixteen sets of lights through the next eight kilometres! The last things she had said was 'If you see a golf ball on a stick then get into the right lane as you'll have to do a u-turn there'. Is that right? We can hardly see as it's so dark and there are all these lanes full of traffic obstructing our view and I'm supposed to look for a golf ball on a stick and give John time to move the R.V across all these lanes of traffic to do a u-turn into several more lanes of traffic and get over to the left lane to turn into the park! I never did find the golf ball. We both saw the park sign however.(Apollo Gardens-Craigieburn)

When we arrived at reception we were so stressed out that the receptionist gave up trying to tell us where the local shopping centre is (as if we wanted to know!) and the dogs were stiff, confused, hungry, fed up and Jack was desperate for a pee. A guy led us to our site in his golf buggy, which was great because I don't think we could have found it otherwise - directions didn't work for us any more! We have to have an 'en suite' site which means we have a lovely new shower/toilet/vanity building right outside our door. It has a heater and outside overnight light. So we now have three toilets in all! We still haven't needed to use our portable one. There are two fields here for dogs to run free and one is right opposite our van. They are having a hydro bath installed for dogs and have a pet-minding service! They wanted to 'sight' the dogs on arrival to ensure they are friendly and both dogs were given a biscuit. John and I didn't get one! Mind you, I was too busy draping myself over the wood-burning stove in reception at the time. 'Look John, a fire - a real fire'. It was so nice to see a fire - one that's actually lit I mean. We have them at the Gold Coast for show, not to actually use. Our chimney pot has plants growing out the side of it! Santa can still get down it somehow.

Anyway, our first task was the dogs as we felt so sorry for them. That meant following them around whilst they investigated where they were as they seem to have to know prior to having a pee and then it was their dinner, toilet again, walk and John had to line the back of the Ute with the tarp cover adding newspapers on top to keep the dogs warm overnight.

At last - the kettle was on, blinds and curtains closed, hot showers and a snack. John had two snoozes before bedtime and today we are staying in the R.V as we cannot face any traffic or roads. It's cold but fine with odd periods of sunshine and I'm catching up with this. After this I'll have to download my photos and having written this, I have been reminded of where the photos were taken. John's managed to disconnect the five electric wires attached to his mirror and we now have to find a truck supplier. However, the most urgent matter is finding a Vet to get the dogs checked over and annual injections done and because both of them have been a bit sick this week although they are very lively. We feel that a day's wait will do them more good than another dose of travelling in the Ute - even if it is only a short distance - they need to rest and recover too. It's now the 4th June. Hello Melbourne - the top choice for backpackers around the world (Sydney has lost top place this year apparently, coming in second). We have to face the traffic again on Sunday whether we like it or not as we will be visiting my daughter at her home. I'm going to turn up with a bag of washing because the kids always do it to me!

CHAPTER FORTY-NINE

We received an email about a friend's trip to Holland and the lousy weather when our friend was there. It made us laugh as the temperatures were the same as they are here now in Melbourne. He asked why people want to live there – well just come here to Melbourne and ask the people here! I have absolutely no idea. This is only the first week of winter and there's rain plus strong, very cold winds but I believe that we are going to get a bit of relief tomorrow with the highest temperature due to be 15C .

Saturday

That was wishful thinking - highest today was 13.9C (57F) but I'm not sure where - perhaps in a kitchen in the city. Callie was sick as soon as she got up this morning, twice. We took the dogs to the Animal Hospital for their annual jabs and after a bill of well over $400 (with substantial reductions) I came out close to tears as she had to have blood tests for pancreatis and we have to wait until tomorrow morning to find out if she needs to be admitted to hospital. She cannot understand why we won't give her any dinner. We had no idea she was in such pain and as the Vet said, it was quite obvious that she wanted to bite him but held herself back when he examined her stomach. She's had an injection to ease the pain for now. She's still cold and hungry though. Whilst we were there a cat screamed and that finished me off! We had planned to leave here on Monday as my daughter has said she will come to us (wherever we are) for the long weekend and we are catching up tomorrow. Tomorrow we'll know what's what.

Sunday

Vets - two particular results were looked at, one of which was sky high and the other normal. Callie could still have pancreatitis, a blockage in the gut, gastro-enteritis or a problem with her liver! It was a very tough decision as to whether to leave her there on a drip or take her out with us for the day because the Vet obviously though she would be better left with them. Above the din of the crying cat I said that I felt Callie would be less stressed with us! We have ensured that she drinks water but she's not allowed to eat. She's pretty miserable about that but is still running around during the day. It was 3.8C (38.84F) at 7.20am according to the news and according to our friend in Sydney, who phoned today, 0C there at 1am. My daughter was out in Melbourne last night at that time and said it was so cold it hurt and she lives here! Anyway, Callie's had one x-ray and has been given 'beads' and has to have a second x-ray tomorrow to track the beads to see if she has a blockage. We're still hoping she doesn't need an operation.

We eventually caught up with my daughter at lunchtime and I enjoyed seeing her unit at last. We all went to a huge and very beautiful park and the families and their pet dogs were out in force, because of the sunshine. We walked over quite a large timber suspension bridge and ordered three Devonshire teas and watched the ducks and geese arguing over the bread that the children and adults were tossing around. Gee, geese can get stroppy can't they? One of them wound itself up so much because it thought it hadn't had its share, that when some bread was chucked at it, it didn't notice as it was too busy throwing a cackling paddy.

Off we went to give the dogs a romp and it was then that we faced a leap off a wall to a level below that was just a bit too big for me to feel comfortable about. I can only jump off from the left leg thereby landing on my right. However, I already know that I am facing a second operation on that right knee and I always take care not to jar my damaged spine so I was thinking about sitting on the edge of the wall before dropping. That's when Sir Galahad approached from the lower level and with a flourish he picked me up. Acting like a hero, John, who often pictures himself like Errol Flynn in those old romantic movies didn't quite carry it off though as he just as quickly dropped me on my back and within seconds the dogs were licking my face. My daughter wasn't much help as she reckons that she was rendered immobile with hysterical laughter the minute she saw the dogs run up to me whilst my legs were still in the air, as she guessed what they were going to do!

John was quite stunned and was rapidly thinking up excuses and as they were both so busy I got up and found that I appeared quite whole, albeit with a rather wet, sticky face. The dogs were prancing around with excitement thinking that this was a new game as there were no balls or sticks available. A new game called 'toss Lisa'.

Whilst still testing my legs my daughter asked me where we will be next weekend. You would think that after all these letters she would realise that we have absolutely no idea. I just looked at her and said 'Do you fancy Adelaide?' to which she responded 'That's an eight hour drive away!' She has four days off and wants to be with us for her holiday. I managed to stall her off by saying that we do not know what's happening with Callie yet. It's 23C at the Gold Coast right now - my perfect temperature! The tenants want to break their lease as they've bought a house, we have no gas hot water heater in the van and now the 12volt lighting system has found itself a fault and we only have one 240v light which is in the bedroom. Cooking by torchlight is not fun. We have to have the T.V on with the sound off to give us some light. And my daughter wants to know which way we are going?

I reckon somewhere where it's warm, perhaps where we could walk to the beach at the Gold Coast! Perhaps even in our home area adjacent to a park, with a swimming pool in the back garden. A place with a proper kitchen, good showers, a toilet that doesn't need emptying and a washing machine that doesn't need feeding with cold hard cash before it will work. Instead of sitting in our van not wanting to go outside because it is too cold, we could walk on the beach and swim again and could hang the washing out to dry again. Where the dogs wouldn't be locked up in the back of the Ute to keep warm from 7pm to 8am! What about going home John? Isn't that rather a good idea? I happen to think it is.

My daughter will be moving soon and we are going to have to find a postal service as she will be staying on in Melbourne temporarily with some friends. We need to get the repairs done. We can always go off again later - we're free to do what we want. This is supposed to be a holiday, not an endurance trial!

CHAPTER FIFTY

Our en suite toilet is right outside our door and we stop and consider how we're going to make it those three steps from one door to the next because of the cold! John will stand there saying 'Towels in the bathroom, I've got my dressing gown on, do I need anything else?' before he makes a run for it. John puts his coat on before going out to open up the back of the Ute a couple of times in the evening in case the dogs need a pee and invariably they jump out with excitement and then jump straight back in again as soon as they feel the outside temperature! The more I think about this the more ridiculous I realise it is. John, of course, wants to go on to Adelaide. It's only two degrees warmer there and getting colder. I want to go to Adelaide too. In fact the more I read about it the more I want to go as it sounds absolutely beautiful. I want to enjoy it though. I want to come back. I want to see Phillip Island properly too. I also want to go to the Eyre Peninsular but without being blown off the beach by the wind and to drive to Adelaide via the ocean route starting at the other end of the Great Ocean Road - the part we missed out on when on a previous trip and the coastline of South Australia. Winter is not the time to do all this!

Monday - Callie does not have a blockage but despite the injection yesterday to stop her vomiting, she did as usual, not long after getting up and despite having had no food for three days. She's now on two different lots of tablets and we are still caring for her ourselves instead of agreeing that they admit her. However, if there is no improvement by Wednesday, she'll have to go on the drip and stay in. I told them I wanted to try her with some food as she's vomiting acid which can't be doing her much good and I am now trying lean chicken chopped up in rice. Her blood test was not good again. Despite the fact that they have not charged us consultation fees for the last two days, the costs have now risen to over $700 with pills, injections, x-rays and blood tests. Thank goodness we have the time to look after her ourselves as it would have cost us so much more had she been kept in hospital.

Today has been a lovely sunny day which gave us chance to get outside! This is due to end by Wednesday with a cold front due and rain. John went out but I dog-sat and did the washing and went through the piles of post that my daughter gave us yesterday. The good news of today is that the lights work again! John found three more fuses and we at last found the blown one! We have realised that this was from a faulty connection at a caravan park that we stayed at and we tried to find a polarity tester prior to leaving as suggested by a book we read but everywhere we asked, nobody had ever heard of it. If you know where we can buy one of these testers so we can check the park's connection prior to us plugging in, please let us know as it's caused us chaos and we don't want to have a repeat performance. We still haven't made a decision as to which way to go as Adelaide still tempts. We watch the weather forecasts keenly but they never tell us what we want to hear. That lovely town of Sale that we passed through a week ago was -3C last night - stuff that!

If we did return it would be to find three of the readers of this diary absent as one will be in Japan and Thailand for a month and another couple will be in Lancashire, U.K. for two and a half months with a side trip to Madeira. I have to keep up with everybody, taking their names off the group email address list for the holiday periods and trying to remember to put them back the week they return!

My calendar is filling up with other peoples holiday dates! Which reminds me, we really enjoyed hearing about the different protocols of marriage in Holland from one of John's workmates and we could visualise the splendid surroundings. Incidentally, we need a Kiwi interpreter here please as John is having a lot of trouble with the Kiwi receptionist. He came back to the van this morning saying that she keeps calling him Mr Tumms and he was trying to ask directions to Epping but she thought he wanted a place somewhere here called Uppan (I cannot even spell the pronunciation that he came out with). He was getting most frustrated with her apparently but they were both talking about the same place!

We had a yuk sort of day although weather was beautiful and Callie wasn't sick! John has been running around amidst 8 lanes of trucks trying to find a new wing mirror and after two days we have had two recommendations - order one from America or get it mended! We could get one that doesn't match but don't wish to do that and we want to reattach the electric wires as both mirrors are electrically adjustable. We enjoyed looking at smaller Winnebago vans today and found one that we really liked but they want $133,000 for it! We told the guy in the showroom that we need to get the mirror and gas heating fixed and he came up with a company very close to our park in an industrial area, who specialise in caravan and campervan repairs and the guy there that John spoke to has agreed to look at the mirror and the gas system tomorrow morning, as long as we take the rig to him. So tomorrow is the day we must decide what to do - if he needs us to stay here for parts then we will stay on. We had almost made a decision on where to travel to next and were very much in favour of carrying on to Adelaide but then we heard the weather report and it is so gloomy. John had left me at what appeared to be a large shopping centre but it turned out to be just K Mart and Coles - no coffee shop, no chemist, no newsagent etc. I was stuck there for a couple of hours whilst he had gone towards the city for the repair shops that he'd been told about. We both got home fed up and tired to find that birds had dirtied all over and down one side of the R.V. including the windows so John had to wash the R.V. I had to cook up more food for Callie and when I took her for a walk it was obvious that she was not feeling too good either. Jack tried to play with her as usual tonight and she tried to bite him which is so unlike her - usually she nudges his face and eggs him on. It was just one of those days.

We received a lovely email from a lady at the park at Cowes on Phillips Island. I had written apologising for booking in for two nights and only staying the one (the other night's money was refunded) and she suggested that we should return in February/March because the seas are calm then and it is absolutely beautiful. The lady who wrote was doing volunteer work for the coast guard that night and she can remember the strong winds and said that it had been so bad that we had done the right thing in leaving and getting away from the coast. This information is just in case you might have thought I over-reacted! But in hindsight I was right, although John thought I had panicked a bit - he had agreed that we move. Wednesday and Callie was sick again today.

Friday. My daughter has now joined us for the long weekend, we have a new Australian hot water system, the mirror has been repaired, Callie has stopped being sick and the weather has been cold but sunny. We are leaving tomorrow so now there will be three vehicles in tandem! There is no longer any debate about the direction to take - we are heading northwards towards warmer temperatures!

We had decided on our first town to stop at only to find that all the parks were fully booked. Another search and we got accepted at another park a little further away. Then tonight on the news they said that the very place we were going to had had an outbreak of Legionnaires disease and five people have already been admitted to hospital today and they are checking three 'air towers', whatever they are, in the town. Apparently the people who have been admitted have not been to the same places in town. We have now varied our route yet again.

My daughter enjoyed 'Mum's cooking' tonight (nothing extraordinary but as she said, because 'you can't beat your Mum's cooking') and I have enjoyed being a Mum again. I just wish I could see my sons too. We really have no other news as we haven't been into Melbourne! We have been there before of course, without the dogs! All we've done is sort out repairs to our R.V and have stocked up for our long journey via the inland route. It's been a very pleasant park to stay in and the local caravan 'doctors', as they call themselves, have been extremely efficient, friendly and reasonably priced and the local Animal Hospital extremely good so we are very pleased that we came to this area. We have also learnt that Callie and Jack are not fast enough to catch the rabbits! The park that we are now heading to have dogs, peacocks and a pet hamster running around the park so we'll have to keep the dogs chained but we are looking forward to getting there tomorrow for a change of scenery and to get away from the traffic! I am going to send this tonight because I fear that there will probably be times when neither phone will work. There appear to be some stretches when all we might see is a petrol pump.

CHAPTER FIFTY-ONE

Sunday 13th June - **Wangaratta**

I'm alone as the other two are playing golf. Well I think they are because I told them that if they couldn't get a game, they could only return to collect the dogs and then they'd have to scoot off again! Three people in this R.V is too much, even if it is big. I thought they'd never leave, so at 11.30am I stood in the middle of the van and contorted my body, with one leg stuck out, an arm supporting me and the other in the air and said 'Anyone want to come past me again?' When my daughter and I bumped bottoms last night I said 'Hands, knees and bumpsy-daisy' and then found out that she had never heard of the song. John and I gave her a rendition, all actions included. I told her that I should have taught her that when she was a child and told her my Mum used to say it, the same as she used to say that we should sit at the front on the top deck of a double-decker bus (very bumpy) because 'It's good for the liver'. I fear I have been sadly lacking in the eduction of my children.

The first night, my daughter slept in John's bed and he in the lounge because we knew she'd go to bed a lot earlier than us. My back was really bad and I didn't want to take any prescription drugs and I found I couldn't lie on my left hand side at all. After an hour, I finally dropped off which was about 12.30am. Next thing I know, my daughter is shouting 'Mum, you're snoring'. John tells me I snore but quite softly and rather rhythmically! I couldn't get to sleep again for another hour and normally I would have got up to do some exercises and get a drink of milk but I couldn't because I'd have woken John. A nightmare night ensued with her waking me up about six times! She woke me up so soon after dropping off at one point that I actually heard myself snoring! So last night we decided that she'd start off in the bedroom and then when John and I came to bed she'd swap with John and move into the lounge with pillow and quilt in tow. However, I couldn't wait for John to go to bed, but I couldn't sleep as I was too frightened that she would wake me up again! There was no point in John sharing a room with her because he snorts and splutters and wakes the neighbours at times. Eventually I heard John open up the double bed and she woke instantly and moved. When John finally climbed into bed I breathed a contented sigh of relief but just as I was about to drop off I heard 'Mum'. John answered her softly but no response.

'Was that her?' I asked John

'Yes'.

'What's up?' I called out.

'What's this noise?' she answered.

Now you can't stay in bed with the door closed when you get asked that. Rain on the roof? The possum that I had heard land on the roof earlier? The control box that cycles on and off, which I now love because when it makes that noise I know we'll have lighting in the van? I had to get up. She was on about a clicking noise that I'd never noticed and that occurred every 20 seconds or so.

John got up and said it was under the dashboard and he had no idea and went back to bed and so did I.

'I can't sleep with this?' she called out. I was losing it and getting angry and got up. 'What are you doing?' I asked her as she was leant over the front seat with a coat in her hand. She was piling anything she could find onto the dashboard to try to muffle the noise and when I caught her at it she started giggling.

'You're acting like a three year old' I said 'and Daddy's getting cross' (she's 25!). With that we both collapsed into fits of giggles probably due to our utter exhaustion. She finally put some toilet paper in her ears and we all went to bed. John and I snored away uninterrupted for the rest of the night. John got up around 9am and I struggled to get out of bed by half-past! The poor dogs must have been desperate for a pee as they were locked in the back of the Ute.

So, if you buy a van, don't be in too much of a hurry to invite people to stay! The noises and idiosyncrasies of your 'home' could drive other people nuts! At one point during the night, John had found her trying to cover up all the floor lights because she didn't know where the switch was to turn them off!

There is also another very important point to consider if you are thinking of asking a friend or relative to stay with you for more than one night (please note that my daughter is not the cause of this rumination). You may be unlucky enough to invite someone who does something that drives you insane and as you have about a forty percent chance of getting someone who will, it is a serious consideration. All females will know what I'm talking about. It is the eternal question of which way around is the right way when placing a new toilet roll on its holder. Like most wars there is no joy of knowing that there is a correct answer as no-one is right and no-one is wrong. So you must always ask all guests, before you invite them, which way around they hang it unless it's only a one night visit because you can put a new one in place before they arrive and if it is the wrong way for them, let them struggle to find the first loose piece. If you are really unlucky you'll get someone who hangs it the 'wrong' way and leaves the empty one on the floor or even worse, leaves both on the floor.

We had a very easy journey here as we stayed on the same main road all the way and there wasn't too much traffic. We are the other side of the Great Dividing Range but although the road climbed a little, it was very gentle and basically we cut through the range. The park is not that big and it is packed out for the long weekend. When I saw where we were supposed to park I said that it couldn't be done and that we'd have to leave. John managed it beautifully and people were coming up to me saying that it was the best parking they had ever seen and isn't he confident. By the time he had finished there was a crowd of about twenty watching. We settled in for a three night stay but John had forgotten to open up the tap for the grey water to drain and the first night it filled up the shower and then overflowed, all over the carpet between the bedroom and kitchen. We have had one heck of a job trying to get it dry but I think I'm finally winning with a fan heater blowing on it, now that I'm alone in the van and there's no 'traffic'. We had also believed that we were going to get a site with a sewer hole for the black water but unfortunately not. Our tank is three-quarters full! We can't let that overflow and are trying to limit the toilet for night use only.

By the way, we're in Ned Kelly country. This is where he and his family and gang hung out. I've looked at all the spots on the tourist map and boy, did he get about! Not bad when your only transport was a horse!

Hello, they're back! 'Rained off' apparently so no golf but although I feel crowded out, I will hate it when the weekend is over and we have to say goodbye to my daughter again.

CHAPTER FIFTY-TWO

DUBBO - 16th June

We left late from Wangaratta as we broke down inside the caravan park as we were driving out. Faulty choke apparently but we thought we had an electrical problem because of the rain and went off to find an auto electrician. First we found a mechanic though, who came to the park with us to check, found and fixed the problem and charged us $5! I thought they'd been a mistake! Only $5! By the time we left it was 11.45am. Trying to find the road to Wagga Wagga we had an argument via UHF phone as John was insisting that I should have turned off at a sign he'd seen. In the end I stopped the Ute and got out and shouted through his window 'That was **Walla Walla**, not Wagga Wagga'! How do these places get their names! We did pass through one very, very pretty town but we can't remember which place it was - we think it was Coolamon but we're not absolutely sure. Anyway, we didn't reach our proposed destination. We were driving at nightfall with 'Beware kangaroo' signs everywhere so had to pull into a tiny, tiny park at **Ardletha** (between Narrandera and West Wyalong).

We needed mains power so that we could put the electric fan heater on! I got up at 7.20am but we still didn't get away until 9.30am! I can never get over why it takes us so long. I think the dogs take up a fair bit of time. I immediately dressed, had a quick coffee, put the fire on and the hot water and took the dogs for their walk. I actually wore a 'beanie' and gloves! I'd bought them as a bit of a joke for $3 before we left home.

Then they needed feeding, a quick slice of bread and jam for me and another decafe coffee. Pull up all window blinds, make up a flask of hot water, put bathroom things away, toaster, fire, T.V aerial down, put breakfast dishes away - I tell you, the time flashes by. John did put a little petrol in the R.V and that took a few minutes but it's still ridiculous. The journey was uneventful and boring - endless fields and trees and very flat terrain. It's becomes quite exciting if you hit an intersection, go round a bend or cross a railway track! We saw a road sign for Brisbane - quite incongruous but then we were in a place called Marsden apparently, which is also a suburb about half an hours drive out of Brisbane in Queensland. However the scenery couldn't have been more different and when we came across Bland Shire we thought it aptly named. I was surprised to see a field of de-fleeced sheep - in this weather!

At **West Wyalong** I got chatting to a 'new' local who had just moved there from Gosford. I asked her why she'd moved there but apparently her daughter lives there. They've bought huge acreage and now don't know what to do with it. She doesn't really mind the weather but she's a Pom who used to holiday at Skegness so it's understandable! Anyway, with a British northerner's usual kindness, she has told me where her house is and if we pass through again we must call in for a cup of tea. I would too, because unlike Aussies who are always inviting you to a barbecue but never say when they are having one, she really means it. (John reckons I'll offend our friends but as I told him, you lot don't do that or you wouldn't be our friends!) We meet people at other BBQ's and chat for an hour and when either party leaves they say to us 'Nice meeting you, you must come to a BBQ sometime'. And we say 'Yes' and we never see them again. I have tried saying 'Yes. That would be lovely. When, where and what time?' It doesn't work of course because they say 'I'll get back to you on that' and you know they don't even know your name, let alone your telephone number! I never invite anyone to a barbecue as we haven't got one any more!

I originally arrived in Brisbane on a Thursday and met a lady on the following Tuesday morning at the local newsagent. She said 'You must come for a coffee' and when I asked 'When?' she answered 'Now, of course'. And I did and thus started a friendship. She was a Pom. A few weeks later I started helping out at the school tuck shop and an Aussie lady said 'You must come for a BBQ' and she continued to say that every month for eight months but it never did eventuate!

Anyway, this lady I met at West Wyalong - she told me that despite the weather it was shearing time and her son was shearing now and they don't care that the sheep get cold in winter as it 'Just has to be done'.

Half an hour before Dubbo and the journey changed because of the trucks. We'd hit road works which meant that everyone had bunched up and the bunch included about seven huge trucks, cars plus cars towing caravans which drove the truckies mad! One got so mad that he tried to overtake me (I was following John and we were travelling at 110ks) on double white lines, on a bend and couldn't get past before a car came the other way. He sat on my tail. Other trucks were passing the caravans and each other, plus there was one slow car (90ks) causing havoc. In the end I passed John and whatever was in front of him and got away from them all and I have to admit I did not know that my car could go so fast so easily but refuse to give you details for fear of incriminating myself! John got so fed up with the truck that he pulled over - boy, that driver was a mad man. The other truck drivers were good - it's just a matter of giving them some consideration and getting out of their way!

Anyway, we're bedded down for the night and it will be 3C here tonight. It was frosty this morning when I got up. We'll go a bit further yet on the Newell Hwy but I cannot wait to get down to the coast where it is so much warmer. Last weekend my son told me he was 'toasting' himself in a comfortable 23C at Browns Plains in Queensland. We've done over 800ks from Melbourne now but need to go a few hundred more. We were going to go all the way to Rockhampton this way but its damned boring and cold. John agrees we may as well enjoy the scenery on the way!

Dubbo Zoo - we are supposed to go to it because I'm not sure my son will forgive us if we don't! We're not sure we want to though! He warned us that it can get up to the high 40's in the summer but did not tell us that it gets so cold at the beginning of winter! We also missed seeing 'The Dish' today as we just wanted to reach Dubbo. We've already decided to stay at least two nights so we'll see. It would be nice to see some sunshine instead of heavy, grey clouds as far as the eye can see. Mind you, it's excellent weather for the ski resorts as apparently they are getting good falls of snow and the season is already up and running. Sydney has had another sunny day and they are praying for rain. My Aussie friends may wander why I go on about the variables of the weather but my overseas friends and relatives may be surprised at how different it can be in our different cities versus the mountains and the plains. We are only about 500ks inland from the sea 'as the crow flies' and all we see is farmland and fields. Of course, the roads don't run the same way as the crow flies, unfortunately!

CHAPTER FIFTY-THREE

17th June (I'm not sure what day it is cause every day is a holiday)

It was -1C last night and our windscreen cracked! Insurance job - they like to hear from me regularly and must have been missing my calls. Trouble is we can't find a replacement windscreen! Our windscreen now has a coat on tonight because John is trying to keep it warm with the Ute tarpaulin cover! We have a window open at the front so it doesn't get too hot inside (because of our heater) whilst so cold outside. It's a curved window. We have two separate windows to the front but it's on the driver's side and tinted and has to be specially made. Apparently it won't shatter but could continue cracking. The windscreen company is going to try and find out how to source one for us but we won't get it done here.

It's a pity as Dubbo is absolutely lovely. The town centre is attractive, interesting and there is quite a lot to see around here. In better weather we would happily stay for about 3 weeks but it's getting colder by day. Callie was stiff this morning - it's hopeless. We are in a lovely park with a large amount of green space in front of our van for the dogs to run free on - we're all happy here - during the day that is. We have to go to the windscreen place again tomorrow so that they can drill the screen to try and stop it cracking further and then we'll have to get moving the morning after - we are even considering tomorrow depending what time they finish! A couple of more stops further north and then we'll turn right - towards the coast.

Saturday 19th

Where are we? It's pouring with rain - let me look at the map. Ah yes, we're at **Armidale**. Where was I the last time I wrote? Oh yes, Dubbo. Well we did leave the next day as it was -1C and we had the two front windows open to equalise the temperature of the window - the curtain did not help to keep the cold out much! We got the hole drilled and left about 1.30pm. What a nice place that was. We must go back when it's warmer. We left via the Mitchell Highway to Gilgandra, then the Oxley Hwy to **Coonabarabran** where we stayed the night. Actually that's not quite right. I went on the Oxley Hwy but John went straight on! Anyway, we arrived at the campsite together and it was so cold that the dogs shared the van with us. They couldn't believe their luck and immediately lay down and didn't move all night. John got up to get a drink of water from the kitchen in the middle of the night and he said that Jack kept putting his big paw on his foot so that he couldn't go back to bed. It was due to be -3C but John braved the cold night air to go to the Skywatch Observatory just 2ks out of town and he thoroughly enjoyed it. I watched an old episode of Mother and Son and rocked with laughter.

So this morning we set off for another 290km run and it was a dream journey. We stopped at **Gunnedah** for coffee and **Tamworth** for lunch and John, who was leading, had no traffic in front of him for the whole journey. About half way through yesterday's journey, the scenery changed and we were back in the hills and dales of rural New South Wales. Today we climbed up and over part of **The Great Dividing Range**. At one point we could see the range across the open fields on three sides of us and the sunlight was glancing down the sides of the range. I had beautiful music playing and the sky was multicoloured with patches of blue, fluffy cotton ball clouds and sheer dark grey streaks and the total vista looked like an oil painting. We travelled for miles surrounded by so many changing colours and I felt deeply moved by the beauty of it. If all our road journeys were like this, I would forever want to travel. John broke the spell. I was breathing in the wonderful aroma of God's own country and thinking that it was so much more beautiful than road train fumes when the VHF radio came to life with a worried voice asking me 'Can you smell something foul?'

'No. Only manure'

'Oh, thank goodness, I thought there was something wrong with the vehicle'.

Today we have changed our route and instead of going to Narrabri to experience the hot springs, we left Coonabarabran via the Oxley Hwy (towards the coast) as we were fed up with the road trains that we encountered today. Tomorrow we had planned to head to Glen Innes but we have been told that it will probably snow there tonight. The only other route is The Waterfall Way and that's not advisable with the R.V. Must go, Parky's on T.V (for those in England - the Michael Parkinson shows are screened here about six months after you see them.)

Sunday

We drove through SNOW today - that white stuff. We had just left **Armidale** and I called John on the UHF 'What's that on the windscreen. Is it snow?' He didn't get chance to answer before it was obvious that it was. I found it highly amusing for some reason and couldn't stop laughing. No, it wasn't hysteria. There we were trying to get to warmer parts and I can hardly see John in front of me. I had to stop to shut the dog's rear window and Jack stuck his head out as usual and by the time I got to him he was black and white! I took a photo of the snow as I cannot recall how many years it is since I last drove through it! It was before I emigrated because the only snow I've seen here is on the tops of the mountains in the autumn when we went to the Snowy's but there wasn't any actually falling then. Anyway, snow stopped and we hit a patch of sun, then rain, then snow again - every 500m it changed. Then the snow got serious again. At one point it was snowing and sun shining and I had to put my sunglasses on. John's voice came over the two-way 'Isn't it pretty' and that sent me off into a fit of the giggles again. We passed **Ben Lomond** and **Llangothlin** and I begin to wonder if I've been beamed back to the U.K. I noticed that the cows don't bother to lie down in snow and were busy eating frozen grass. We were still climbing higher and higher. I saw a sign for **Ben Lomond Range** 1410m above sea level. It was somehow madcap and exhilarating to be driving in such conditions. I screamed down the two-way 'John, please put your headlights on so that I can see you' but he didn't respond and then I realised that I had been screaming into my tape recorder!

We passed a sign saying 'Great Dividing Range' and I realised that it was the first time I'd ever seen that sign and it reminded me of my lovely geography teacher back in High School in England so many years ago. We went over the **'Clarence River Overflow No 1'**, then No 2 quickly followed by the Clarence River. Now poetry flies into mind and I recall that the only other good teacher that I ever had was my English teacher! We drove over one of those old bridges 'clackety-clack'. It was quite long and single lane. I was nattering into the tape recorder and crawling along looking at the river when I realised that people were waiting the other side. A driver waved - I thought to me but he was waving at Jack who had managed to squeeze his head through the narrow window gap.

Half an hour before Casino we stopped for a coffee as we had just completed our climb over the range. We looked at the tourist map and realised that we had to go over another one, the next being the **Richmond Range**. We had to drive slowly because of the road and the sun was shining through the trees, the sky was blue and the beauty of northern New South Wales filled me with contentment. It is just so beautiful. I framed a thousand photos in my mind but couldn't stop as I was following John and we now had traffic behind. Creeks, gullies, dams, rustic old sheds and old barns with corrugated iron roofs gone brown with age, post and rail fences that look as though they were built when the settlers first arrived, almost falling over but not quite, the patterns in some sheer rock faces, the colours of the trees and some with bare trunks, devoid of foliage and looking stark against such a gentle backdrop. The hills, valleys, the cattle and horses, the signs for organic crops and seeds again which I haven't seen for a long time, pumpkins or bulls for sale! We arrive at Casino to find that we've missed 'Beef Week' and also an agriculture machinery show but who cares because I can smell a cup of hot coffee. And so we travelled. From Melbourne in Victoria to northern New South Wales and 'as the crow flies' we are only about 60-70ks from the Queensland border and almost all in email to you. Easy wasn't it!

CHAPTER FIFTY-FOUR

Tuesday 22nd June. **CASINO MOTOR HOME VILLAGE**

Oh what lovely sunshine - we are wallowing in it during the day. The first day Callie and Jack didn't know what to do with themselves! Callie (who gets so cold) kept lying in the shade and Jack (who gets too hot) was lying in the sun. Then Callie started moving in and out of it every ten minutes and they both panted continuously. That night it was zero degrees yet again - such a contrast to the daytime. Thank goodness we didn't stop at Glen Innes as they had -8C that night! The temperatures are only about 17C but it feels fine to us and the sun quite hot enough. We all need to acclimatise before going north. So we set everything up knowing that we had a lovely week of not going anywhere. The following morning I noticed that the black water was registering between three quarters full and full! We had passed the dump point on the way into the park! So we chucked some stuff outside on the table and packed the rest up and drove there to empty the tank and then put everything back again. Dogs were bemused as they were only in the car for 10 minutes instead of two hours - just for a tour around this park!

We received a phone call this morning from Dubbo and the news was that we could get the windscreen and they would phone the Lismore branch. Lismore phoned and said that they wanted to see the vehicle today. So we packed everything up yet again! John went to Lismore and I went shopping in Casino in the Ute with the dogs.

It's the monthly get together this weekend at the motor home village - barn dancing on Thursday night, free sausage sizzle on Friday night and dinner dance on Saturday night with disc bowls on Sunday. Three wonderful days of relaxation, hot during the day with good breezes. The Casino Headquarters is on a vast tract of open land (the old airport) and catches all the wind but when shopping in Casino yesterday we found it rather too hot. Not complaining though!

I discovered my feet again this week - I'd forgotten all about them as I haven't seen them for so long! It was when my feet became so hot that I dug out my thongs to wear again. For the last few months they have been hidden in socks and trainers, socks and Ugg boots, under the bedclothes or in hot water. I said 'Hello' to them. I noticed that I had broken a nail completely in half and had never realised it. I apologised to them and told them I'd pamper them a bit from now on.

John's gone to golf today and I'm cooking a beautiful, fat organic chicken. I managed to find a butcher near the cemetery (Frederick Street if you come here) who sells very good meat and all his beef and lamb this week is organic too. You should see the thickness of the rump steaks I bought! Not at all like those bought in the supermarkets. I had defrosted this chook overnight and was going to put it back in the fridge but got up at 7.30am, put the water heater and fan heater on and went back to bed and neither of us awoke until 9.30! The van was so hot! It's being cooked immediately so that we don't get food poisoning.

Well we opted out of the Barn Dance but we did go to the sausage sizzle night. I've already told you that I'm not good at 'small talk' in these types of social gatherings and usually do the washing up but the caterers were in the kitchen so I had nothing to do. However, whilst we were eating outside we were asked if we wanted to have the live music outside or inside and everyone opted for inside, except for us! However, that gave me something to do as I volunteered to clean up the tables outside! Well, our friend Harvey stayed outside too and by the time I joined him and John the discussion was scrambled eggs and custard. I thought you might like to try it! Harvey was saying that he doesn't buy milk and it used to cause him problems when he cooked scrambled eggs in 'Scruffy' (the name of his van). However, he now adds some custard as it gives it such a nice yellow colour. So there we are - I thought you needed to know that.

The lady in the next van to us was telling me that she has been to **Nimbin** twice this week. For those in England, Nimbin became famous when the Age of Aquarius festival was held in 1973. Anyway, it has stayed a hippie town as so many people who attended stayed on or return often. One of the original co-directors of that festival still lives there. Our new neighbour went to the candle factory and the museum and Rainbow Power Company. It has become famous throughout the world as it was pioneered by the hippies in town. So for Nimbin 'read' hippies, organic food, natural fibres and tie-died clothes, bead bracelets & necklaces etc, hand-made candles. However, it is most well know for the purchase of dope!

I first went there many years ago, to a settlement outside of town where about 16 couples bought a heap of land and tried living in a communal house. (I can remember the name but won't reveal it as they do not want 'sightseers'). Anyway, they didn't like living together and decided that they'd all have about ten acres each and build homes. They kept the original house for the telephones and washing machines and there was a roster system to man the phones and milk the cows etc.

Circumstances had caused us to miss meeting up with friends at Byron Bay en route the night before and we had got hopelessly lost, ending up at the town of Lismore on the other side of Nimbin. So we drove north again on the Nimbin road and it was now dawn. The sun rose and the mist cleared to reveal calves and lambs gambolling about the fields and the wild flowers and grasses were waving hello with excitement of a new day and the arming temperature. The soft green of the fields and the rolling hills enveloped us and neither of us spoke because of the sheer beauty of the scenery.

Having made enquiries from the only person around in town we eventually found the right gate that led to the homes but there were miles and miles of dirt roads going off in different directions. We asked some kids and they just pointed through the bush not realising that we actually needed to know what road as they don't use them.

When we did arrive I was overawed by the beauty the place and the land and will never forget my visit. After greetings were over and explanations given about our getting lost Pam suggested that we had a sleep as we were obviously exhausted having been up all night. She took us to a separate two-storey building where there were bedrooms upstairs and she offered me the large bed on the huge balcony which was reached via the main bedroom. I lay down gratefully but couldn't sleep. Surrounding two sides of the balcony were tree tops and a myriad of brightly coloured birds flitted from branch to branch singing and twittering to each other and I was enthralled. I was warmly bathed in the sunlight as I watched and listened. After a while I sat up to look at the view over the end of the balcony and there below was Pam with her three little girls, all with long blond hair and the four of them were collecting salad and herbs from their organic vegetable patch for our dinner that night. They were all naked, all beautiful to look at and the scene so perfect that it brought a feeling of peace and joy to my whole body and mind that I hadn't felt for a very long time. I was literally in the 'here and now' and wasn't able to let any other thoughts intrude. I can still 'feel' that peace as I recall it – so perfect, so natural and so beautiful. I lay down again as I didn't want them to see me watching them but I never did sleep but felt totally rested as though I'd slept for hours.

Ever since then, when we have been house hunting I have always felt that 'something' was missing and ever since, I have always wanted a large balcony off an upstairs bedroom with tree tops either side and a view beyond, plus a large outdoor bed for summer.

Pam's land (I've changed her name) included a section of ancient fig trees and they were awe inspiring. The guys were swinging off the vines shouting 'Tarzan'. It was truly ancient rain forest. We had gone for the picnic races which happen annually and is a chance for everyone to get together for the day. A lot of the original people were professionals and had busy lives on top of building their homes and growing their own vegetables etc. We had a wonderful stay. It was blazing hot and the water-holes were icy cold but we splashed and swam for as long as we could in them. I just loved it there. To me it was paradise. Pam told me that she was going to move to Lismore for a few years, so that her three daughter's could get used to town and roads as they had grown up not having to worry about such things and they had their own bus on site to get the children to school. However, no-one there sold their places so I presume she still owns it. I lost contact with her but often think of her wonderful home and land.

I had another trip to Nimbin which was totally different unfortunately. I stayed in the hotel in the town and I had a room with a balcony over the front door of the hotel. In the early hours of the morning there was a loud banging on the door and a man was shouting 'It's Jesus here. Let me in'. I heard another male answer but I won't repeat what he said. I remember lying in bed giggling and thinking 'This could only happen in Nimbin'.

Every so often there is a drug raid. I was sitting in the Aquarius café the night before waiting for my organic/vegetarian delicious meal when the whispers started. I whispered to the female friend I was with 'What's up?'

'Cops are on their way'.

The police had no chance of finding anything with the bush telegraph that works in that area. I got a 'nod' when a civilian-clothed man walked in. Everyone knew he was a cop and there was no sign of any drugs. The next morning it was business as usual which means that if you walk the length of the very short main street you will be asked about five times if you need any dope (there are various terms). My friend had actually gone to buy some the night before and she had had to drive about two hours driving distance to get any, as that is how far the news had spread.

When I left Nimbin, I had to attend a Jazz Festival at the Gold Coast (we lived in Brisbane at the time). By the time I had got back onto bitumen roads my white car was grey with dust and so was I as I didn't have any air-conditioning and had had the windows open. I was going to a high class hotel and I parked the car at the seafront as I did not have the courage to use the hotel parking. I crept into reception hoping that no-one that knew me would see me and asked the receptionist where I could immediately get a hot shower. She gave me a quick glance over and handed me the keys to the beauty salon which was closed. I found a lage spa bath and stayed in it for an hour! I came out beautifully dressed and wearing high heels with my hair blow-dried and my make-up in place and as I reached the bottom of the wide staircase there were my two friends and I joined them for lunch. What a change of environment! I kept thinking of where I had been that morning and how I looked in comparison to the present moment and had to keep myself from laughing all through lunch.

One does not have to travel far to gain wonderful experiences that stay with you a lifetime - just be prepared to accept unusual invitations. When my friend had said to me 'Do you want to come with me for a drive to Nimbin?' one Saturday afternoon, I said 'Yes' before she even told me to bring an overnight bag 'Just in case we stay'. I envisaged I could end up on someone's slab floor for the night and it was only when I found myself alone, although I did actually bump into another friend and we spent some time dancing in the pub, that I decided I'd feel safer with my own room at the hotel! I wonder where these people are now and what they are doing. Visit Nimbin. It's an experience.

When we leave Casino we are going to stay with my son near **Murwillumbah** on the Saturday night and will park on the river bank and plug into his place for power.

CHAPTER FIFTY-FIVE

Parked by the river, sun shining, fishermen in small boats, fishermen on the banks, an old wooden boat that has been restored and now operates as a tourist cruise, kids on a houseboat shouting out greetings, and opposite, resplendent, towers **Mt Warning**. I called out to John 'It's so wonderful to be 'home'.

'Yes it is. As soon as I saw the sign for Tweed on the highway I thought so. This area is so beautiful.'

We had driven from Casino to Lismore and then turned towards Bangalow and the scenery had been stunning. We had to go under a bridge in Lismore which was 3.4m and our rig is 3.2m - without the air conditioners/roof hatches etc on top. John stopped and I was shouting down the two-way 'Go, go, go', as there were many cars stuck behind me. I can visualize his cringing appearance as he crept forward. He made it of course or we wouldn't be here. It is so good to be back, if only for a couple of days and it's wonderful to be staying with my son.

I have just spent a very frustrating hour trying to sort out why a photo would only print in black and white. I thought there was something wrong with the printer or the ink and even went as far as replacing the colour ink cartridge. It was a picture of the snowstorm and a deciduous tree. If you ever try to print a similar photo don't worry if you have problems as there isn't any colour!

We had a lovely stay with my son but I was surprised at how busy and noisy it can be parked here by the river. We had some fishermen there that night trying to catch a shark! Tourist helicopters fly en route to Mount Warning and back to Sea World on the Gold Coast and then there is the river traffic. We decided to put the van in a local caravan park so that we could go off and leave it without having to worry as there were so many people passing by. So we went to the **Chinderah Lake** caravan park on Sunday and as soon as we had parked the R.V we set off in the Ute with my son to go towards Mount Warning for a roast lunch at the pub at **Uki.** A lovely day and my son only left us when he realized that he was about to fall asleep! He still gets up in the early hours of the morning and goes to bed about 8pm. Seemed strange and sad to be already saying goodbye to him and he suggested to John that I need a holiday and we should settle somewhere for a month. John has now said that it is up to me when we move and where we move to.

At the end of the first half of our trip there has been a change in outlook for John. He loves the hinterland and doesn't want to camp near the sea all the time any more. He's also slowed down a bit, thank goodness. John's enjoying the life on the road but doesn't like going too far in one day. He likes the change of scenery and enjoys exploring new areas, once the van is parked. Conversely, he loves the familiarity of this area. As for me, I'd be just as happy to go home now. I'm tired, in fact I feel like I've run a marathon, which I have! This 'holiday' is too long for me.

On Monday-Wednesday inclusive, we'll be at **Tanah Merah**, where there is one of the very few parks in Brisbane where dogs are welcome. It is also easy to get to as it's just off the Freeway that we'll be on to travel north. My other son will be coming to see us here so I'll have seen all my kids within a couple of weeks - not bad when touring around Oz! Seeing them is far more exciting than travelling. The park is opposite the Logan Hyperdome just off the Freeway so it's very handy for us. We will have three days to enjoy not having to pack up the van. My x-work mate with whom I have the crazy conversations will also be visiting. We are so looking forward to catching up with family and friends. John's friend who writes the Jazz articles in the Gold Coast Bulletin has already promised to come and visit us despite working full time and editing his second book which will be published in September. Not on Sunday afternoon though as that is when his live Jazz radio program is transmitted! Busy lives some people have.

We have just realised that the school holidays have started which makes life difficult for us when we leave Brisbane to travel north. John wants to have a look at Hervey Bay again but we doubt that we'll get in a park there so will probably phone the one at the Glass House Mountains, at Beerburrum and see if we can stay in that area for about a week. It's a lovely area and we tend to fly by it on the new road and miss it nowadays. Also it's central to Caboolture, Bribie, and Caloundra and just off the highway. As soon as the nights are warmer we'll be looking up our information for off-road places and then we won't need to bother very often with caravan parks. Just occasionally, to recharge everything and to do a big wash!

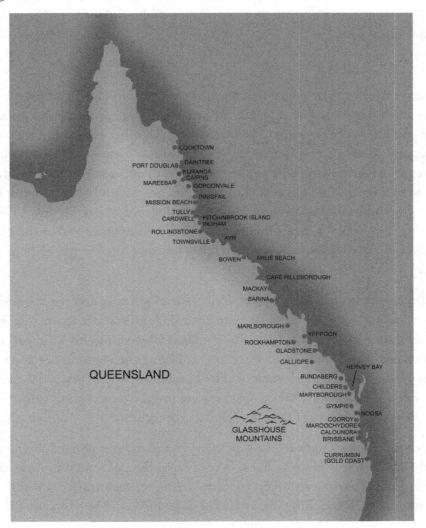

CHAPTER FIFTY-SIX

We're in Brisbane at Tanah Merah. We've just completed setting up and have had lunch and my son is coming to dinner. This is my son who rarely travels far. Huh! He's just booked a ticket to Adelaide on Wednesday as he's going down there to try working with a close friend who has his own painting business. So he'll be there before me! If we'd gone on to Adelaide we could have caught up with him there! John has just asked me how I feel about having three children in three different States!

I need to face the grocery shopping within the next 24 hours which means summing up the courage to face the Logan Hyperdome, do our pile of washing and face repairs to our new water heater! We connected the water on arrival only to find that it is pouring straight back out of the overflow pipe and won't stop. My son is taking our dogs out for the day tomorrow - not us - the dogs! How about that - we're being left behind! They are going to visit his dogs and the kid's Dad and his dog! Huh. And I'm left with the shopping and washing! It will be very odd without the dogs outside our door.

Wednesday

Well I didn't have time to even notice that the dogs weren't around. I had just put two loads of washing in the machines but hadn't yet made my bed when my phone rang and it was my daughter with heaps of good news. Meanwhile, John was using the other phone and was on hold to our mortgage company. John's mate appeared at the door calling 'Hello' with John saying 'Hush' and behind his friend was the guy to mend the water heater. By this time we had flooded the ground outside and had planks of wood to get to our door! Not good with stringent water restrictions in place! Our poor friend backed back out and said 'You appear to be rather busy, I'll wait outside' and I'm shouting 'No, come in Baz' and my daughter's on the other end of the phone trying to get my attention to say that she will hang up but I couldn't hear in the bedlam of people and dogs woofing.

Kettle on and everyone in their right places, John's friend relaxing and water heater man hard at it and my son turns up with one of his dogs and our dogs go ecstatic again with joy. He picked up their leads and they went even more ballistic and clambered into his 'dog' car. I settled down to catch up with our friend's news and when he left I hung the washing out and prepared to go to the shops as I hadn't even had a biscuit to offer him but my friend phoned to say she'd be here in half an hour and it would have taken me that long to get over the other side of the main road and to have found a parking space, let alone find a grocery store!

Another lovely visit, then straight to the supermarket and my son phoned saying the dogs were a bit confused and when would we be back. With two trolleys of food we returned and he came back with the dogs. By the time we'd said goodbye to him we were stuffed. Piled the dry washing back into a basket, put all the shopping away, fed dogs and said I was too tired to cook dinner.

We had toasted chicken and pineapple sandwiches, tidied up the van and had just sat down when some more friends arrived. After a wonderful evening, they left at 11.15pm! I slept in until 10 o'clock the next day!

I did the last lot of washing and hand washing this morning and here I am on the computer. John has broken a tooth so is looking for a dentist, also going to the Post Office to get our mail redirected to our friends who were with us last night as they have kindly said they'll forward it to us when my daughter moves, gas bottle needs filling and we need a water reduction valve to fit to taps to stop our overflow pipe from blowing again. Apparently the water pressure is too high in this park and it still leaked with a new valve, even when the tap was turned down. A handy hint for camper van owners as this is a fairly common problem - just one we didn't know about!

We so enjoyed seeing my son and our friends again as we hardly ever have any interesting conversations face to face with people any more. Conversations revolve around 'Where are you heading?' or 'Where have you been or awning covers and the fact that there's a local RSL in town where we can get cheap meals and for five dollars we'll get a raffle ticket for a meat tray, so many games of bingo with tokens for the 'pokies' and such like!

With John's mate we not only discussed family matters and work but found out that he has a second radio program now on a Wednesday night and he's doing his index now for his book as it's ready for publication and may well be made into a film and he explained to me what I need to do to get books published and how to 'sell' books to publishers.

With my friend, who looked so different and so pretty with her hair grown longer, it was Real Estate and mutual friends and contacts and her dogs and investments and with our evening visitors (who are the same generation as my kids) it was their upcoming holiday in New Zealand, their new investment home and their four wheel drive and soft-top sports car and their dogs!

I marvel at the accomplishments of the younger generation who have two incomes and no children. Obviously they both work hard for what they have and are not on extraordinary salaries (she does two jobs with her second job taking up her weekends) but when I was a year older than her I had nothing. Well I had three children and a trunk of their toys and our clothes but at one point that was all I had. I didn't even have a home for a short time.

I also realized that I was thirsting for some decent conversations and laughter! I do miss that 'on the road'. It also reminded me how lucky we are to have such good friends who drop their lives at the drop of a hat and come and see us immediately. No-one had much warning as they hadn't received my email on Saturday and some haven't even read it yet so they all thought we were still in Dubbo!

I was hoping to catch up with my daughter's best friend today and see her new baby but until I know what's happening with John's dentist appointment and I've been to the shops, to get the things from shops other than the supermarket (health shop for example) I'm not sure when I'll have the car. We are not that comfortable staying in a cramped park with the dogs, right next to the toilets and laundry and although we have been made very welcome here we are no longer used to the sound of the traffic!

We have not done the normal tourist trips at the Gold Coast of course and neither have we visited Brisbane. If we didn't have the dogs I'd be tempted to catch the bus at the Hyperdome and go into Brisbane. Perhaps for the Friday night markets at Southbank or just for a walk and coffee around the gardens and beach and lagoon, perhaps a tourist bus around Brisbane, another trip up the river in the ferry or the Sunday markets at Riverside. It would be nice to walk along the river in the Botanical Gardens too. I must go back to the Art Gallery again - it is so pleasant there and there's no charge to go in.

I hear there's a good new show starting soon at the Cultural Centre which reminds me that Jupiter Casino at the Gold Coast also have a new show. Have you been to Sea World to see the polar bears? I can recommend it - they enthralled us. It almost tempted me to buy a season ticket when I last went there so that I could go and see them regularly. I like Seaworld best although my foster-daughter preferred the Currumbin Sanctuary when she and her daughter were out here. The last tourist park I went to was Dreamworld - I went on my own when John went to the car racing at Willow Bank and I had a ball. I even visited the Big Brother House and was fascinated at the placing of the cameras. Movie World is o.k. but Seaworld is my favourite.

There is so much to see here and travelling makes you appreciate what we have on our doorstep. Why do we normally wait until we have visitors to go and see all these places? John and I used to have weekends in Brisbane when we lived at the Gold Coast before and we must do it again as it is a great city. Those new to Brisbane can pick up Brisbane Visitor's Guide at some caravan parks and the information centres and it has a list of cruises and tours in the back. At the Gold Coast you'll stay with us!

CHAPTER FIFTY-SEVEN

Saturday

Glass House Mountains. It doesn't take long to look around here as unfortunately the area is getting ruined with brick and tiled houses which are breeding out of control. The mountains are fascinating as is the legend surrounding them and there are a couple of good lookouts as well as many walks. Yesterday we looked at all the local villages as far as **Landsborough** and found that the main town is **Beerwah.** We have seen all the mountains from virtually every angle. We both agreed that we loved the Moss Vale area so much and all those beautiful villages, that what we see here in this area pales into insignificance. However, today we went to **Caloundra** and stopped at Moffats Beach and Shelley Beach and had a very relaxing day with a picnic lunch and weekend newspaper. The dogs enjoyed examining rock pools again and so did I. We had a coffee 'al fresco' and tied the dogs to a public bench at the end of the seating area but were asked to 'tell' them to move to the other side of the bench because of the health regulations. We were told the Council is very active in enforcing the rules and I amused a neighbouring couple by standing over the dogs telling them that 'Rules is rules and the Council insists that you sit on the other side of the bench'. The dogs listened intently but didn't budge. Callie's forehead wrinkled as she struggled to make out what I was saying. I saw a chain which stops pedestrians from crossing the road and attached them to that but Jack kept creeping under the bench to get nearer to us so we all pretended not to notice.

Anyway, I was reading the Courier Mail (which is quite interesting when you haven't seen it for months) and the Arts Council had a list of events between July and December in the paper and it reminded me of so many events that we are going to miss. However, I would have missed them anyway because I always plan to go to them every year and somehow don't get around to it! Last year I even marked them on the calendar but still didn't go and very often it is because John doesn't fancy whatever it is that's on. That's going to change! If we can be a tourist around the rest of Australia then we can be tourists at the Gold Coast and in Brisbane. We actually went to more events at the Gold Coast when we lived in Brisbane than we do now!

I have never been to The Valley market in Brisbane nor the annual Fiesta, nor the writing festival, nor the International Film Festival (and John loves films). I cannot recall the last time we went to a Jazz Festival or the Riverfestival (yes, it is all one word) in Brisbane nor the Last Night of the Proms and I've wanted to go to the Woodford Folk Festival for years. I see that Andrea Bocelli will be at the Brisbane Entertainment Centre and the Brisbane Powerhouse Theatre (another place I've never seen) will host Flamenco Fire - music, dance and tapas. Have you ever experienced live flamenco - if not I can highly recommend it as the sights and sounds invade your body and soul. Mind you, I was always in Spain when I experienced it and had always had a few drinks! This is not an advert for Brisbane. I'm wondering if you are like us and rarely join in local festivals and act like tourists. I'm not talking about a walk on the beach or in a park at the weekends. If we were to do all the things on offer at the Gold Coast, Brisbane, Sunshine Coast and surrounding hinterland we could have a diary full of varied and entertaining events. So why did we need to go touring to realize that we can learn and discover so much where we actually live?

But will we be tourists when we return? I doubt it unless we have visitors staying. Do we need to live somewhere else to enjoy the area we now live in? When I think of the Gold Coast I think of the traffic! We have met some visitors from England, staying here in this park. Today they've gone to see Australia Zoo (just up the road) and are hoping to bump into **Steve Irwin** (the 'Crocodile Man'). We met him years ago when he used to do the croc show and the snake show and he was just as mad then. Anyway, there is a young girl and her boyfriend and her Mum and Dad. The kids landed in Perth (they offered no comment but loved Esperance), travelled to Adelaide (Simpson Desert boring, loved Adelaide), Melbourne (liked but not the weather), Sydney (again no comment) and Brisbane (loved). They summed up the above a second time by saying that in Australia, so far, they have loved Brisbane and Adelaide and the coastline of New South Wales is very pretty. They too will be going to Cairns, like us, and then right around via Darwin and back to Perth. The daughter lives at Twyford and the parents at Windsor so it was great for me to catch up with news of those areas in the locality of where I lived from the age of nine until I married when I was twenty.

We are delighted with the cost of petrol here. We have just paid thirty cents less per litre for it than we did in Melbourne. Considering Queensland only gets an 8c per litre subsidy provided by the State Government and we are now in a rural area with little competition it really does seem crazy.

Callie appears to be better although she does have times when she starts to walk slowly and we think she's in pain. She has not been sick since Melbourne and she is beginning to tease Jack again and to gamble about. Dogs never like a sudden change in diet and I think she's improving as she's adjusting to her new tinned food and dog biscuits and we are only feeding them both once a day instead of half the amount twice a day as we used to. I decided to do this so that she has a long period between meals to give her pancreas a break.

Another lazy day tomorrow and then off we go again on Monday and this time I don't mind moving on as we have had the time to relax here and I've caught up on filing old touring leaflets and have swapped my clothes again so that the winter ones are stored and the summer clothes are back in the drawer. When we change the quilts over it will be good but I have accepted that this is a very early winter with unusually low temperatures at night (I wake up cold nearly every morning and this morning I was shivering) but the further north we go the better it will get. The daytime temperatures are beautiful and have reached 25C at times.

I read today that the ski slopes have twice the amount of snow as they had at the same time last year and that they are in for a bumper season. Everywhere else seems to need rain. This drought is really very worrying for our economy and I'm sure that those of you who live outside of Australia have no idea how bad it is here. I saw a photograph of one of the major dams that supplies Sydney with water and it is now dangerously low despite the water restrictions.

It was so noisy at the Glasshouse Mountains, with both the parks there having the main road outside their doors, plus trains at all hours that we decided to leave for northern Queensland and set off for Childers.

CHAPTER FIFTY-EIGHT

CAIRNS FROM LAKE MORRIS ROAD

For those of you abroad, **Childers** is where the back-packing hostel was deliberately burnt down killing and injuring so many, mainly young, tourists from all over the world. The place has changed as it is so much busier than I remembered, probably because of the wonderful reputation that the locals gained due to their compassion and assistance at the time. From what I've read I believe that at least one backpacker stayed on permanently and many of them return to see the people they became such close friends with. There is a new hostel now and there is a memorial to those who died but unfortunately the place was closed, as was the information centre by the time we'd parked the van and returned to town. In case you stop here, they close at 4pm during the week. We had a lovely dinner at the Hungry Hippo café and the staff were very friendly. I had quiche, chips and a huge, wonderful salad for $6.50. However, a lady who worked at the park made life uncomfortable for us and we won't go back to it but there is another park.

As soon as we arrived we were told there was no room but another guy overruled that decision and there was indeed plenty of space. In the morning I saw her fiddling with the tap near the laundry where our hose was connected. I asked her if there was a problem and she accused us of having a faulty hose and having wasted water all night. I turned off the supply and went to talk to John. He insisted there had been nothing wrong with it so I went back to check the fitting and found the top ring undone! I tightened it and turned it on and it worked just fine with no drips. I told her someone must have undone it whilst we'd been out for dinner the night before and it was fine but she didn't answer. John was about to nip to the bank to get some more cash as they would not accept a credit card the night before and she asked when we were leaving as she wanted to put the sprinkler system on - it was spitting with rain at the time! Would you return? What a way to run a business!

FREE FORESHORE POOL IS PACKED

Not far from there, at **Gin Gin** for example, we saw some great off-road camping sites and they seem to be very popular but we had to go much further north before stopping for the night. With the aid of information I'd saved from our club web site, we headed for free parking behind the hotel at **Marlborough** (hot showers $2 and a good menu). By this time it was dark and it was so quiet it hurt my ears! In the morning John realised he would not have enough petrol to get to the next town so he went into the shop (other than the one shop, a police station and the hotel there was little else there) and asked if there was a petrol station in town. He was told that he'd have to go back 30ks or onwards for about 130ks before we'd see a petrol station. So we drove out of the hotel grounds, glad to leave the dust behind (due to the drought) and around the corner there was a petrol station! He told them what he'd been told at the shop and was told that there is rivalry afoot - something about it being a BP town and his was a Shell or something. We filled up and set off north only to pass another petrol station a few kilometres further along and another before the next town. Neither John nor I can understand the mentality of people such as that girl in the shop. We had arrived in the dark and the petrol station looked closed for good because there were no prices on the sign (nor were there the next day) and perhaps she thought we were stupid not to have seen it when we arrived but she must be a pretty miserable person to be so unhelpful to tourists. We'll not go back to that town again of course! At least it was quiet there though! I thought that 'country-folk' had a reputation for being friendly!

Next stop was **Bowen** where all the parks were full and many vans were still turning up looking for spaces. We were directed to the show grounds where there was heaps of space and power. Again the grass was bare and it was a dust bowl and John kept getting grit behind his contact lenses because it was very windy. At $5 per person per night it was cheap for us but a couple turned up with three young children and when they heard they left. I don't blame them as a charge of $25 per night was outrageous - the Council should not charge for children. That is a normal charge for a four star park. The guy who took our money asked us if we needed a receipt as he didn't have a receipt book with him. Considering that he was meeting each van, I can only wonder! However, he was very friendly and helpful and we were grateful to fill our internal tank up with fresh water and have power for the night at such a cheap rate. The dust made us move on in the morning, after John made a quick trip for groceries. We also saw some large land releases for more houses, so Bowen seems to be growing at a rapid rate - probably because of the lack of land at Airlie Beach and corresponding high prices. I like Bowen and we will go back. It's a laid-back town with so many beaches and when we first visited we were actually staying at Airlie Beach which is so stunningly beautiful. I said to John at the time that Bowen would be the next place to take off and it would be a very good place to buy an investment home. At that time the house prices there were dropping, whilst rising at every other coastal town in Queensland and you could still buy beachfront property at ridiculously low prices. However, the rents were so low then that it did not seem feasible to invest.

(Footnote: I have since read that the Council charges $10 per night per van at time of writing this, so if you are asked for more, contact the Council.)

CHAPTER FIFTY-NINE

BARRON FALLS

We were doing short stopovers en route to our final northern destination with the idea being that we will return very slowly and that the rising temperatures in the north will push us home - the correct way to travel! About 21ks past **Townsville** we stayed for two nights (in order to get three loads of washing done) at **Bluewater**. The park is actually about 5ks before Bluewater and it is a very large park with fairly new and very friendly owners. There is heaps of room for the biggest of R.V's and there were quite a few there. One was a coach with enormous trailer box on the back to house their four-wheel-drive vehicle. The overall length must have been over fifty feet. Apparently it is very thirsty to run (diesel) because of the weight and travels at around 40kph up hills. They are thinking of upgrading at some point to something with a bit more grunt. The owners are a young couple who sold their house and this is now their life. They have been travelling for ten months now and, like us, were amazed at the NSW coastline. She found it similarly exhausting as there was too much to see every day. They haven't worked so far but may do some fruit-picking which seems very popular. There were a lot of fruit-pickers camped at the Bowen Showground. By the way, there is absolutely nothing at Bluewater itself - not even a house that I could see!

We left the motor home at the side of the road at El-Arish and went to look at **Mission Beach** and to check out a park as we intend to stop there on our return journey. Apparently a Canadian visitor once said it is 'Utopia with mod cons' and I'll go along with that description. I know of someone who came out from England and once she saw the area returned so often that she ended up in buying land there and building a house. I had heard so much about it that it has been a long held dream of mine to visit the area and I knew I wouldn't settle down in Cairns unless I'd at least had a quick look as we passed the turn-off.

We arrived at **Innisfail** as it was getting dark and pulled into another Road Rest stop with free cups of coffee. In Australia they are called 'Driver Reviver' and are funded by the Transport Department to encourage people to have a break on long journeys so they don't fall asleep at the wheel of their vehicles. They are manned by volunteers and we visit them frequently! It was pretty good so we camped on the grass for free overnight and were soon joined by three other campers in two vans. After packing up in the morning we had another free cup of coffee before setting off!

Then it was a short hop to **Cairns**, where we stopped in town so that I could visit the farmer's fruit and vegetable market and then have a quick drive around to refresh our memories. We were amazed at how much it has changed since we were last here and it is absolutely stunning now. The changes are vast but so well planned and the new lagoon and beach is only a small part of those changes. There are now outdoor cafes everywhere and the place is buzzing with vitality. There are a lot of new buildings but they've retained the parkland opposite the backpacking hostels along the Esplanade. Everything has been upgraded though and it looks bright and clean yet still has the same casual characteristics that charmed us so much before. We had not seen the Convention Centre, nor the Casino and there are far more high rises but they are mainly at the southern end of town around that old industrial area that used to look so sad. We didn't recognise the road into town as it is now built up with light industry and it was bustling with activity. We were happy to see that the place we've stayed at before in Sheridan Street is still there and still doing budget accommodation. I have happy memories of our stays there.

We have finally settled in on our site at **Lake Placid** and it's a late Sunday afternoon and we have already decided to take a run to Cooktown in the Ute and stay the night in a motel - sometime during the next two weeks. It is raining and very cloudy but we don't care as there is a beautiful lake one minute's walk away (part of the Baron River) and we can swim in the cool clear water there or in the huge tropical pool in the park here. A two minute walk takes us to the Lakeside licensed restaurant which is open seven days a week and boasts some very cheap lunches and dinners in the most beautiful surroundings. We can hire boats there, aqua bikes, paddle boats and surf skis. We can also go white water rafting and I kind of fancy that.

The park is beside the **Barron River National Park** yet we are five minutes to a large local shopping centre. We are only 5ks from the Kuranda railway station (a steam train which takes you through scenery which leaves me speechless), 2ks to the Sky-Rail terminal (also to Kuranda) and about 13ks on good straight road to Cairns. There are beaches galore to visit too of course and we will obviously visit Port Douglas again. When I first went to Port Douglas many years ago with a friend, there were a lot of empty shops for lease and I remarked that it would be a good investment to own some land in the main street - that turned out to be an understatement! The next time I visited the prices made Brisbane prices look like peanuts! At that time I was a single parent on a pension and felt very frustrated that I didn't have the money to invest!

CHAPTER SIXTY

Cairns is a vibrant city - or so it seems and if it wasn't for the weather it would be wonderful to live here. What a contrast to Melbourne where we were only a few weeks ago and where we were so cold. In fact it's not that long since we were in a snow storm in New South Wales and now we are in the tropics. This, of course, is the best time of the year to visit but I do no think I could cope with the summer humidity, particularly in January. 'The green season' (monsoonal rains) usually starts about November and goes through to around May. I might handle it up to the end of October but would have to hibernate in an ice-box until April again! I wouldn't like having to wear mesh suits to be able to swim in the ocean because of 'stingers' (jelly fish) and I can only assume that the netted areas for safe swimming get packed out. Even today with grey, heavy clouds and rain, the lagoon in Cairns was very busy and it's only about 25C. I wonder what summer is like!

BARRON FALLS 2

Still, as with everywhere, I suppose you get acclimatised or there wouldn't be so many people living here and so many thriving businesses would there? Also, with the Daintree and Cape Tribulation just up the road it may be worth putting up with the summers. Oh, it is good to be back. We are surrounded by leaflets with so many wonderful things to do. Yesterday was a leisurely day for us as we only looked at the Barron Falls Hydro Electric station which is just up the road from us. Today we went to **Trinity Beach** to have lunch - paradise and then on to have a look at the beach at **Yorkey's Knob**. After two days of relaxation I feel like a new person. Mind you, I've also been sleeping on top of my soft, feather down quilt and it is so lovely for my back that I've slept really well! Today, I've changed the quilts over but I've folded the down quilt and have placed it under my bottom sheet! I'm like the Princess with the pea!

We have also booked a ticket for the Skyrail which stops twice and takes up to 1¾ hours to reach **Kuranda**. As well as the stop at the Barron Falls Station (like the steam train), there is another called Red Peak Station with a boardwalk through the rainforest. The cableway is 7.5ks (4.7 miles) long with the tallest being 40.5 metres (133 feet). Red Peak Station at 545 metres (1788 feet) is the highest point. The towers were placed by helicopters so as not to disturb the rainforest (someone told me that it was actually cheaper to do it that way but it sounds good when you read it on the leaflet). It costs $50 return or $35 one way with no pensioner concessions. So instead of paying out $100, plus boarding fees for the dogs whilst we do it, we have decided that John will go up on it whilst I drive up in the Ute with the dogs and then I'll come down on it. We'll both take the camera of course! I will get to Kuranda long before John, which suits me just fine as I'll have a quiet cup of coffee and soak up the atmosphere and then hopefully find a butcher that sells organic meat. When John arrives, he can sup coffee and look after the dogs whilst I tour the market. We'll probably have a picnic lunch and wander around before I get onto the Skyrail for the return journey. The clouds have gone and it has been a sunny 27C today with cool breezes so we haven't felt too hot.

Wow, Kuranda has changed. The market was a bit disappointing and apparently the best day to see it is still Sunday but there are so many shops there now and it seemed to me that most of the stalls I used to visit have now become shops. There are few ordinary shops and there is no butcher selling organic meat. Instead you see gift shops, art galleries, clothes and cafes galore. It is very pretty. The Skyrail was interesting but did not overwhelm me like the train ride. I have been on the train ride during two previous trips to Cairns and on the train I felt surrounded by the forest and the views and I did not get the same feeling looking down on it. There is a fare amount of land disturbance around all the pylons and certainly at the two stations and I now do not think it is a good idea to have one at Springbrook (Gold Coast hinterland). However careful they are when building, it still cuts a scar through the beautiful forest and must affect the wildlife. I think the original trip up with the back-packer mini-bus, stopping on the way up for the army-duck tour and boomerang throwing and returning by rail is the best option.

CHAPTER SIXTY-ONE

ANOTHER BEACH VIEW

Friday 16thJuly.

We have seen several 'Beware of the Cassowary' signs recently. On a prior trip John, my daughter and I stayed in Cape Tribulation, north of Cairns on the other side of the Daintree River. To visit Cape Tribulation and stand on the beach where the rainforest meets the ocean is an experience not to be missed.

Anyway, I took my daughter for a walk to see if we could find these birds late one afternoon, believing them to be like little chooks or pullets. We crept along these paths through the bushes looking towards the ground and we kept very quiet as we knew that they are shy creatures. We never saw any and when we later discovered what they really look like we were so grateful that we hadn't found them.

The Cassowary is a large flightless bird which can reach a height of two metres and they can weigh up to eighty-five kilograms. Another words, they are a damned site bigger and heavier than me! They have brilliant red and blue neck 'wattles'. They also have a helmet on their heads called a 'casque'!

They are very handsome creatures but do not hang around them as they can also be very dangerous and have been know to attack people. The safest place to see them is at a zoo!

We spent the day in Cairns today but would have preferred it without two poorly dogs! It's like having two infants, with us worrying about keeping them in the shade and have they had enough to drink etc. Not being able to sit and have lunch in an outdoor café because of the health regulations (the inspector was most apologetic but said he'd have to fine us if we sat down) we sat in the park on the other side of the road and enjoyed sandwiches and hot chips. The lagoon is just perfect - so beautiful - but we got told off for walking around the path (about 30 feet away from the edge of the lawn and a long way from the water) with the dogs. I got some lovely photos! We walked around a fair bit of the town and found that the old wharf area is boarded up and that has to be prime vacant real estate but I've no idea what they are planning to do with it. The new area is not so much fun because originally there were several tour company booths and we would wander around, picking up leaflets on the way and then sit and have a coffee whilst browsing and then go and book the various tours. Now there is one large air-conditioned building with what appeared to be about three tour company desks inside and it was all very formal.

We returned to the old back-packers section, with countless eateries and information desks and enjoyed comparing the different tours and finally made a choice at lunchtime. We also got a $5 discount! We have chosen to go out on a yacht to Upolu Reef next Friday as that is the day I have booked the dogs into a local animal welfare group, at Smithfield, who came highly recommended. They will look after them, take them for walks and give them treats for only $20 for the two of them. I have never been on a yacht and have always wanted to go sailing and this tour takes a maximum of twenty people (although licensed for 34) and will give us hands-on experience. Apparently, along with the coral and reef fish, we will see spectacular giant clams. We should see dolphins and turtles on the way. They have a glass-bottom boat and we can snorkel. I have a perpetual ear problem so I can't go scuba diving apparently and John needs a doctors diving certificate if he wants to go as he's over 65 so he's not going to bother. We also get free tea and coffee all day, lunch and wine and cheese on the return voyage. It costs $99 per head which is very comparable to other cruises but is much more personalized. We both hate going out with three hundred other people on boats and coaches so always look for the more individual trips. I've been on medium sized boat trips and everyone wants lunch at the same time and you always get the individuals who compete over who can get the most prawns on their plates whilst the queue behind gets longer and longer! Tomorrow we're off to Palm Cove for the day (very trendy apparently) and on Sunday to Port Douglas.

CHAPTER SIXTY-TWO

RETURNING TO COAST

How to describe the beauty of **Palm Cove**? Imagine a longish, narrow, straight road with the sea on one side and resorts and homes on the other. Add the trees - huge, very old melaleuca trees with branches shading the walkways and road, with any spaces filled up by palm trees. Beside the beach is parkland and edging the pavement on the other side of the road, are the most glorious, luxuriant tropical shrubs. This tropical plant vista immediately pulls your eyes away from the beach. Pavements are built around the tree trunks and resorts have planned their entrances between the trees. The beach is not that wide but it is so long that you feel you have it to yourself. The sea is a brownie-blue (perhaps the water is shallow or the water was mixed with the sand that day because the sea was quite choppy) but when you look out at Double Island or the island called 'The Hat' you see a line where the sea beyond is turquoise blue. It is a hot, lazy day as we wonder along looking at the beautiful resorts, many pure white, with beautiful entrances, the odd fountain and endless outdoor dining. No high-rise buildings here and all the resorts look so stunning that they entice you to enter and stay awhile. At the far end we were surprised and delighted to find a few old private beach homes because it somehow made the 'whole' even more perfect. At the other 'entry' end there is a caravan park! The shops are hard to find with most being under the walkways of private resorts, hidden by outdoor restaurants and cafes but there was one tiny paved walkway with a predominantly bright turquoise blue colour scheme plus touches of pinks and lemon. It is situated at right-angles to the beach and we spotted a Post Office sign and climbed the wooden stairs to the balcony to find another restaurant and a small supermarket. How discreet! Palm Cove is 'Classy' as well as stunningly beautiful and restful. There is no more resort land available so if you want to buy into the area, be prepared to pay whatever is asked! Prices have risen dramatically over the last few years and the only way now is up. If you come from abroad and want to feel that you've sampled the best there is to offer in the tropics I cannot think of a more perfect place to stay. If you want something a little livelier then head for Port Douglas and enjoy the scenic, winding coastal journey on the way, overlooking deserted beaches.

We went to **Port Douglas** after a rather too long, very lazy morning we finally arrived at 2pm which gave me only half an hour for the seafront market adjacent to St Mary's By the Sea overlooking the marina. So you can come straight out of church and indulge yourself! It's held every Sunday morning and boasts wonderful flowers and plants, fresh fruits and vegetable, fruit juice and jars of jams and pickles. However, it is the local handicrafts, artworks, clothes and jewellery that I had come to see. Perhaps it was a good thing that we arrived so late because I spent far too much money in a very short time! There are a lot of jewellery stalls and some of the gemstone and pearl jewellery was amazing. Once a bracelet was on my arm, I headed for a clothes stall. The lady had half packed up her vehicle with her goods when I arrived. I immediately spotted a cool, long cotton shirt which had been hand-painted. 'I'd have to go and get some money out of the bank' I said, hesitating.

'Well I take bank cards' she answered.

My grin grew wide as I said 'You've got the goods and I've got the gold card. Unpack your vehicle.'

We had a wonderful time and I ended up with two shirts and a hand-printed T-shirt and have the joy of knowing that no-one else will ever have another to match, as each one is individually designed. I rejoined John and we headed to a beach so the dogs could have a play in the sea and I rolled up my cotton trousers and joined them for a paddle. Then it was off to the main street where I stopped abruptly when I saw a chalk board saying 'warm chocolate bread and butter pudding with ice cream and raspberry sauce' (or words to that effect because is certainly did not say 'sauce'). An impulse buy. It was good but there were two slabs of this desert which was rather too much and along with the coffees, so was the bill! Anyway, John enjoyed all of his and half of mine. It had been the same the day before in Palm Cove - my sandwich had turned out to be a triple sandwich with about a quarter of a chicken inside and they wrapped up half of it for me to bring home! I asked our present waiter why the servings are so big and he said that Port Douglas might be pricey but offers good value. What a wonderful response!

It was getting quite late and we wanted to go and collect our vehicle and drive down to the other end of the street as we had planned to have a swim at Four Mile Beach and did not have our towels with us. However, we took a detour up to the Lookout and drove up the main street about three times as I wanted to photograph a particular building and it's not easy with so much traffic around. We didn't bother with the swim in the end but we did get to discover that some of the original places that we remember so well are still there - such as the wharf, the old jetty and the Bally Hoo train. However what had been a small main street with a few shops, with a dry field between it and the wharf was now a thriving shopping complex.

The first time I went there we got off the coach at the wharf and I asked the driver where the town was as I couldn't see one. He told us to walk across the field. We weren't sure that he was telling the truth because looking across the field we still couldn't see any shops but we did as we were told and found a few. I needed the Bank of Queensland but there wasn't one and I had very little money on me. Well it has the banks now and the huge supermarket, as it has grown so much, but it has still retained the magic. It's a wonderful place to visit and I would think a fun place to stay. There are many more cafes and bars of course and on this Sunday afternoon there were a lot of live groups playing so you can choose to eat and drink according to your taste in music! The ambience is the same wherever you stop - relaxed, friendly and pretty. No formal clothes needed here. Actually I cannot think of anywhere here in the tropics where you would need such clothes! However, if you want world class resort wear, there's a myriad of wonderful shops in the north and Cairns abounds with them - there's even a Louis Vuitton store there. However, this market was particularly good and there are many more in the area that I haven't yet visited.

A couple of days later we took the dogs to the Animal Protection Society and left them there as a trial run for Friday when we go out on the yacht for the day. They had a large open pen to themselves for the six hours they were there but I'm not certain if there was much shade and they were very thirsty when we collected them. We had been told that they were cleaning the kennels and that they would be moved into one together and Jack would have had shade and water there and with his long, black fur he needs to be in the shade most of the time. Luckily it was very breezy but there was no water in the pen when we picked them up, not even an empty bowl. Jack was a nightmare from the time we picked him up - barking, edgy and almost uncontrollable. It's a worry.

Whilst they were there we went into Cairns. We wanted to enjoy the lagoon but as it happened it was closed until 3pm. None of the guide books tell you that it is closed every Wednesday for cleaning! It didn't matter too much because we had to do some 'odds and ends' shopping and post letters etc and we didn't get there until 2pm anyway but it would be very frustrating if you had children and had promised them a treat!

By the time John tested the waters it was rather too cold for me and that is something that we have been discussing. We have always come to Cairns in August and now it's July and we rarely do swim here because the water, even in swimming pools, is far too cold. We did brave the pool in the park the other day and a lady approached me afterwards and told me how brave I was! At the Cairns lagoon there were many swimmers once it opened but they were all non-English speaking or had white skin (from Europe or Melbourne!!). The tourists were all lying around in the sun desperate to get tans and we were looking for the shade even though it wasn't that hot. We've decided that it would be better to come at the end of May into June when the sea is still warm but we haven't yet found out if the stingers (jelly-fish) are still around then. We'll make enquiries. For us, the temperature of the water puts a damper on white water rafting, swimming at Mossman Gorge or para-flying (you do get the choice of landing back in the boat rather than in the water but that would spoil the fun!) and similar activities, as well as the ocean and the swimming pools.

We found a Swiss café that I'd read about and the pastries were divine - I had a savoury lunch but John saved me a mouthful of his pastry for me to sample. There are so many places to eat that it had been difficult to choose, so we went to this one because it had been recommended. We drove up to the Cairns Botanical Gardens on our way home and have decided to spend some time there on Monday as it appears bigger than we thought. We really enjoyed the atmosphere again in Cairns and John is now wondering if he could cope with the summers! That should ring alarm bells - live here - could we - would we! We have over three months left of our holiday and we agree that this is by far the best place to stay. We are not staying in the city of course as we are at Lake Placid but there is so much to do and so many places to visit. We booked in for a week, stayed a second and have booked in for a third but we'll probably keep extending.

CHAPTER SIXTY-THREE

We will drive to Cooktown next week and stay a night in a motel there, leaving the R.V. here. We will go up to the tablelands via Kuranda and Mareeeba and return via Mossman and Port Douglas. There is not much to see at Cooktown apparently but we have been advised to visit the cemetery! Taking this route between Cairns and Cooktown entails only 35ks of dirt road now and when the road is all bitumen it will open Cooktown up to the caravans and motor homes. If you want to invest in a business when you retire then get ready to head up there and open a coffee shop or trinket shop or anything else that would attract the tourists because I'm sure there will be vast changes and an economic boom in Cooktown. You'd only even need to be open in the dry season and you could travel south during the wet season. We encountered business like that on the Victorian coast that shut during their winter season. A camping supply store wouldn't go amiss, after the coffee shop has started turning a profit! There are five caravan parks there already so the need is there. I'll let you know next week as we're going there on Wednesday.

Remember my not being able to take advantage of that dusty village of Port Douglas - well that was only fifteen years ago and it wasn't that much better twelve years ago. If Cooktown can warrant all those van parks then it needs shops for tourists to look at and places to eat al fresco. I couldn't count the amount in Port Douglas now and every one was packed out on market day and it was the same in Kuranda.

Well I didn't get my day on the yacht, ending up instead at the Cairns Hospital with a very swollen knee. I count myself lucky because a young guy was killed in a road smash that morning and the other driver, also a young man, ended up being air-lifted to Cairns with head injuries just as I arrived. Add to that the amount of people who have been going down with a severe stomach bug in this park, with our neighbour admitted to hospital the day after me, plus another with a suspected heart attack and it really doesn't matter a jot! The dogs were saved the stress of going into the kennels again so that was a bonus.

If you know of anyone whose surname is Morris, tell them to be proud of the name. There was a City engineer here who surveyed the Lamb Range area west of Cairns back in the 1930's. He found a suitable site for a dam in 1935 and we went to visit it today. How on earth he surveyed that terrain I have no idea. It is almost impenetrable and the road that was built was a feat in itself. He wouldn't have been able to move more than a few feet a day as he hacked his way through and if you take into account the snakes, spiders and whatever else is frightening in such a dense forest, just imagine it at night! The area cleared for the dam was 336 hectares and that was after he'd climbed 500m above sea level! Perhaps it was all in a days work when you worked for the Council in those days - can you imagine the reaction of current employers and their Unions if they were asked to do this type of work! Anyway, if you are in Cairns, make a point of taking the amazing winding drive up into the rainforest to see Lake Morris and the Copperlode Falls Dam. You'll need a car or bike, because caravans are not allowed up as the road is so narrow and dangerous! We saw one man running up but that's not an option for me! The scenery is beautiful and there are wonderful opportunities to get a bird's eye view of Cairns on the way.

I've been reading my tourist leaflets again and feel you need to know that crocodiles can wear through one hundred sets of teeth in their lifetime. They have a lot more teeth than we do - over sixty - and I cannot help wondering if they ever get toothache. It could be toothache that causes them to get cranky at times! They can also jump from the water to a height of two metres so don't think you're safe swinging on a rope over crocodile infested creeks! Apparently they are unlike most other reptiles as they are active twenty four hours a day, so never think they are asleep. Most of their food comes from the shore rather than from underwater - you have been warned.

Now for something that you want to tell your overseas relatives about (don't tell them about the crocodiles until they get here). The Great Barrier Reef can be seen from Outer Space and is the only living organism on Earth that can be and it stretches for 2000 kilometres along our Queensland coast. If you stick your foot into a giant clam don't worry because they shut too slowly to trap your foot. Our rainforests are the oldest surviving rainforests in the world at over 140 million years and we have sixty-five rivers running through them.

By the way, camels wear bras in northern Africa, in the Sahara Desert to stop their calves from sucking them dry of their milk. We should all know these things!

CHAPTER SIXTY-FOUR

A VERY FIT CAPTAIN COOK

28th-30th July - COOKTOWN

Our journey to Cooktown was an introduction to the 'outback'. The reason I know this is that it is written in a guide book. We went via **Mareeba**, through **Mount Molloy, Mt Carbine and Lakeland**. If we had a four wheel drive we could have gone via the Cape Tribulation National Park (the Bloomfield Track) and along the coast. Many people go one way and return the other. Many people without four wheel drives have set off along the **Bloomfield Track** only to find that they have to turn back as there are at least a couple of streams to traverse!

The first part of our journey was pretty monotonous but the latter part encompassed some wonderful views and we understood how people from the outback cannot understand how people can live in towns and cities. You can 'feel' the outback - it sort of reaches into your soul. The wild grasses bordering the sides of the road vary from patches of green through to yellow, russet and brown. The trees are various shades of green and here and there are patches of yellow wildflowers and bushes with red flowers.

What surprised and impressed us the most were the mountain ranges. Some of the mountains were so high the tops were hidden in the clouds and thinking back to when I lived in Switzerland, I believe that some of these were even higher than those surrounding Lake Lugano. We eventually hit the dirt track and it was pretty rough in places.

AN ATTRACTIVE TOWN

My predictions in my last letter were correct except for the fact that Cooktown is much prettier than Port Douglas was fifteen years ago. I salute the local Council and the local community because they have done everything imaginable to make the town attractive and interesting. Needless to say we stayed an extra night and it would be easy to stay for several days. There are parks, Botanical Gardens, Lighthouse, monuments and statues, waterfront walk overlooking the fishing boats, the Museum, the Historical Society, beautiful old buildings and the beaches. That's without any bush-walking, wharf or river fishing (Endeavour River or Annan River), reef diving etc. The first night we walked along the waterfront parkland watching the sun set over the water as we did so. We watched a fishing demonstration and would have stopped at the bistro and bar (inside and outside dining) except for the fact that we had just eaten and were ready to unpack and settle into our cabin. We had heard about the amazing sunsets but it was even more beautiful than we had imagined. As for the fishing - throw in a line from the wharf if you fancy large Spanish mackerel, Barramundi, Queen Fish, Trevally and Mangrove Jack. Huge gropers can be seen around the wharf but if you must have a boat, you can hire a tinny there. About 40ks out to sea you can apparently see the black marlin taking your bait, as the waters are so clear. I could tell you more but you'll have to go there for yourself.

BOTTOM OF TULLY FALLS

The following day I walked around the town whilst John went to the Cemetery and I heard that you need to go to the museum, then to the cemetery, then museum again and then back to the cemetery because there are so many stories of the local settlers and the pitfalls that led them to 'rest in peace' that you get caught up with each unique tale. We didn't have the time to do this on this trip but we did explore the beaches and Grassy Hill, which Captain Cook climbed to gaze upon the reefs at low tide in order to find a way back out without further mishap. He must have been a mighty fit fellow to get up that hill, particularly if he was dressed in his depicted uniform. He apparently had a good time at Cooktown, got along with the Aboriginals and stayed for forty-eight days whilst repairing his ship. Their arrival caused a bit of a stir though, especially when some Aboriginals pinched some of their fish and the soldiers raised their muskets. They tried giving the Aboriginals some trinkets but they tried to eat them. How sensible - why would we want things if you can't use them or eat them. I think it's us that's got it wrong (yeah, I know I'm using a laptop right now but I didn't miss it when they weren't invented, did I). Anyway, Cook planted his flag, George III gained a Continent and we're still arguing about the merits of that action today. Cook's crew might have enjoyed it even more in the gold rush era as nearly all the buildings housed either a pub or a brothel - I'm told fifty brothels and a higher number of hotels. However, I heard conflicting stories about whether or not the local Aboriginals were cannibals with one shop owner telling me yes and another telling me no and as I have not done any research on any of the history you'll just have to find out for yourselves!

Cooktown interested us for another reason. It is like a flower bud trying to burst open but not being able to for lack of water or Jack fidgeting when he's about to be let off his leash! Unlike Port Douglas it has not seen the arrival of a Christopher Skase who had the foresight to build his wonderful resort there and albeit that I am thankful that I was not one of his shareholders; I have always admired both of the Sheraton Mirage resorts. I spoke to a couple who run a shop in the centre of Cooktown and their attitude to the place was awful. They sold men's clothing and our conversation went something along the lines of him saying 'We'll never get back-packers up here' with me exclaiming 'What! The place is full of them'

'No, they'll never come because we won't have pontoons out on the reef like down off Cairns'.

'Cooktown is surrounded by reefs and diving opportunities as well as deep-sea fishing'.

'It's bloody windy here too'.

'Well that's good isn't it? It keeps the temperatures pleasant'.

'When the wind drops the sand flies bite'.

'When the road is finished this place will boom.'

'Well we won't be here'.

I looked around the shop and wondered who would buy all his tailored clothing. I had just purchased the last three pairs of men's underpants in John's size and there was one set left that were smaller and then they'd be out of stock. No, backpackers had nothing to buy in this store yet there was no camping store in town that I could see. In the park we stayed at there were so many tents and so many young foreign tourists. They need hiking socks, underwear, tent pegs, candles, batteries and torches, mosquito coils and nets, small gas cylinders, wet weather gear and so on and so forth – not a three piece suit!

The fishing industry is in turmoil and tied up with red tape, thanks to the new State Government proposals. They are extending the New Great Barrier Reef zoning and it will be a bleak future for fishing off Cooktown and Cape York. The new marine park will stretch from Bundaberg to the tip of Cape York. I can only presume that is why the waterfront café, bar, bistro and seafood takeaway, right on the waterfront with a licensed courtyard and veranda is for sale for only $185,000 (walk-in-walk-out basis). It is a bright, modern, large establishment in the most glorious position imaginable and was pretty busy when we walked past. It was so beautiful that I took several photographs of it. Also on the Esplanade was a practically new, commercial building with windows overlooking the river inlet. It was empty but on the street side there was a small launderette incorporated into the building. When we walked around the veranda to look at the water we saw a heap of For Sale signs lying on top of each other but on the street side was a" For Lease" sign. Another commercial building in a superb position. Right in the town centre there is a 506m block with views of the river with commercial zoning, for only $160,000. The road to Cooktown will be completed this year - the potential is huge, there is land selling along one of the beaches for $500,000 a block and yet they are giving their businesses away - and I could cry as we have no ready cash to invest! We met a lady in an outback pub who lives in Cooktown and she told me that 'every business is for sale' and she believes that the couple with the men's clothing shop have only been there for a year.

If the place wasn't going to boom then why would people be buying land at the price I mentioned above? The cheapest housing block in town is $69,500 and they go up very quickly to around $480,000 for a quarter acre block with views. A good residential home could cost $385-675,000 in town with a beachfront property around $725,000. That is not that cheap and all the people who build their homes here are going to need supplies. There are plumbers, electricians, landscapers and building and construction workers ready and waiting and advertising in the weekly news pamphlet. The caravan parks are packed with vans, the road to Cooktown has a continuous stream of tourists already and there isn't even a hot bread shop! The bakers shop in town only supplies pre-packed, black and gold wrapped bread! What is wrong with the local business owners? It is so like Port Douglas was, with prime commercial shops empty.

A good example is the lady I met in a pub on our way back to Cairns. She told me she does trail-bike riding. I asked her if she was very busy and she said she could be but has to do it low key as she hasn't got any insurance! So why hasn't she got in touch with an insurance company and arrange a user pay system, just as we do when we hire cars? Still, there are always the tourists who like it the way it is and we met a couple who said that they hate Port Douglas as it is too 'proper' and I'm not suggesting that Cooktown should replicate it. Go there - it's worth the trip and you may stay longer than you planned.

CHAPTER SIXTY-FIVE

On our return journey we turned off the main road at Mt Carbine and went to **Mossman** and the change in scenery was immediate. It was so green and lush and we enjoyed the journey to Mossman which has grown bigger but not more attractive. We then headed to **Daintree** which has hardly changed at all as far as we could tell and is just as perfect as we remembered. We had no time for a river cruise as it was getting late in the afternoon and we had to get back to Cairns but although we've both done cruises from there before, we would like to do another one when we haven't got the dogs with us. I wonder how the dogs would react at their first sight of a crocodile! Not an option because I know how the crocodile would react at the sight of them!

We'll stay here at Lake Placid until the 11th August and then we move to Mission Beach. We were off to see the Crystal Cascades today after a quick trip into Cairns to collect more post but we're so laid back now that we decided to return 'home' for lunch and leave it for tomorrow. We haven't been up to visit the Atherton Tablelands again yet either and there is so much to see there. Mind you, I do not believe this feeling will last as I'm already getting this little niggle about wanting to work! I want to get my teeth into something - renovating the rest of our house or perhaps even return to work! I get this odd feeling of dissatisfaction that I'm accomplishing absolutely nothing. What a problem worrying about the fact that I have such an indolent lifestyle! How blessed I am.

Well, it's Sunday 8th August and I've got nothing to send you because I haven't written anything! That's because we haven't done anything exciting I guess. What have we done this week, um…? We had a huge row but I cannot recall what it was about. What I can recall was that I was in the shower and was washing my hair whilst we had this row and John stormed out of the R.V. and I heard the wheels of the Ute spinning as he turned it around. I flung a towel around most of me and ran outside to see him roaring off and I was so stunned that I just stood there in front of all the happy campers with soap dripping into my eyes, water running down my legs onto my now dirty feet and realised that other than the towel I was stark naked. By the time I climbed the steps into our R.V I was fuming, incredulous and crying at the same time. Living with your partner 24/7 is not always touring and relaxation! Usually we cope because he will decide to go to golf or I will decide to go to the shops even if I don't need anything – just to give each other some space and time to think. Some men go fishing or play bowls and some women do so too of course and many women do some sort of craft or painting and many sit with other women whilst doing so. It's a kind of 'women's business time out'. Likewise, men discuss the various attributes or problems with their caravans or motor homes as an excuse to get away from their partner for a while. Those that don't escape each other now and again seem to argue and I know this because you can hear them inside their vans nagging away at each other and bickering non-stop.

I love it that we have our time alone when we are driving and what John doesn't know is that if he's in a really chatty mood and the two-way radio is buzzing every couple of minutes, I turn it off and later tell him that it ran out of batteries! However, we still have those times when a divorce seems rather attractive. It's normally over something petty and due to pure frustration, plus usually when we are tired. We are lucky because we have a back bedroom to which either of us can retreat to. We can shut the bedroom door and the bathroom door which means that we can lie on the bed and read and not hear the television in the lounge. We recently heard of one couple who sold an American motor home like ours to buy something smaller and newer and were only on the road three weeks when she decided she'd had enough and they went back home and she would never even get into their new van again. He was on the prowl for another big American motor home!

We did go up to the Atherton Tablelands one day, which reminds me that I have a camera full of photos, so hang on a minute and I'll download them and then perhaps I'll remember! A chocolate biscuit is needed for a sugar hit.

John dropped my packet of chocolate biscuits and they are all in bits. I just love broken biscuits because I can eat as many bits as I like without feeling guilty because I don't know how many biscuits I've actually eaten! A couple of century's ago, I had a Saturday job in Woolworths and they used to sell bags of broken biscuits to the customers. In those days they sold biscuits loose and I would have to go upstairs to get more supplies to fill up the containers around the counter. We all used to pinch a few biscuits whilst doing so but I got moved to the stationery department but not because I got caught eating the biscuits. It was because the customers complained that the biscuits were a bit tough and it turned out that I had been replenishing the chocolate biscuits from the wrong bin and was selling them dog biscuits! They looked the same to me and tasted good.

We went to see the **Crystal Cascades** one morning. I had told the dogs they were going for 'Walkies' and they were so excited. It's not far from our caravan park in the car but when we arrived it was to find notices banning dogs. I get so very frustrated with local tourist leaflets that fail to tell you these facts in advance. We started to walk down the track to see the falls and Jack howled so sadly and so much that I just had to return to them, so I never saw the falls! John enjoyed the walk and the falls which are apparently extremely pretty. The dogs are fine when we go to a shopping centre etc and just wait patiently for us but all they could see were trees and us going 'walkies' and I think Jack thought we'd forgotten them! Why they couldn't have gone along the concrete walkway on a lead I have no idea. I realise that wildlife can smell the dogs but had I left them unaccompanied in the Ute, Jack's howling (which is identical to a wolf) would have terrified the wildlife even more! John dropped me back at the caravan park and took them for a romp in a field.

ATHERTON TABLELANDS

The area is bigger than Tasmania so we were selective about what we would include in one day. We will be able to see the southern end when we have moved down to Mission Beach by going up via Innisfail. We could also have gone up via Kuranda but we've done that route already when we went to Cooktown, so this time we went via **Gordonvale** which meant travelling south along the Pacific Highway a little way. The road up over the ranges from Gordonvale looks better (less bends) on the Hemma map than the Kuranda route but I had read in a local leaflet that it was the worst. Well, thank goodness we never took our R.V. By the time the climb ended I felt exhausted and I wasn't driving. The switchback bends went on and on and on. John took it carefully but Jack became most unhappy in the back of the Ute. Most of the bends had 30k limits and every time we thought we'd reached the top we would get out to look at the view and could see that we still had more to climb. Of course, once up there it is beautiful but I wouldn't choose that route in a motor-home or caravan. The easiest route is from Innisfail.

We went first to see the **Cathedral Fig** tree with roots that drop 15 metres to the earth. It is well over 500 hundred years old and apparently the most visited tree in the world! From there we drove to the Mobo Creek Crater and it wasn't worth the very rough drive. Instead of going on around the lake, we turned back to find the bitumen road again. It would be bad even in a four wheel drive vehicle.

Next stop the beautiful village of **Yungaburra** which is 720 metres (2376) above sea level. They have eighteen Heritage Trust listed buildings and it is the largest National Trust village in Queensland. It is well worth a visit. By this time we were delighted to come across the Lake Barrine Teahouse. We have been there before and I remembered their wonderful scones. Lake Barrine is an extinct volcano and the teahouse has been owned and operated by one family since 1927. During World War II it was a convalescent home for soldiers and I'm not sure that they would have wanted to get better and leave too quickly because it is so serene and is indescribably beautiful. I have no idea how to do it justice. John agreed with me that he has never tasted such perfect scones either so I can recommend their Devonshire teas! We went on to Atherton and just drove around to see if it had changed at all but it hasn't and we didn't stop. However, if you've not been before a 'must see' is the Crystal Caves mineralogical museum in the main street. You should also go and see the Mt Hypipamee Crater south of Atherton.

We headed on through Kairi and down to Lake Tinaroo again to see the dam. It was created in the 1950's by damming the Barron River and has more than 200 kilometres of shoreline and the world record barramundi at 124cm long, weighing 38.75kg was caught at this lake and you can fish for them all year round. It was time to return home and we went via Mareeba and Kuranda. A lovely day enjoying wonderful scenery with the dogs even more exhausted than us!

The rest of this week has been lazy with the usual shopping and washing and me making a shade-cloth screen to hang off one end of the awning (how I wished I'd packed my sewing machine!) so that the dogs and I can keep out of the sun. We've also talked more with the people around us, particularly to those that have lived here for a while. One of the owners here has just sold a house in Thailand and lived for many years in Hong Kong and an English lady has a piece of land up the road but is not sure what direction to take at the moment. Another guy here works seven months at a time for a mine and spends the other five months travelling but hasn't yet ventured outside of Australia but would like to visit Rome and the Pyramids. Some live on the road permanently but most are on holidays and come from the south to escape the winter temperatures in Victoria and South Australia.

We have been discussing what to do with ourselves in the future and are getting absolutely nowhere! Do we buy a smaller van, do we go to Europe, should we do a house swap with someone in Europe or go to Canada first and swap R.V's (they would expect something like ours). I still want to go to Spain and Portugal and that hasn't changed since I was nineteen years old! I love Spain - the people, the smell of it, the lifestyle - I get off the plane and breathe in the air and I'm in paradise! Or should I go back to work for a while in which case, what on earth is John going to do with himself all day!! I'll be happy to just get home, see my kids and enjoy Christmas!

CHAPTER SIXTY-SIX

Tuesday 10 August

Tomorrow we leave Cairns and although we are both ready to leave, we are both surprised at how melancholy we feel about it! It is purely the surroundings of course. Our site at the caravan park is extremely cramped and normally we wouldn't have stayed for more than one night, yet we have been here a month and it seems like a week. I will so miss Lake Placid and the knowledge that Cairns is just down the road. Today we had a last look at Palm Cove and it still stuns me with its beauty. After the dogs had exhausted themselves on the beach we went for a coffee and a wander around the shops and when we returned Jack introduced John to a Londoner and his beautiful Asian wife and teenage daughter. Jack is never lonely and we often return to the Ute to find people drooling over him and asking 'What breed is he?' In this case, they had been awaiting our return to find out. It was nearly dark and the wind was quite strong and I huddled in the car whilst they chatted. The car was almost on the beach and I happily viewed the islands as the lights came on around me as I eavesdropped on the conversation. They have sold their house in Sydney and have bought in Palm Cove having first checked the whole of the coastline from Sydney until they found their nirvana. I'll drink to that. Palm Cove is Paradise.

MISSION BEACH

For my friends abroad - we are about 130ks south of Cairns but will not get to Townsville for a while yet.

Well I have a new regard for the Cassowary (that giant bird I told you about). I now believe the female Cassowary to be a bird of outstanding intelligence and now wish I'd long since got my act together like they have. The females live alone and then run amok around May/June having a bit of 'how's your father' with several males of her choice. She usually hatches three to four very pretty eggs (olive green with pearl lustre) and then leaves the male to incubate them for 48-50 days during which time he has to fast. Oh, I love that! To cap it off he has to rear them for the next eighteen months. She's off swanning around the bush having a fine old time. The male doesn't have a lot of choice because she's about 60kg and he's only around 35kg so he doesn't argue. Local leaflets here tell us that if you meet one, don't run away but hide behind a tree and wait for the bird to leave because they can be dangerous and have a deadly inner claw. Apparently one crossed the main street in Mission Beach the other day with its baby.

17th August

We have decided to stay a second week because our first week has been a bit of a blur. I was so excited when we arrived because I was going to track down an old friend. We went down to the beach and stood in awe at the beauty of our surroundings. It is truly magnificent - even better than the beach at Palm Cove because the sea is turquoise and there are a range of islands off shore, the most well known being Dunk Island. It is an absolute tropical paradise with the trees reaching their huge branches over the sand as though trying to reach the water so there is never the problem of finding shade.

We then went to the information centre as I had been told that a lady there would know where my friend is living, together with her son. First I heard she was ill, then that her house is on the market, that she was back in England and finally that she is in hospital. I spoke to her son here at length (I now had his new telephone number) and he is in Cairns. When I finally spoke to her in hospital she was so doped with morphine that conversation was impossible as she could not comprehend. She has cancer of the spine and has a very short time to live. I was totally devastated. I wanted to say 'Thanks. Without your friendship I could never have managed all those years ago.' I wanted to say 'I will never forget my visit to your home in England and the fun we had and sorry to hear that your Mum and Dad have died because I liked them a lot'. I wanted to say so much but all I heard is how sad and bitter she is over some family trouble and I was devastated that she will die with those feelings. She had corresponded with me weekly for eighteen months when I was going through a very bad period and she was back in England, but I haven't been there for her. It's not all my fault of course as it takes two to keep in touch but whereas she has been coming and going between England and Australia for her parents and her operations and treatment, I have made no effort at all. It was her daughter who got boxed by the kangaroo and we were together when I heard that shark siren on the beach (which everyone ignored). I will remember her how she was - laid back, smiling and laughing, our times in Bundaberg, Rockhampton and our trip to the town of Seventeen Seventy and how she literally had me collapsed on the floor, crying with laughter when I visited her in England. There is so much truth in that saying 'It is better to have loved and lost than never to have loved at all' because I have so many wonderful memories and they are nearly all wrapped up in laughter.

The morning after I finally reached her by telephone, I awoke feeling 'heavily' sad that I had left it too late to sort out our reasons for our dormant friendship as there had been some misunderstandings on both sides and then I received a phone call from one of my kids with a problem. Every parent will understand when I say that I felt frustrated as I could not help and somehow listening just didn't seem enough. The problem is temporarily solved (without our assistance) but not being able to talk face-to-face is difficult and it confirms that I am too far away from my kids. I suppose the lesson learnt is that however much you fall in love with a place (and we have with Mission Beach), nothing compensates for not being around for your family and friends. And it doesn't matter if you escape to a paradise like this with no cares in the world other than 'Should we go to the beach or sit outside and have another cup of coffee?' because you take your life and the people you love with you in your heart and mind.

We always knew that whilst touring, if there was an emergency we could fly back but there are other times when you are needed. I had thought that a phone would do but it's not enough. This has to be taken into account if you are thinking of doing what we are doing and are going to be a couple of thousand kilometres away from home and you get a call asking 'How far away are you Mum?' I feel like telling them all to have a holiday and come and see this place.

CHAPTER SIXTY-SEVEN

The trees tumble down onto the beach, the sand is white, and the sea is blue and green. There are four villages connected by fourteen kilometres of beach. There are dolphins and turtles, tropical fish and a whale was seen yesterday, plus the closest access to the Reef in North Queensland. There are over two hundred types of birds, sixty percent of all Australian butterflies and fifty-two different mammals. They also have one of the largest frogs in the world - the white lipped tree frog - which I have yet to spot. Then there are all the walks, sporting activities, sidewalk cafes and the Sunday market.

A GOOD VIEW OF RAFTING SECTION

We went to **Tully** last week. It is Australia's wettest town and boasts a giant gum boot which you can climb up, to get a good view of the town. As we are not into fruit picking, fascinated by sugar cane nor get excited about field upon field of bananas, there's not a lot that attracted us. However we went up the Tully River to watch the people doing white-water rafting. There must be a rush of rapids at the bottom because everyone clambered out of the rafts with grins from ear to ear and when we asked what their journey had been like 'Wicked' was the usual response. Unless you are actually going to do it yourselves though, it probably isn't worth the fairly long drive to the end of the road where, hidden beside a parking bay, with no signs, is a pathway down to some rocks which you need to traverse to get a good look at the river where the rafting starts upstream. This we did and Callie slithered off the rocks into the water for a swim but we had to keep her on a lead so that she didn't get washed away!

Yesterday we went north again towards Cairns to visit a couple of coastal communities and to shop at **Innisfail** as we are finding the local prices a bit steep. Driving north, we turned off the main road at Silkwood to Kurrimine Beach which has about three caravan parks. The road leading to **Kurrimine** (mainly sugar cane vistas) boasts the Murdering Point Winery and the Murdering Point Rifle Range - no doubt there's some local history attached! Kurrimine beach is quite pretty and they have a café, seafood shop, pub, shop and a visiting mobile vegetable van! I was delighted to see a small Real Estate Agency which is only manned part-time and thought of my friend. She could come and live here and have the office to herself as it is manned from the main office at Innisfail and she's looking for a change.

Next stop was Cowley Beach and the road leading to it was prettier with glimpses of a river, more trees and hills. It consisted of a few houses but had no shops at all. When we reached Innisfail we enquired about a beachfront block we had seen at Kurrimine and we were told the owner wanted $1.2M for it. After I'd stopped choking I said that it must have gold beneath the soil. We have seen absolute beachfront homes here at Mission Beach from about $800k with in-ground pool, walk straight through a few trees to the sand. (Note that the prices boomed just after we left the area.) A house at Holloways Beach (Cairns) was advertised last week as 'Well-appointed cottage plus self-contained flat' for $775k. It's obviously not big but it's modern. It shows a view of the back of the house/patio and a view from the patio to the ocean. Between the edge of the patio and the beach are a few ferns and a couple of palm trees - about three feet to the sand! There are several homes here for over a million dollars of course but they are magnificent.

I really liked Innisfail, which is the largest town on the Cassowary Coast. Basically it is a sugar town but it is also a big fishing centre, a fruit picking centre and has a heck of a lot of bananas. We had bypassed it before and it seemed very uninteresting from the highway so it was a huge surprise to me to find a large, pretty town with riverside walks. We also went down to the beach at **Flying Fish Point** but it wasn't as pretty as it was nearer town because where the ocean meets the river it is beautiful.

In the town itself the river winds off in a couple of directions by the bridge (Innisfail is at the junction of the Johnstone and South Johnstone Rivers) and my camera is full of photos again. The parking facilities and shops were excellent too. The best part of town for me though was when we went over the bridge to explore East Innisfail. We explored nearly every road! It looks as though it must have been the original town because there were so many old Queenslanders on the hill. In fact the roads left and right of us seemed so inviting we drove up and down them - they rise and fall, some quite dramatically steep! The houses seemed really old and some had exquisite stained glass windows. Then we found the river further back and it seemed that wherever we turned there were more and more Queenslanders. I was so struck by the casualness of the siting of the homes in this area.

Imagine a large, very green block of land and three people standing around saying 'I think I'll build my house there' and the others pick their spots too. It matters not which way they face and nor do they need dividing fences, nor care whether 'my house is better than yours'. They just erect a Queenslander and I suppose they take it in turns to cut the grass every now and again. Got a dog 'No worries' as they are free to roam but we saw some lazing under trees, presumably in their own gardens. There didn't appear to be any defined front gardens with just beautiful lush green grass everywhere and some old trees providing shade. The whole area seemed like this - casual. It was so refreshing and like going back in time about a hundred years. We only saw a few fences in the whole area and they were just low wire ones and very unobtrusive. If only we could all live like this instead of trapped behind our six foot dividing fences or brick walls and worrying about whether we'll get good neighbours when we move. Here they just seem to assume that they must be nice.

It must be a nightmare if a house is on the market because goodness knows what a surveyor makes of it! I don't suppose the people care a toss what bit of land is theirs because they all have plenty of space. As is always the way with me when I really love a place - I forgot to get any photos! I still haven't remembered to take any of Mission Beach town centre because it is so pretty I am too busy looking at it! Anyway, back to where I was - abutting this area there is acreage and I suppose some of it is farmland but we couldn't explore further as we had to do the shopping and were getting further away from the town. It was a lovely day.

CHAPTER SIXTY-EIGHT

PRETTY EVERYWHERE

Today has been 'business' as we collected our post yesterday and there was such a pile of it and the dogs needed washing which means I have to shower and wash my hair too by the time I've finished with them. It's quite a long process. We also got off to a late start because we keep chatting to all these young back-packers from the U.K. It's all late nights and a lot of laughter and we love it and it makes us feel as though we've been in an old people's home up to now with all the 'grey nomads' around us. We don't really get going until the evening when older people usually want to go to bed!

The Post Office had mislaid post sent to us some weeks ago. This package of missing post finally turned up but so did another package from the Post Office which we hadn't been aware was missing. It had all been readdressed to our home and had been caught in the new redirection to our friend's home in Brisbane. Along with all the new post that they had received it was quite overwhelming.

I've caught up on my photo printing tonight. We have so many on the computer and it takes ages to decide which ones to print but we have some wonderful photos and are already enjoy glancing through our album. They also scroll up on my screen-saver on the computer but as soon as the random selection starts rolling John and I forget the work we were doing and say 'Oh, do you remember that place' etc. John often says 'Where's that?' and I pretend that I know but I'm reading the small print on the top of the screen as I have a worse memory than he has for names. It is so relaxing to watch the screen but it's almost impossible to comprehend that we have actually been to so many beautiful places. It would be easy to forget without such a visual reminder.

It has been very hard for me not to keep busy all the time and to learn to truly relax but I was lying on the settee the other afternoon doing absolutely nothing and thought 'I feel really happy'. That's when I realised that I was at last 'doing nothing' without feeling any guilt at all. I knew we had slowed down but I'm usually thinking about the ironing, washing, shopping, cleaning, dogs need a bath or a walk, diary, photos, batteries that need charging. If I'm not worrying about these things, I'm reading or doing crosswords or watching the news whilst cooking. Because I'm so used to doing at least three things at any one time (whilst even doing crosswords I'm thinking about other things), I have never sat outside in a chair sunbathing like other people do outside their vans.

Today I tried to relax and do absolutely nothing again when John was at golf but a young man came up before I'd even got the lounge chair unfolded to say that he missed his dog so much (back in Canberra) and could he stroke my dogs! Half an hour later I escaped back into the van to find my water jug had been overflowing most of that time! By the time John returned I was preparing dinner whilst feeding the dogs as well as watching the news and soaking some hand-washing! Old habits die hard. It's now 11.39pm and I still haven't had a shower!

We went into Mission last night for a dinner and unfortunately it was absolutely lousy! I find the attitude of those who work with the public here a little odd (excluding the wonderful help we received at the Information Centre). Think John Cleese in Faulty Towers and you get the picture! They do not really seem to appreciate the tourists at all. A waitress was boasting to us about how rude she had been to a couple the previous evening. The customers had sensibly walked out but the waitress seemed to find this quite amusing! At least she was friendly to us but we found the owner extremely arrogant and rude. He also obviously doesn't really want many customers because he turned 19 customers away when we were there. He cooks a set amount of meals - always a roast - and serves meals until he runs out of vegetables. Apparently there was a heap of meat left over! At 9pm he sends the waitress home. The lady in the local paper shop was brisk and businesslike but to the point of rudeness. You wouldn't want to repeat a question for fear of being reprimanded!

In the middle of doing my washing in the van park they put up the price by 60c. I had my knee in a bandage and didn't want to walk back to the van but when I asked them to lend me $1 the two owners just looked at me and another guest stepped in and helped! For the sake of 60c they really annoyed me and it is that appalling customer service that negates any goodwill with guests. The next time we washed, we took it around the corner where the prices were cheaper and the washing came out better as it had hot and cold water instead of just cold! People astound me at times. However, the area is just so beautiful that I could have stayed longer if it hadn't been for the fact that everywhere we went we were constantly reminded of my friend's illness and the fact that she should have been here in glowing health. How I suddenly overwhelmingly miss her beautiful smile.

CHAPTER SIXTY-NINE

So today we moved down the coast to **Cardwell** which is a new area for us as we've not been here before. Offshore is **Hinchinbrook Island** which is the largest Island National Park in the world. Then there is the reef off shore. The Shire of Cardwell covers 2,900 sq km of mountains, tropical islands, rainforests and plains with almost 70% being World Heritage listed, National Park or Crown Land. The Shire appears to include Mission Beach, Tully, Dunk Island and Hinchinbrook Island and the town of Cardwell itself of course. The Poms discovered it in 1864 which was very unfortunate for the Aboriginals as they lost a lot of their people with the introduction of European diseases. It was the first port in north Queensland. Again we find the rainforest coming right down to the beach, about 4ks north of town and we have a list of places to explore.

John took the dogs for a lovely romp in the sea today and then further along saw a big sign warning of crocodiles! I'll stick to the pool even though locals tell us they aren't often around at this time of the year! I don't know why I'm surprised as I know about the 'salties' but in Cooktown, for example, there were signs around the inlets but we were able to swim on the beach that we went to. If it gets too hot we'll go and look for the Five Mile Swimming Hole about 8ks south of town. Apparently if we go on the forest drive we'll also find fresh water at the Spa Pool and Dead Horse Creek (Callie can look for bones!)

26th August

Today we're off to explore. The town of Cardwell mainly meanders along the seafront and it's really quite uninteresting. I found and a greengrocers shop though that I was very impressed with as the quality of the produce was excellent. The local people here have been very friendly and helpful.

We went to look at Keith Williams **Hinchinbrook** 'sprawl'. Not quite sure how to describe it! It's like yet another Gold Coast upmarket waterside estate. It doesn't exactly impress but it is built around a harbour which is always attractive. The surrounding views are majestic but the whole area has these views so you don't have to live here to get the benefit. However, there are some high, water-front blocks.

The rest of the town is on the other side of the beach road without direct access and all along the front is a grassed area. (I am generalising with this description as the road does vary). Behind the town is a vista of forests and mountains and out to sea are islands of varying sizes as well as Hinchinbrook Island. We were looking at this vista on the first wet day they have had for weeks and the clouds blocked many of the views unfortunately. We could not see many of the islands and we could only see parts of the ranges. We persevered and went to the forest to visit the various lookouts. I was disappointed to find that we were travelling through plantation forest rather than natural forest and I only saw one of the lookouts because of the difficulty of the climb to the other three, with my knee. I had been hoping to try to get it operated on in Townsville and the doctor at Mission told me he could arrange for me to see a specialist within three weeks with the operation within the following three weeks and I was considering booking ahead but then he mentioned the 'after-care'. I was thinking I could be like Jana

Pittman but for some reason that I can't understand, he doesn't think that I am as young and as fit as she is and reckons I'll need weeks of physiotherapy. Therefore I'll wait until I get home.

We visited a real estate office and picked up their leaflet to find out what houses, land and commercial properties cost. There are many homes in poor condition so I was surprised to read that the prices have gone up 35% in the last year and equally surprised at some of the prices being asked. What really shocked us though is the fact that it seems that every commercial business is for sale! Before John looked at a pamphlet that I'd picked up I said to him 'The towns for sale'. When he looked at the commercial list he looked at me in amazement and also said 'Is it ALL for sale?' Yet again I wonder what is going on in this Shire.

We are seeing mosquitos again (all the mangroves probably don't help) but they are midgets in comparison to those we encountered in New South Wales. John also saw Dugongs in the sea today and a local told him he saw one giving birth last week and how she pushed her babies out of the water to make them take their first breadth. There is also an old crocodile that cruises up and down about thirty metres out to sea, sixteen feet long, which the locals have named Bismark. Apparently he's pretty well behaved! We walked along the pier but all we could see were jelly fish - lots of them! We're moving on tomorrow but we'll come back one day without the dogs and hopefully when the sun is out and take a boat trip around Hinchinbrook Island. It takes a whole day and we have been told that around the other side of the island the scenery is majestic with craggy rocks - quite wild and beautiful. Well the R.V is on the move again tomorrow as we head back down the coast again.

We stopped at the Casual Cassowary Tea House about twenty minutes south of Cardwell to get a good view of Hinchinbrook. John made the mistake of asking which tea they recommended and was given a list so long that he told them to serve him with whatever they recommended. He wasn't so sure that he'd done the right thing when he saw the bill! However, we received very friendly service. Incidentally, you cannot drive up to the top, where the tea house is situated with a caravan, so if you have one leave it at the bottom. We drove up in the Ute as it would be a slow, steep climb if walking but the views are extensive.

We didn't stop at **Ingham** and nor did we take the road to Lucinda which John would like to look at but stayed on the main road until we reached Rollingstone (still part of the Hinchinbrook Coast). **Lucinda** is well known for the fishing lures made at the Lucinda Lures workshop. Lucinda also has the world's longest off-shore loading facility at 5.75 km long!

CHAPTER SEVENTY

BATH TIME FOR DOGGIES

LOTS OF ROOM AT ROLLINGSTONE

There is a free rest area at **Rollingstone**, it was fabulous. It is a vast area with parkland which is floodlit at night, barbecues, toilets and cold water showers right next to a lovely creek. The shop is only a few minutes walk from there. We settled in really well because of the scenery and clear, fresh water creek. Here we at last met up with people who live permanently in buses and motor homes and spent a lot of our time chatting and comparing vehicles. The reasons they have sold their homes and businesses for a life on the road were varied and interesting.

One elderly couple were just on holiday as she has had heart by-pass surgery and she has a heap of grandchildren who are always calling in at their house and she can't get any rest!

I watched a lady doing her washing and was so intrigued I went over to talk with her. Two buckets, one quite large and a huge plastic funnel on a pole with some holes punched around the middle. She stood there pushing this funnel down into the bucket which pushed the soapy water through the clothes with remarkable force. The clothes got rung out and put into the other bucket for rinsing and again the water was forced through with the funnel. It took little effort and her husband helped her hand wring the towels out and hang it onto the rope strung between two trees. It took half the time of an automatic washing machine and appeared squeaky clean.

Another couple sold their business within three days of testing the market and then sold their home at the Gold Coast. They have not been travelling very long. They bought a bus and have converted it themselves (currently spent up to $45,000 but it is still an ongoing project). We talked of money and budgets and theirs was so simple. It went something like this - $150 a week for food, $150 for travel (petrol etc), $20 for insurance and registration, $50 savings for emergencies or trips abroad and $20 for something else which I cannot remember but probably phone. Total $390pw! Their capital is in shares which have shot up from just over $1 to over $6 in the past six months. He's on a Veterans Affairs pension and they manage just fine. They don't have the endless bills we house-owners have. In five years time they are off to England and will tour the Continent. In the meantime they will go back to Asia for their holidays. So they do not regard being on the road as one long holiday as we have been doing. It is their home and a way of life and holidays are a separate matter. When they stayed for six weeks at a relative's place recently they saved an extra $150 a week on their fuel bills which will go towards holidays!

It's just that having owned a home and business and to change your lifestyle so dramatically and to end up with such a simple budget leaves me wondering about whether our complicated finances are worth it! It's like going back in time to when people had a tin with sections and the cash would be put into the different sections for the rent, electricity and housekeeping bills, plus the necessary savings 'for that rainy day'. Some people used cups or jars or tea caddies and many hid their money under the mattress or behind a brick in the fireplace. John has a foolscap page with print so small (in order to get the necessary amount of lines on the one page) that I cannot read it even with my glasses on! I cannot make head nor tail of it yet here was this lady itemising her budget in under a minute as she pointed to the fingers and thumb of one hand, there being only five budget items!

If I had extra cash I'd renovate my kitchen but I realise that it is I who might be regarded as the one who is crazy! I have a perfectly good kitchen already. When I get to the stage when I rely on my memories would I remember the kitchen or the trip to Vietnam! It is a matter to ponder over. This reminds me of some jokes I read the other day.

'Not one shred of evidence supports the notion that life is serious.'

'My idea of housework is to sweep the room with a glance'.

I also liked 'Men are from earth. Women are from earth. Deal with it.'

The beach nearest Rollingstone is Balgal Beach and what a wonderful spot that is, with its vast tracts of sand stretching from the ocean way up into the river inlet. There, beside the beach, was another free parking area for vans, although much smaller and packed out. A cafe with covered outdoor dining served excellent fish and chips along with other food and ice cold beer. It is also a shop and caters for the fishermen. We were very impressed. One lady told me it was the first time they had free camped and isn't it just wonderful? She and her husband had been looking for a caravan park and had stumbled on this beautiful free camping spot. She was carrying a toilet roll! She explained that she had seen someone take their own paper and thought you had to supply it and I assured her that it is provided free! Her husband had already enjoyed a game of golf at the local club.

CHAPTER SEVENTY-ONE

TOWNSVILLE - 30th August

We arrived yesterday and went into town late afternoon and I am stunned at what a wonderful place Townsville is. The city is fabulous as is The Strand along the front with all its foreshore parks and gardens. There is a vast area with exciting things for children to do and two free pools to swim in for both children and adults. We met a couple in the caravan park who are from England and who went back to live in England for seven years before returning to Australia again. They went all around Australia and have just bought an acreage property here because 'Townsville offers so much'. I don't know how long The Strand is because we gave up walking and drove down it in the end!

Townsville was proclaimed a City in 1902, along with Brisbane and Rockhampton. However, Townsville has retained all its old buildings and has done them up and they are truly magnificent and we saw so many beautiful Queenlanders close to the town and along The Strand.

As for the history of Townsville, if you rely on the Townsville guide book you will get most confused! On 6th June 1770 Captain Cook sighted the area naming Cleveland Bay, Cape Cleveland and

Magnetical Island (now called Magnetic), the latter because the island affected the ship's compass. The first European contact happened in 1812 when Allan Cunningham landed on Cape Cleveland. 'A further 45 years elapsed before Townsville was founded in 1864'. Now either I can't add up or the guide book has an error! Further reading confirms the following: In 1864 a northern port in Cleveland Bay was founded and was named Townsville after Robert Towns. On September 16th 1901 the Australian flag was officially raised for the first time in Australia in Flinders Street, Townsville. Yes, in Townsville - not Sydney or Melbourne.

Apparently the night-life is pretty good but doesn't commence until after 10pm and is really starting to rage about 2-3am with some clubs open all night and there appears to be two main areas of night clubs being Flinders Street East and Palmer Street. Then there is the Casino and Entertainment Centre. There is so much to see in the daytime that we'll be too exhausted for the night-life!

Having spent the our first full day catching up with domestic duties we were due to go exploring today but John has gone down with that extreme stomach bug which hospitalised so many people in the Cairns park. It's so rare for him to be ill. I'm trying to keep away from him which is rather difficult with our space! I keep spraying the door handles with disinfectant and now he doesn't know if he can touch anything! To be continued....

It was a weird week in Townsville as John was only really on top of his stomach bug on the day that we left and I also caught the virus but was not as ill as he was. It was an amazing experience for me as John didn't want to eat and that has never happened before! Suffice to say that we both lost weight!

We saw most of the scenery that we wanted to see and spent one afternoon touring the suburbs finding only one modern housing estate and the odd modern home amongst thousands of Queenslanders. I realised that when faced with only Queenslanders to look at, I felt quite different about the brick and tile! Usually of course I am the other way around. We also spent more time walking along the Strand, which was only completed three years ago and looking at some of the beautiful old buildings in the city.

John also spent an afternoon exploring the river. The only trouble with Townsville is that it is a fair distance to other attractions, whereas there was so much to go and look at when we were in Cairns. From Cairns we could choose to go to the Atherton Tablelands or North to Port Douglas and there were all the other trips that we talked about to dams and lakes and places such as Trinity Beach or Palm Cove etc. Townsville is also noted for having very little rain so the areas that are not irrigated are very dry whereas Cairns is so green. We did have some rain one night here though - it sprinkled for about five minutes and it was such a shock that the power failed!

CHAPTER SEVENTY-TWO

BOWAN 6th September

MOTHER BEDDOCK LOOKOUT

We arrived today having spent last night off-road. It was a 20hr rest area with parkland, next to a service station and adjacent to the Pacific Highway. Five other vans soon joined us for the night. It was quieter than the van park in Townsville as we only had the roar of the passing traffic, which actually wasn't very heavy, and the piercing whistle of a train around midnight! At Townsville we had continual roaring traffic, sirens and the airport quite near, along with the thunderous roar of the RAAF planes which often took off after darkness. They were so noisy that I'm sure we could still hear the roar by the time they were probably flying over Asia! We, therefore, did not enjoy staying at that van park and would not go back.

Fathers Day was also a bit of an odd day as John's brother-in-law died the day before and we received the news when driving into **Ayr**. We stopped there again in the beautiful park where we'd stopped on our journey up to Cairns and thought and talked lot about Ron and his family. He should have died last year according to his doctor (cancer) but decided he was going to live to see his 70ᵗʰ Birthday, celebrate his Golden Wedding Anniversary and to be at his Grandson's Wedding. John last saw him before Christmas and he was definitely not going to make it through the holiday period but he was so determined. He was there for all three occasions and then let go. The power of the human mind over human body never ceases to amaze me.

Also, I spoke to all three of my kids and I felt rather grumpy that they all seem to be going through career upheavals at the moment. All three are questioning where they are going. I thought that at least one of the boys intended to stay put for a few years but apparently not. I want them to all be settled so that we can go daft and run away when we want! It's our turn.

My son's birthday is this week and he has decided that his needs are quite different now to what they have been for the last ten years. This equates to the amount of money he earns and his future. My other son is going through a similar phase with his business and my daughter may change careers completely!

Now when kids are going through such changes it is to be hoped that their parents are there for them to offer advice and wisdom gained through their extensive years of experience. However, my poor kids have a mother and step-father running around the country wondering whether to sell their home and move to the southern highlands in New South Wales, buy a beachfront property in northern Queensland in the hope of making a quick quid or whether to leave Australia and become gypsies in Spain! As they have no living grandparents or any relatives in Australia their concerns all fall upon their Dad who is back in Brisbane and who would really rather like to move as well! Well, we are surrounded by beaches and we will have plenty of time to walk by the sea and ponder the meaning of life and what advice, if any, we should be giving our kids! In truth, I doubt they want advice though but they might have if they had a solid, reliable and dependable mother which is what I always intended to be when I gave birth to them!

My dream was to be the perfect mother with the perfect marriage and my children would grow up in the same home all their lives and I would always have the right words at the tip of my tongue when needed to offer advice or guidance or sympathy. They would receive the best education that money could buy and would have the chance to try out every kind of pastime imaginable and learn many skills. They would obviously pass all of their exams with distinction, be able to follow any career path they chose, would be able to holiday in Aspen in the ski season, wallow on our yacht in the Caribbean with their friends in summer and trek South America or Africa or wherever else they wished to travel, whilst we funded them. Money would never be a problem and I would have the time to take them to Paris or Rome or wherever because by the time they reached their late teens I would have the perfect home with a full-time housekeeper and cook. That was my plan anyway.

We are told so often by 'successful' writers that we must have a plan. Well I had it. I think the problem is that I forgot to write it down. That must be the reason that I haven't accomplished one single item on the above plan. I honestly did try to be the perfect wife, mother and housewife and when they were very young it was absolutely wonderful but then when things went wrong, like my Dad falling ill with cancer and my little foster-daughter coming and going and finding out that our local Council had decided to demolish the house we had bought and were so lovingly restoring, I just couldn't keep it up any more and fell apart both physically and emotionally. I have tried to put myself back together again but have never truly succeeded and I think that I must have regressed to being a teenager again because I always felt safe. My teenage years were the sixties and I lived about forty minutes from London and life was whatever you wanted to make it and it could change (and did change) from one month to the next. It was a time of teenage confusion, great highs and lows, discoveries, being scared yet having the courage to try new experiences, gut-wrenching distress accompanied by endless tears when relationships broke up and excitement when the next new relationship began. It was a topsy-turvy exciting time but I always had my elderly parents there at home to put me back together and older, married brothers and their wives to go to for advice. So that is my problem. I need parents and I haven't got any and sometimes I wonder if I have started to lose the ability to know how to be one again!

Still - I look at Mick Jagger and Rod Stewart and wonder if they ever feel any guilt at their failed marriages or other antics and whether their kids think it's just normal because they have never experienced parentage like ours. Most of ours were so grateful that they had survived the second world war, were used to being thrifty having lived through rationing and had truly learnt values that would stand them in good stead whatever hardships they had to deal with in life. I swung like a chimp from one branch to another with each branch representing a different way of living. I'd live on a commune, I'd convert to the Catholic faith and become a nun, I'd marry Elvis and live in America, I'd work in third world countries assisting the poor, I'd marry a very wealthy man and never have to do any domestic work in the house or I'd marry a Spaniard or Portuguese man and learn the language fluently and be beloved by all his family and stay at home raising all our babies but would never expect to live in a house bigger than two rooms. Then again perhaps I'd join the merchant navy and see the world, or I'd become a nursery nurse or a continuity girl at Elstree Studios. Of course, I'd definitely go to Art College as well.

Well, I nearly did a few of the above and I did work in Switzerland, as a maid of all things and doing all the housework and I nearly married a guy from the continent but he was Italian. I wanted to marry a Portuguese guy but he didn't want to marry me and I ended up as a secretary, married an Englishman and soon after had a mortgage! Are their any sensible, stable married couples out there who are probably now in their late seventies who would like to be my role models and put me back on the straight and narrow so that I can again be a good parent as I once was.

CHAPTER SEVENTY-THREE

So, where were we, or rather are we? Oh yes. Bowen.

This caravan park is on the beach front with foreshore parkland and is almost within walking distance of the town. Outside our entrance is the harbour and as I adore watching boats jostling about trying to keep to their own allotted space I am in heaven as I walk the dogs down the long harbour road every morning. As well as the normal toilet/shower block they have a block of bathrooms which we can use free of charge. It's been hot here today but there is a pool on site as well as the sea and I think we are going to enjoy it here.

I am reading a book about Spike Milligan at the moment. Colonel Bloodnok (The Goons) is talking to Seagoon and reveals his Regimental Oath:

'Open your wallet,' he tells Seagoon 'and say after me, "Help yourself."'

Please read this to anyone who is thinking of starting a family in the future!

Friday 10th

MURAL AT BOWEN

We left Bowen this morning. We had intended to stay another night but the van park owners laid into some young Irish back-packers this morning at 7.15am (whilst they were fast asleep in their kombi van and tent) and I became so incensed that we left! I had heard the two girls talking in the shower block and thus knew that they were Irish but no-one else had heard their voices, not even the people in the van one metre away from them. The girls were accompanied by a guy (also Irish) and he slept in the tent. The Irish tend to speak with a soft lilt anyway but they have to have been the quietest backpackers that I have ever been amongst. Apparently the night before last, they cooked dinner in the camp kitchen and sat down to eat it at the table provided outside when one of the owners approached them and told them they couldn't drink beer with their meal and to take it outside the park!

Last night they were eating and not drinking and were told to take their dinner outside the park! They went to the parkland opposite and decided that they would take a beer each to have with their meal. The police turned up saying there had been a complaint about them drinking in a public place. The poor guys walked back into the park and the owner gloated that he had reported them! They went to bed and got woken this morning by both owners and the woman was screaming 'I've had enough of you. Get out and never come back'. She was banging on the kombi van and the girls must have been terrified. Then she started shaking the tent. I happened to be walking past and stopped in astonishment at the owner's craziness. The permanent park dwellers drink non-stop and are quite noisy in a friendly kind of way and a couple of them came back last night at 12.15pm in high spirits but apparently they are acceptable! This morning there was an empty carton by the resident's bin, so they had consumed a lot of beer last night. I hate to see discrimination in any form and I do not know if it was because they were young, back-packers or Irish but they picked on three of the quietest visitors that we or our neighbours have ever come across. I asked them not to take it personally and I too would be leaving and not all park owners are like it! I suggested that they come to Airlie but they want to see a bit more of Bowen and had looked at another park yesterday because of the way they were being treated, so they are moving there and then they will come to Airlie. The park is on the market I believe so I hope someone else is in residence before we come back here again!

Well, we covered all of the beaches around Bowen - Edgecumbe Bay (by the town), Queens Beach, Queens Bay, Kings Beach, Rose Bay, Grays Bay, Horseshoe Bay and Murray Bay - and they are all different. Many have views of the North Head Lighthouse on its small island, Stone Island (bigger) and the very large Gloucester Island further to the east. We forgot to look at Coral Bay, the 'alternative dress' beach (read nude).

We went up Flagstaff Hill for the 360 degree views, up to Mt Nutt and John climbed up to the Mother Beddock lookout which is a big, roundish rock balanced on top of a hill. We also visited the Mullers Lagoon (in Bowen) with its 176 species of wild birds but there were so many there that we could not relax as the dogs were disturbing them too much. I like the town very much and love the laid-back country atmosphere and it is hard to imagine that it was once considered for the trading and administrative centre of north Queensland. However, with that role in mind, the town was laid out with wide streets and I love them. It is north Queensland's oldest town having been established in 1861.

We also photographed some of the 24 murals that are painted on the walls of the buildings around the town. These depict scenes from settlement through to the present time and we were surprised at how very good they are, though we knew that some were painted by well-known artists. Guided walks are available if you turn up at the library on Wednesday mornings.

Obviously the Aboriginals lived here long before the town was built and there were four main tribes. Charcoal from an ancient campsite near the Nara inlet is thought to date back 2500 years. I had intended to visit the museum but it will be something to look forward to in the future (when we do not have the dogs in tow). One of the most interesting stories is about a James Morrill who was shipwrecked just north of Bowen and he lived with the aboriginals for seventeen years. Apparently when he eventually saw white settlers he frightened them with his appearance and the aboriginals were sad when he left them. He spent his remaining years in Bowen and was buried in the cemetery here in 1865.

There is another of those slab huts next to the museum and I would have liked to have seen inside it but it's too hot to leave tho dogs tied up outside. This one has been furnished too and I enjoy looking at the period furniture. I have the ability to 'feel' myself living in those surroundings and it is as though I have been transported back in time and the things around me are familiar and are mine and I get the urge to sweep the floor or fill the pail. It's weird but I love the feeling. That brings to mind a visit to the dungeons of Nottingham Castle when I was a child and how terrified I felt. I cannot watch any film or programme with violence because I 'feel' the violence and I put this down to no T.V as a child and so much reading and having to use my imagination. I was reading by four years of age and into hard-back books by six and when my father gave me a gift of Grimm's Fairy Tales at six it so terrified me that it set me off on years of insomnia as a child! I thought they were true stories!

CHAPTER SEVENTY-FOUR

AIRLIE BEACH

We arrived here just before lunch and as we drove through Airlie Beach I realised that we are back in 'Paradise'. This is our third visit here and it is so beautiful that it still takes my breath away. To be continued…….

p.s Sunday - I have been feeling unusually flat. We are surrounded by National Park with palm tress swaying outside of van windows and a swimming pool a few metres from the van. It Is 27C with a light breeze and clear blue skies. A bush turkey keeps wandering past in front of Jack and a huge, very beautiful peacock roams around us in the afternoon. We also have possums and so many varieties of birds fluttering about and at the front of our van they feed the lorikeets every afternoon. I couldn't even be bothered to get off my bum and look at them yesterday afternoon! Told John there must be something wrong with my head to feel so dissatisfied with life and my surroundings and told my daughter on the phone that I feel like seeing large green fields and must always want what I haven't got. Kicked my own butt and told myself I am a spoilt brat and set to cleaning the fly screens, oven and anything else that I hate cleaning. Tidy van, tidy mind?

ANOTHER OF SHUTE HARBOUR

I started to worry that when we return and have got the house back to normal I might get itchy feet again as I have gradually been getting used to this lifestyle. Then I worried that I was not satisfied as I have already been to Airlie before and was I blasé because this is not a new area to discover? Then, as I was scrubbing the oven I suddenly realised that for the last two nights I have taken the book on Spike Milligan to bed with me and have read a fair bit of it before going to sleep. It continuously describes his manic depression in some detail! No more of that book for a few days as I was obviously absorbing that too much!

Despite my mood, I did stir myself enough yesterday morning to go into Airlie and we followed the sound of a beautiful voice. It was a lady singing at the foreshore markets. I love the market atmosphere so long as the market is not too crowded and this was right at the edge of the beach so we were able to walk alongside the markets and the dogs could have a swim too. I bought some very fresh fruit and vegetables and we had coffee and doughnuts whilst people watching and then sat under the palm trees looking at the yachts gliding across the ocean. It is such a picturesque area. I then made a roast dinner (I hate lighting the gas oven pilot so rarely do roasts) which meant that I had to stay in to keep an eye on it! So now I am back to feeling normal and have the bonus of knowing that I have a heap of cooked organic chicken ready in the fridge. Life's good!

We have the weirdest water here in Airlie. I make an instant cup of coffee and when I pour the boiling water in the cup it froths up! I refill our small water bottles with filtered water but am finding it tastes soapy - not nice. Water filters are an absolute must if travelling like us but still don't guarantee sweet water.

At Bowen we had been parked next to a new 30ft Swagman, top of the range motor home with leather upholstery etc. I forget how much it cost but it was a lot more than our home is valued at, at the Gold Coast. Yet they did not have hydraulic ramps for levelling like us and had to check the levels by eye. The owner told us that they cost $11,500 and are an 'extra'. He also didn't have a built-in water filter. I think I'd forgo the leather upholstery, plus a lot of the fancy fittings and order the ramps instead if I could afford a rig of that price.

Anyway, John called me outside not long after we had arrived as Callie was acting strangely. She had her tail tight between her hind legs and was terrified and kept looking at the Swagman. I laughed and said perhaps she could smell the leather as it was still warm! Anyway, they had a tiny dog and they came to warn us that they were just popping out and the dog might whine for a few minutes as they were leaving it in the van. Naturally the dog did whine and Callie hid under the van. When he returned I asked him to introduce his dog to Callie so that she could see that it was friendly and happy but after he had done so, Callie was even worse and kept sniffing the ground where the dog had been standing. When we took the dogs for a walk, Callie would give the van a wide birth and if she was off her leash she would run around the other side of our van.

When we were talking to the guy later he told us that their dog had to learn a lesson so that they could get out occasionally and that she was fine in the van with the windows open and he sometimes left the air-conditioner on for her as well as the T.V. He then told us that she had arthritis, was very old and had a brain tumour. I couldn't help myself saying 'Isn't it a bit late to teach her a lesson then?' He wasn't very friendly after that. Callie could obviously smell the poor diseased dog and as she communicates with Jack in some way, the other dog must have been communicating her distress to Callie.

So we checked some parks out here at Airlie and we saw their van in a park that we wanted to stay in, next to Club Crocodile (where we'd once had a holiday). There was plenty of room so we would be able to park a long way away from them. When I went to the office, I said that we had a 'big rig' and was told they refuse to have them! I asked why not and she said they are too heavy. I didn't say that they already had one in the park but I realise now that if I had said 'I have a Winnebago' instead of big rig, they would probably have said they had plenty of room! That Swagman and trailer/second vehicle would have weighed much more than our van. Thinking she thought we had an old bus I did manage to say 'No, ours is not heavy as its aluminium-framed' but she couldn't get rid of us fast enough. She also said they take up too much room but I had driven around the park and the single sites were plenty big enough and we're on a single site now with a van behind us. I had thought I'd seen it all with tourist businesses but am again amazed. Discrimination about what kind of motor home is allowed is really taking things a bit far! I'm now glad that we're not staying there because of her attitude but am in a quandary as to what to say when I phone other parks! I usually say that we have a Winnebago motor home but now I am afraid that I sound like a snob when doing so!

The next people to turn up next to us back at Bowen had a fifth-wheeler. They are becoming very popular because they sit over the top of a Ute or rear tray of a four wheel drive and lock in. Therefore, when you arrive at the park you unhook it and you have a large caravan (5th wheeler) and your separate vehicle to drive around in. It's easier than towing a trailer with car on it. Inside, you go up a few steps to the bedroom area, which sits over the top of your vehicle tray. Well these people had a top of the range four-wheel drive and had built the fifth-wheeler themselves. They had gone to America and when they got home he built his own, working eighteen hour days for a year to complete it - without any plans whatsoever!

It was stunning and had a slide out extension. He said he drew a rough plan on his driveway! He had built it from the chassis up. He had designed every bit of it and the quality was better than any motor home that I have seen. The windows were fabulous and door (storage) latches - everything was of the highest quality and to the rear he had a door that lifted up and out came his boat. I told him that I appreciated the amount of research he must have done as it takes so long to decide on any part you need for a motor home and you may find yourself sourcing parts from all over the world. He said that he had had to get some parts from America and yes, it was really hard trying to decide which make and model and that he had to order far in advance as the caravan industry always supplied him after they had met the caravan dealers needs.

They were travelling with two English friends who have been unsuccessful with their applications for emigration. They leave the country every six months and then return and they carry on touring. The owners will leave their van wherever they happen to be at Christmas and will fly back to their home in Western Australia for Christmas and then return and carry on. They reckon we're 'infant travellers' as we've only been on the road for seven months. This latest tour will take them over two years.

CHAPTER SEVENTY-FIVE

MIDGE POINT (100ks north of Mackay, 37ks south of Proserpine)

Well we were heading for a four star park but first looked at one on the highway by the river and then on the way to Midge Point we found the one that we decided to stay at and we have so much space around us, it's glorious. It is about half an acre to the next van, about an acre to the showers, shop and pool and our side windows give us a 180 degree panorama of bush and ocean. The beach is about 1½ acres away and we can see the Conway National Park on the other side of Repulse Bay. It is very picturesque. We can also see the Repulse Islands National Park. There are seventy-four islands all together that dot the Whitsunday Passage. Most are pine forest and rainforest and most of them are National Parks. Eight of them have resorts and we will see more of the islands when we move on to Cape Hillsborough and then to Mackay.

This area is part of the Whitsunday Passage. The first detailed survey of the western shore of Repulse Bay was made in 1843 and 1844 and the main boat used was called Midge. There is a hill called Midge Mountain (although it's only a tiny, conical hill).

The young woman in the office here told John that they have only owned this park for six months and I'm sure it will become very popular because she is so friendly and you really don't have to cook. She cooks the normal burgers and chips and serves hot pies but she also told me that she had a joint of beef out ready to cook if I fancied a roast dinner that night and that she cooks a roast most nights for people. The shop is well supplied with basics and newspapers and she is going to order the milk that I like. We had booked a four star park but it only had a small shop and what really put me off is that we were told to take our dogs to the beach for walks and to bury the dog dirt in the sand. I had visions of me lying back in the sand with the smell of dog dirt wafting around. I not only felt sick at the thought but it is also very dangerous for small children because they can pick up an eye disease from it digging in the sand, as children do.

It was good to talk to our friend from Sydney yesterday. I was still laughing as we drove out of Airlie Beach. It was his response to John's question about whether he is saving a lot of money as he wants to buy a motor home. His outburst of laughter had me laughing even before he answered that he is writing his over-expenditure off this year as 'Establishment Costs'.

Now that we are here, what are we going to look at? Well there is the small town at Midge Point down the road although we didn't see any shops yesterday. There is also the Laguna Quays Resort, which I've heard of but have no idea what it consists of other than a golf club! The view is so beautiful that we just sat and did nothing most of yesterday afternoon. We were gloating at the space we have - absolutely revelling in it. I was the one that wanted to leave the park at Airlie and move on. I was feeling claustrophobic. I told John I couldn't take any more trees because we were so surrounded by vans and trees that I felt I couldn't breathe. It was also noisy because helicopters took off from a field very close by, taking tourists on ten to thirty minute flights over the Whitsunday Islands and the local area. Then there were the light planes which were probably taking people to the islands. The planes also took up those people that fancy jumping back out again with parachutes. The birds were extraordinary but even the big cockatoos got a bit too noisy at times. I needed space and I am rapt that we found this place.

I did manage to do some hand washing yesterday and got such satisfaction out of doing it, that I set to and did the weekly wash by hand today and am amazed to find it much cleaner than normal! It is only since being in Australia that I have constantly had a washing machine. In England I used launderettes to start with but when we moved to Wales I did all the washing by hand even though we had four children under six and my daughter was in cloth nappies. My husband thought it fine not to have one until the day he was faced with a growing mountain of dirty clothes that he had become responsible for because I was in hospital. I returned home to find a brand new washing machine!

When we returned to England a few years ago I did it by hand again until we moved into the flat we rented but even then I only bought one because I knew that my daughter and son were going to join us. Thank goodness I did buy it because my son got a job the day after arrival as a dustman! Luckily he found a driving job quite soon after that but his first job provided an unexpected bonus. He rescued some extremely good art books which he gave to me and a limited, first edition poetry book (of some very famous 19th century poet who's name I cannot recall as I'm not that interested in poetry) which he has kept. He has the same love of books that I have. I keep coming across 'book exchange' at these parks but I cannot make myself give away any book that I have purchased. However, I read the other day of a scheme that has taken off around the world where you do pass on books. If you find a book in a telephone box or on a park seat, look inside. It may have a message telling you that you can read the book but to please leave it somewhere in a public place for someone else to find. Apparently they are tracking these books and they are travelling all over the world. One of the most popular places to find them is at airports so please check inside before handing any books that you find into lost property - they are not lost - they are looking for a new reader. What a wonderful idea.

No, there aren't any shops at Midge Point. There is, however, a delightful Post Office. This consists of a garden shed with some Post Office boxes outside and a letter box. We entered the garden to have a look in the shed and the house owners came out and asked if we needed help. We admitted that we were 'sticky-beaking' (Australian term for being nosey) and I said I thought it was wonderful in its simplicity and I wish I had my camera. Apparently it is much photographed by tourists. We posted a letter to a friend and I asked how often they get picked up. Apparently they take the post daily to town (I presume Proserpine). I asked what services they provide and was told stamps and small parcels only. So you can work at home for the Post Office here! Apparently, people call at their house to check on post on the way home from work.

We had read the local paper in the morning and had found out that Laguna Keys has a new Japanese investor and that the five- star hotel is to be refurbished and a whole heap of capital works completed, including shops. It covers a vast area and people get about in golf buggies. We went to check out the golf club, saw a sign to the Conference Centre, saw a lakeside area where they hire out water sport equipment for guests, a sign to a residential section and ended up at the harbour. It was there that we discovered that an international airport will be completed by the middle of next year which will boost the whole area - Bowen, Mackay, Airlie Beach and this resort. Also in the pipeline in years to come will be a Police Station and other services also based within this resort.

So it seems that Midge Point will stay much as it is now and all the major services for the whole area will be contained within the resort. There are plans for a pub and petrol station at Midge though but we were told not to hold our breath for it as the airport was supposed to have been completed two years ago. The lady who told us all this bought a five acre block here within the last year and it has just been valued at ten times what she paid for it! Mackay airport is not an international airport, so the nearest one at the moment is Cairns, which is too far away to bring overseas tourists here. Now that there is Japanese investment, there should be a huge influx of tourists to this part of the coast. On a later trip we found the van park closed so this did not happen.

I had a 'shocking' morning this morning. I had been to the shop with a small spiral notebook in hand, to get the address of the Mackay Post Office. Then I went to talk to the horse. We had a good chat and although I felt a bit 'odd' a couple of times all was going well until the metal wire of the notebook touched the fence! I didn't know it was an electric fence. All I know is that I dropped the grass I was holding, my right arm was hurting and I had a pretty severe burning pain in and on my stomach - presumably where my other hand had been holding the notebook. It's been at least half an hour and I'm still feeling a bit light-headed but an ice-pack has helped my stomach which now has a large, slightly red area on it. I'm hoping that with a jolt to my brain like that, I will now become a genius at remembering names, faces and telephone numbers or perhaps become a gifted artist. I'll even settle for being able to learn how to read music easily and so be able to learn to play the piano without forgetting what I learn within twenty-four hours.

There was a couple here with a small child who moved on this morning. They had a truck which housed their boat and small tractor. This tiny tractor had big rubber wheels and they were able to roll over the uneven ground and stones in order to tow their boat down to the water. The truck towed their caravan. They are heading north into the heat and are leaving here because it's not easy to get their boat into the water. I asked them if they were going to Airlie Beach next and suggested Bowen for fishing but he told me that he would just continue driving until he'd had enough and then they'd set up camp again. I find this sort of touring so odd. I wonder if it is so that they can say that they've been all round Australia.

CHAPTER SEVENTY-SIX

There was an article in a magazine that John saw before we left and he kept it. It gives examples of how you can get right around Australia. You can apparently do a 'Quick trip - 25 days being 17,000ks' (that's 486ks per day, every day and I'm not sure what you'd see other than tarmac).

A suggested leisurely trip of 60 days being 24,000ks.

'Around Australia - the works 120 days, 35000ks.' (A later round trip took us over 11 months).

Apparently you can do New South Wales in 15 days covering 4000ks and Queensland in 24 days being 6000ks. And so it goes on and all I can say is good luck to anyone who plans to take just over three weeks off work to go around Australia! There is no way in the world that we could get around Australia in three weeks unless we flew!

It would not be a 'trip' but a marathon. The longest we have driven per day on this trip is about five hundred kilometres and we were exhausted and ended our drive in the dark. Previously we had driven about 1100kl sharing the driving from Shute Harbour to Brisbane when on a short holiday because we had to back to work. When you cover those distances, on the average roads provided in Australia, it is very tiring. If there was an eight lane motorway all the way around it might be different but either way you'd see hardly anything of Australia. The kind of distances that this article suggested would hardly provide time to stop for a toilet break, let alone time to eat and drink. I find it very odd that people would even want to do it. It's not as though we drive slowly either, unless the conditions warrant it and we usually cruise along at the speed limit.

John's gone to play golf at the Turtle Point Gold Club at **Laguna Keys** and I must hang the sheets out - how mundane! I ran out of patience with my hair yesterday. I still had the back section feeling brittle from the hair dye I've been trying to grow out, so out came the scissors and I cut off about five inches in one swoop. I was very surprised to find that it looks quite stylish and it feels and looks better than it has done for years. Yes, I do have some grey hair but I'm lucky that it is still mainly brown and I don't mind the multi-coloured look. I also found a night cream for my face which appears to be reducing my wrinkles! So all in all, I should look quite good right? Wrong! I look like a spotted dick (for my Australian friends - this is an English desert, not what you are thinking). I have bites all over my arms, neck and ankles again and my figure is a 'splodge'.

You sit in a car and drive to your next stop, get set up, eat dinner and then feel exhausted. The next day you get back in the car to go sight-seeing. Every so often you get out of the car to take a photograph or to look at the view and maybe you call in at a shop to get some milk or similar. You force yourself to sit around under your awning with a book or just looking at the view because that is what this life is supposed to be about, right? You may go for a lazy swim in the pool and take one of the daily walks with the dogs, which cannot be hurried because they keep stopping to sniff at everything. I tell you, the most vigorous exercise that I now get is washing John's socks by hand!

My body won't know what's hit it when we get home and have to get all the furniture back out of the flat and empty and clean up this van. I'll be up and down our two small sets of stairs all day long. I'm sure I'm going to be shocked by the cleaning too - all those floors again and three bathrooms! On top of this, my daughter will be moving in and Christmas will be approaching. Hopefully my body will cope with all the action it so sorely needs!

Monday 20th September - **Cape Hillsborough**

Actually, we're not at Cape Hillsborough according to the locals because we are staying at a park called Haliday Hideaway at Haliday Bay. It's a beautiful spot which is probably why the park has been sold for development! It will operate as a park for about another year. We did go further along the road to the Cape Hillsborough National Park but, of course, we cannot stay there with the dogs. That has changed in the last few years, apparently due to the 'Greenies'. At one time you could free camp at the parkland on the front, right next to the beach but now you have to stay within the resort/caravan park there. I recall seeing photos of it years ago when my friend (who is now ill in England) camped there and they were often surrounded by Wallabies. There are several beautiful beaches here and we first stopped at Seaforth where there is another camping area next to the beach. It is operated by the local Council who charge a fee and there is water but no power. You can also camp free by the beach at Smalleys Beach but it is a small beach and the camping area is very small whereas there is heaps of space at Seaforth. Ball Bay also has a Council camping area but we haven't been there yet. This was the only place that we could stay at with the dogs.

We have the bush turkeys again and wallabies, bats and possums. It is a very old park and the manager warned us that the amenities are basic. There is one washing machine, toilet doors that do not lock and the showers have a curtain that wraps around you whilst you shower and there are no doors. However, as I do not use the amenities I couldn't care less and I love it here. We have to leave on Wednesday as it is booked out because the school holidays started last Saturday. There are swimming enclosures here and at Seaforth and next month the stingers will appear. We went to visit the Sunday markets yesterday but they only run between eight and eleven and by the time we got there, they were over! Apparently they'd sold out of fresh vegetables anyway. Next Sunday they will have a big market which unfortunately we will miss. We got off to a late start because I'd got up late and then we were nattering to our neighbours. However, we had a walk on the beautiful beach at Seaforth and then went to look at the resort near our caravan park because they have a nine-hole golf course.

We were looking at the menu as we were thinking of returning there for dinner that night, when we were told that they were serving beefburgers (not my favourite form of food). I looked in the restaurant and saw it was a buffet and this included salad so we decided to stay for lunch. I ordered a wine and John a beer and then we started piling our plates with salad, beautiful home-made crumbly burgers and added a bread roll. Then I collected a couple of plates with apple strudel and had fun operating the ice-cream machine (and I don't usually eat ice cream either). We took the lot outside and sat at a shady table with the golf club to two sides, the bar on another and the beach in front of us. It was so good. John returned to the restaurant to help himself to a bowl of fresh fruit salad and we finished up with coffees. Total cost came to eighteen dollars including the drinks!

John walked the dogs back along the beach whilst I drove the Ute back to the park and after returning I decided that I couldn't go for a swim because I'd sink! I fell asleep and eventually woke up at four-thirty and made my bed! It has to have been the laziest day that I've had on this trip. It is a beautiful area with lovely beaches, turquoise sea and National Park and it is a place you must make the time to see if driving this far north. Just don't expect to stay here after next year if you have dogs with you. Next stop will be Mackay.

Before moving to Mackay we went to look at **Ball Bay** and went back to Cape Hillsborough, where we had lunch. We absolutely loved Ball Bay, possibly even more than **Seaforth** and **Haliday Bay**, although the beaches are all beautiful. There is so much waterfront parkland everywhere and at Ball Bay it had that laid back casual look whereby the houses had been positioned wherever the owners felt like putting them rather than all in a line - I'm not sure how to describe it but it's magical. The beach was huge and we were the only people on it. There are so many old beach homes still around, some fairly new and others that have been modernised but all settle back into their surroundings as though nothing has changed since the first settlement days.

Point Midge and this area are very different to Lake Placid and Cairns but all three areas have been highlights of our trip in Queensland to date. Having said that, it will be nice to get home and swim in the sea without worrying about crocodiles and the stinger season. We are definitely adapting to a much quieter life than the Gold Coast though and John is not sure how he will feel about the constant traffic when we return.

CHAPTER SEVENTY-SEVEN

I had a word with Anne who manages the park we are staying in and asked how often she goes to Mackay to shop and she said usually once a month and it takes half to three-quarters of an hour to get there depending on the cane trains that can hold you up. She has a bread-maker and freezes milk and she gave me a few tips on that, such as do not freeze the one litre plastic bottles as they blow their lids, nor the two litre ones as they bulge but the one litre cartons freeze beautifully and should always be defrosted in the fridge and never in water (as I've witnessed before). Her freshly-baked bread is costing half of what I pay.

We have been rather tempted by a private advert about an eight hundred metre block of land on the beach at Midge point. It has a habitable hut on it at the moment with power, water and air conditioner and it's for sale for $350,000. It is absolute beach front with room to build in front of this beach hut. We had a giggle over offering a contract with five thousand deposit, subject to the sale of a property, subject to our lender agreeing when neither of us have jobs, subject to searches, subject to planning permission with a settlement date at least ninety days after all of the above and subject to anything else we could possibly think of so that the International Airport is finished before we buy and then we can sell it for a profit and boost our superannuation! I suggested that we ask the owner to swap the land for this motor home and we could off load everything into the hut and drive home in the Ute!

When we had been at Seaforth we had been parked next to a couple from Forster, NSW and the four of us could not stop talking! A quick question turned into conversations that lasted up to three hours! They were going to Midge Point and then will go inland to Longreach to visit the Stockman's Hall of Fame and it will be interesting to hear about the road conditions and scenery for future reference. Someone came up to them yesterday and warned them not to go to a van park at Midge Point where their friends were told to bury their dog dirt on the beach! I told her that we hadn't stayed there for that very reason but how silly of the owners of the park as word is getting around quite rapidly.

....

THIS IS ALL OUT OF SEQUENCE SEAFORTH BEFORE MIDEGE POINT THEN SEAFORTH AGAIN – DOESN'T MAKE ANY SENSE AT ALL

MACKAY 23rd September

Parked our van yesterday and realised that although there are fields on two sides of us directly outside our van (as we chose the very back of the park, away from everyone else) we are near an industrial estate. Our first chore was to stock up with food as we were out of nearly ever basic item. This morning I had a quick trip to the doctors for a prescription, John replaced the Ute door handle as it had broken and once I had the washing out and dried we set off to look at Mackay town centre, the Marina, the beach (where we enjoyed coffee and carrot cake at the Lifesaving Club). On the way back we saw two sign posts leading to the same road - one said 'Cemetery' and the other 'Waste Disposal' and John said that you'd have to hope that the funeral director didn't take the wrong turning once he was on that road. I replied that it could be handy if you wanted to keep the costs down and it may be that indeed they are one and the same place!

I found it odd that I didn't recognise the town until it suddenly dawned on me that I have never been to Mackay before! We drove on to the Northern Beaches. First stop was a place called **Bucasia** and we were impressed as it was very pretty. Then we went to **Eimeo** and instantly fell in love with the village. It is very rural with so many beautiful old trees, beautiful beaches and sea inlet. On top of a hill was a pub with stunning views. I took so many photos of Eimeo because at every turn it was so pretty. I've got to the stage where I don't even look to see if there is a shop but I don't think there were any, just lovely old houses, old country lanes, parkland to the foreshore, rocks, bays and boats.

BEAUTIFUL BUCASIA

I told John this morning, before we went out, that this trip is messing around with my head. I now hate shops and traffic, love quiet, small villages and would rather be on a deserted beach than viewing the towns along the New South Wales coast that I previously thought were so wonderful! I used to mention that this or that town had all the services and shops that are 'necessary' but now I would rather there was only a village store and so long as I can get to a major shop within about fifty kilometres to stock up now and again I can manage. I am, therefore, not enjoying being in Mackay and it was for these reasons that I was so delighted to find Eimeo today.

I am also beginning to enjoy this lifestyle more and more. That kind of worries me a bit but I'm not really sure why. It's rather unsettling to feel like this as I'm also looking forward to getting home as I've said so often. I keep hearing how great Darwin is and now I want to go there. It's taken me a long time to settle into this way of life and it's crept up on me whilst I have been consciously planning for our return home, my daughter arriving, seeing my sons and thinking about Christmas. I keep telling myself how lovely it will be to have our own pool, sleep in our king size bed, and have a large bathroom and kitchen and not to have to worry about the dogs bowel habits! I can wake up and enjoy a cup of coffee without creeping around quietly so that the dogs do not realise I am up because as soon as they hear me they wake up and howl with excitement at the expected 'walkies' and I cannot relax because I know they are now desperate for a wee! We have also been very lucky in having very few wet days but the storm season should start in November and I'll be much happier in our solid brick home then. I just wonder if I am going to get bored with our 'normal' life and if I will be able to settle down.

Friday

John started chatting to another elderly traveller with a dog this morning. His fluffy, white dog would not leave Jacks bottom alone and he was longing for his early morning wee (we're talking about Jack here not John!) In the end he couldn't wait and the dog still wouldn't move. When John got back he was telling me that this guy had told him that his dog was a 'self-cleaning dog' which I thought was hilarious. Apparently they only have to bath it twice a year. I told John that I had been watching out of the window and Jack had just peed all over it! When I went to hang the washing up I saw the dog being dried with a hair dryer - I do hope they bathed it first! When was a self-cleaning dog invented anyway?

We are going to leave here on Sunday to find somewhere further south on the coast. As we only have one day left here before leaving, we are going to take the opportunity of getting up into the Eungella National Park tomorrow. It covers 51,700 hectares so we'll only see a bit of it!

We got our post today. It was sent Express Mail and took two days to get from Brisbane to Mackay Post Office - so much for guaranteed overnight delivery! Anyway, I received a club magazine and was reading an article on someone's trip to the Elsey National Park and apparently the park ranger explains that 'there are freshwater crocodiles in this section of the Roper River, however they are known to be harmless to people if not interfered with' …. Anyone want to volunteer to test the truth of this statement!

CHAPTER SEVENTY-EIGHT

Apparently our club now has 40,000 members and they expect that number to double within five years. You won't be able to get anywhere fast on our roads if this is the case! They will be blocked with motor homes and vehicles pulling caravans, all crawling along as the owners are touring and have no need to hurry. Vans will be packed into caravan parks like sardines in a tin and they'll be standing room only in the swimming pools. Off-road camping will have a whole new meaning with people jostling for the last bit of space at the overnight rest areas! As for the Driver-Reviver stops where free cups of coffee and tea are available - well the volunteers will be so exhausted and stressed that they'll have to form a Union to gain better working conditions! I wonder if we'll have room for any overseas road tourists and back-packers! The road-train drivers who have deadlines to meet will be going ballistic. It's quite a horrendous thought. Perhaps we should continue our travels now and get right around Australia whilst we still can in relative comfort and then 'retire from the road' and revert back to plane travel. If petrol prices go up much more it might be cheaper to fly anyway.

When we were north of Mackay we were discovering the **Hibiscus Coast** and now we are about to head south, known by the locals as the **Serenity Coast** - what pretty names. Today we travelled the Pioneer Valley, heading inland and up the (very steep) Eungella Range to **Eungella**. On the way there we turned off at **Mirani** and travelled round the **Kinchant Dam** until we found a lovely spot for a coffee. There were toilets there and barbecue table and benches and around fifty very young kangaroos! John leapt out the Ute and got the rear window shut before Jack saw them and started barking which alerted both the kangaroos and Callie. When Callie saw all those bouncy animals running away she nearly burst with excitement. However, one decided to hang around so we had to keep the dogs on leads until John took them down to the dam for a swim. It was so hot here today and we find it odd that it seems so much hotter in and around Mackay than it was further north. It is cooler at night but much hotter during the day and it has been rather uncomfortable. We thought that when we reached the top of the range we would find it a lot cooler but it wasn't. At least it was reasonable enough for us to be able to enjoy our picnic lunch though.

On the return journey, we turned off at the small town of **Pinnacle** to look at the Teemburra Dam. We didn't go to the Finch Hatton Gorge, Eungella Dam, nor see any waterfalls, mainly as there is so little water about because of the drought.

When we were in Cooktown we learnt about the problems the fishing industry is facing and we followed the news all the way down to around Townsville. Now we're discussing the cane farmers. Recently we heard that the sugar yield is much lower than expected because there has been no rain and here we are right in the heart of sugar country. We saw so many cargo carriers lined up out at sea the other day and were told they were waiting to go into port to collect the sugar. The cane cutters, trains and sugar refineries are in continuous operation at the moment as it is harvesting time. The mill chimneys belch out thick black smoke and as you pass, the air is sweet with the smell of sugar. There seems to be some sort of rota system because every farm that we saw had been partly harvested, with some fields already replanted, some ready to be turned over and some waiting to be cut. We also saw a harvester in action and what enormous machines they use! However, we also saw some fields that had been replanted that are already drying out too much and the farmers are desperately hoping for rain soon. What we had heard on the evening news but had not thought much about suddenly became very real to us. We wandered about the realities of being a cane farmer whilst travelling around two hundred kilometres today. All the small towns we passed through rely on the sugar industry as does the train engineering company we saw. The port is also kept busy with the sugar transportation. From what I could see the area relies on the sugar industry, mining industry and tourism and the scenery was disappointing today because the ground is so arid. Suddenly I long for rain!

Sunday

GRASS TREE BEACH, SARINA

We headed off for Sarina which was only about 27ks further south from the park we were staying at! However, we wanted to get as near to the beach as possible. We knew that there are a couple of parks in Sarina that take dogs but the area didn't inspire us much so we headed for the Information Centre and they came up trumps. A small park, right on the beach at **Armstrong** beach and we turned up to find a very large site right next to a path that leads directly to the beach. It's wonderful and everyone is so laid back and friendly. We had no sooner arrived than we were told that everyone was getting together for a barbecue that night around the campfire. We spent most of our time chatting to a Welsh couple who live in Perth. Today we have pottered around and tomorrow we will have a look at the various beaches around here. The beach here is endless and so is the distance to the water unless you happen to catch the high tide. We heard it late last night! The dogs love their new play area as much as we do.

Whilst travelling down the highway there was a large billboard with a picture of a crashed car and the words 'I wish he'd crashed at a friends'. My first thought was 'Congratulations to whoever thought that up' because it's clever and hits you in the face but then I wondered how many parents have actually said those very words. I could almost feel their shock and pain and I wish there were more of these signs around because it certainly makes an impact.

28th September

Today we had a quick look at **Sarina** town and then went to look at some beaches. Sarina Beach is lovely, Campwin Beach is not worth the visit unless you want to go up to the headland, Grasstree Beach is beautiful and then we went to Hay Point because we were advised to! Unless you are interested in the shipping of coal, it probably isn't worth it but we found the contrast interesting.

Sarina Beach is a Dugong sanctuary. Dugongs are air breathing mammals that can grow up to 2.5m long and weigh up to 300kg. They look a little like very fat dolphins but have very different faces/noses. They look like they've been in a fight and have had their faces squashed! Their numbers have declined over the last ten years because of the diminishing seagrass, mesh netting and shark nets and boat strikes. Sarina Beach is obviously a haven for boaties as we saw two boat ramps, plenty of parking space and beautiful bays. There were about thirty vehicles with trailers parked there but I have no idea where the boats had all gone to so you'd have to ask the locals. Other boats were moored near the beach. It is well worth a visit. We have also visited Freshwater Beach which is not far from this park. A lot of house blocks have been sold there and there are a few homes already existing. Other than that there's just beach and bush there.

CHAPTER SEVENTY-NINE

Rockhampton

Our last month of travel - for a while anyway! We were sad to leave the park at Armstrong Beach because we met some lovely people, not least the Managers of the park Peter and Denise. We also met another couple who live at Emerald Beach in NSW which is near Woolgoolga. Denise told us how, unbeknown to them, the park had been advertised for sale on the internet this year as four seafront blocks and was snapped up by an investor for $800,000 - what a steal! The owner turned up one day to tell them it was sold and they had to leave within the month! To cut a long story short, the new owner subsequently found out that he had bought a caravan park! What a shock! He phoned Denise and Peter and decided to keep it as a going concern and asked them how much money they wanted to manage it. All they wanted was free site rental, free phone calls and fifty dollars a week to clean the amenities! The amenities are spotless and pretty with little pots of flowers and pump-action soap etc. It probably takes her over ten hours a week to clean them. The owner received $2000 in receipts the first time she made a deposit and he is over the moon! So would I be. Peter has even done the accounts for free for the previous owner for several years.

The highway journey to Rockhampton is not much fun. Actually that's rather a generous observation as it's a nightmare! We were travelling at 110kph and all the cars and semi-trailers were overtaking us. I believe I only saw two overtaking lanes over a 334 kilometre stretch and what with the caravans and road trains we had some pretty tense moments. The road is also very bumpy and I advise anyone travelling between Rockhampton to Mackay to ensure they are not tired.

Our first stop along this highway was to drive down to look at **Carmila Beach** as we had been told that it is worth a visit. It is if you have a four wheel drive but we made it along the sand roads in our Ute and even through some very soft and fairly deep sand without getting stuck. You can camp down there for free. We came to a park and John walked the dogs along the beach and around the headland. I walked across the park to meet him on the beach and as I came to the top of a rise I experienced one of those moments that you know you will always remember. The soft sand, the blue/grey water close to shore where it is shallow, a huge band or turquoise coloured water and another band beyond of deep blue. Dotted around near the coast were sandbanks and I was looking at this view through a whispery veil of tree fronds which were a green/grey colour and were feathery. It was so stunningly beautiful.

Our next stop was at an overnight rest area which was also a driver reviver stop. We were offered free electricity but had already set everything up. However, John had a shower in the caretakers cottage and we enjoyed free coffees and date biscuits. We had a good site, right next to a barbecue table and overlooking the very dry creek! Every creek we have passed recently has been bone dry and dead animals and carcasses have lined the highway. The crows don't have to fly as they can walk to their next feast? If it weren't for the trees you would have to rely on your memory to recall the colour green. It really is a miserable journey.

We settled down for the night but couldn't sleep for trucks pulling up on the main road (they were not allowed in the rest area itself). The truckies obviously used the amenities and seemingly, so did every car driver on the road that night. They came into the rest area pulling up outside our van with lights left on, car doors banging, shouting to their mates and we'd wait for them to leave. Then another truck and more cars and then the truckies who had arrived first started leaving (after approximately three hours of sleep). On and on until at about 3am I felt that I would be quite capable of murdering the next driver but luckily I fell asleep. When I woke up in the morning I felt sick with tiredness which I found rather amusing as it is a driver-reviver stop! We stopped again further south for a quick lunch of pies and coffee which were so appalling that the dogs had my pie and I tipped the coffee onto the grass! A couple of kilometres past this garage we saw a sign reading 'Real Coffee Yummy Food.' If you are driving south and see this sign and are hungry I advise you to stop here! No doubt the owners of this establishment have heard complaints about where we had stopped!

At last **Rockhampton** and that is where our hearts began to lighten. So many trees and shrubs and flowers along the centre of the road and as it is now spring in this part of the world, we saw many spring blossoms. We travelled straight through as we were heading for a park on the south-west of town, at **Gracemere**. It is a rural area with a village centre and the park has large, shady sites as well as a very large pool. It is also cheap. We booked in for two nights and found that we love this city and the beaches so much that we will willingly stay here for a week.

Rockhampton straddles Queensland's largest river, the Fitzroy River. It has the lot - urban, rural and seaside towns. This is known as the Capricorn Coast (as it is situated on the Tropic of Capricorn) and between Yeppoon and Emu Park there are thirteen stunning beaches. We started at **Yeppoon** yesterday and returned via Emu Park (which I love) but realised that we need to start early in the day and return to the coast and do part of this coastline at a time, stopping for a while at each place.

It was quite a shock though to realise that it is thirty-five kilometres to the coast from Rockhampton and we are situated outside the town centre so it is further for us. We did a fair distance yesterday as we first went up **Mt Archer** to see the views of the area and to walk the dogs. Unless you want to go there to use the barbecue facilities and spend the day there, I wouldn't bother though as you are so high up that you cannot see the area well enough for photographs when there is a heat haze below you! Rockhampton is hotter than further north or south and yesterday was forecast to be 35C whereas at our last stop further north it was 29C. We felt the difference when we first arrived and sat inside with the air-conditioning on for most of the afternoon! At the moment the breezes are helping us to manage and we have plenty of shade.

Rockhampton appears to be a very large city and history records the Archer family arriving in 1853, setting up home near a lagoon west of the Fitzroy River, first named Lake Farris, now Gracemere, which is where we have temporarily set up home! Around 1858 gold was discovered sixty kilometres north of Rockhampton and also near Bouldercombe and at Mount Morgan.

It is the 'Beef Capital of Australia' with about two and a half million cattle within 250ks of Rockhampton (not counting the six bull statues that we keep seeing around town which represent the six main breeds). Apparently you can ride a bull at Lee Kernaghan's Great Western Hotel in the centre of town but I'm not sure my back would stand up to it! The saleyards are here at Gracemere and apparently it's worth a visit on a day when the cattle sales are held.

Besides cattle, there are over twenty national parks, we can fossick for gems on the largest sapphire fields in the Southern Hemisphere and see the unique bush architecture, visit the Carnarvon N.P and visit the gorges, sandstone formations, waterfalls and Aboriginal rock art. We could visit the islands (I've previously visited Great Keppel Island), visit the Capricorn Caves (but we've done that before too), visit the Dreamtime Cultural Centre or the Heritage Village (apparently well worth a full day visit) or go to the Botanical Gardens overlooking the Murray Lagoon, which includes a zoo and a bird aviary with free entry. There is also a Japanese Garden there. The Botanical Gardens has recently been heritage listed and there are the Cliff Kershaw Gardens which we passed on the way and will be returning to as John spotted a stunning waterfall there. Then there is the Cooberrie Park Flora and Fauna Sanctuary and there's also the Riverside Park with boardwalk. Two blocks of buildings in Quay Street have also been classified by the National Trust and we can take a one hour self-guided walk. Rockhampton has many historic buildings.

How long can we stay! There's too much to see but we are limited with the dogs so will have to return another time. We will probably spend a lot of our time visiting the coastal towns so that we can tire the dogs out on the beaches and John wants to walk along the river in town again. I've seen very little so far (John's in town at the moment) but from the little I have seen I like this area lot.

CHAPTER EIGHTY

Well, it's 1.20pm and my daughter left Melbourne yesterday morning and has just arrived at her Dad's at Browns Plains! She says she's 'stuffed'. Apparently she had hardly any sleep last night at the motel where she stopped because a lot of 'grannies' were staying there and they wouldn't be quiet. She told them she had to be up at 4am (she had already driven for twelve hours straight and hadn't arrived until 7pm) but they put the television on at 10pm and she agrees that she shouldn't have even been driving today. I couldn't and wouldn't have done what she's done and I'm just happy that she's arrived safely!

I asked a local when it last rained here and she had to ask someone else but I never got an answer as neither could remember! We went into town this morning, stopping first at the wonderful parkland that we had seen when we arrived. The waterfall is so pretty and there are so many acres to explore with a scented garden, slab hut, monorail and rapids to look at. However, by the time we had seen the waterfall we were so hot that we wanted to get back into our air-conditioned vehicle. We drove into town and parked by the river and went to vote. As 'absentee voters' we can vote before or on Saturday and we wanted to get it over with. We had to vote for the House of Representatives and for the Senate. John dislikes the Australian way of voting for your party of choice and having your preferences automatically distributed. However, when he was told that he would have to number all the boxes from one to fifty for the Senate candidates if he didn't let the party choose them, he nearly flipped, I finished my voting and turned to find him sitting at a large table reading all fifty names so I sat down and unpacked my picnic lunch, which amused the voters walking in and out of the door beside me! We returned to find two hot dogs but couldn't find any shade and we ended up sitting on a path under a bridge which totally confused the dogs as they could hear the cars passing overhead. Once they had stopped panting we put them back in the car and toured the town in the car. The shopping centres are outside the city so driving around the centre is comparatively easy and there are so many old buildings, some of which are very lovely and trees everywhere. There are also many old houses that look like they are falling down as well as some modern homes.

We drove out to Gracemere again before returning to the caravan park and John looked at the photos in a Real Estate window. You can still get an acreage property here with a house on it for around a hundred thousand dollars. If you were self-employed and wanted your first home I reckon you couldn't go far wrong here but you'd have to find an acreage property with bore water. Next stop was the park swimming pool.

No idea what day it is - I'll look in the T.V. Guide - It's THURSDAY

How do I describe yesterday. Putting it mildly, it wasn't good yesterday morning but we escaped to the coast and had a lovely day. Jack, Callie and I were almost at screaming point for different reasons, so first stop was the beach where we all went barmy with delight. We were the only people on it. We started at **Keppel Sands** and ended up in **Yeppoon** and saw so many beautiful beaches and were surprised at how different they all were. We also looked at a couple of caravan parks but didn't like them much. The first had a lake but it seemed hard to walk to the beach from there and the other park was just disappointing.

I had so many phone calls yesterday from people with problems but the last call, whilst we were by the beach made me laugh. My son called and although he had no idea I'd had so many calls about problems he said 'Is that the advice number?'

In the morning, another friend was having serious problems with a housemate who has bipolar disorder. What a cruel disease that is. One of the other calls was from the insurance company advising us that they have doubled our premium for this van - why am I surprised! We returned from the coast to receive yet another call which wasn't a happy call. Why are some days like this?

On top of this, we have been battling all week with a noxious neighbour - the first we have encountered during our travels. When we arrived she said 'You have spoiled our view' and I was too stunned to answer but John thought she was joking. When she started to move my washing on the line I got more confused. She wanted to know what washing machine I had and did I have a sink strainer and all manner of daft things!! She and her husband sit there all day and just watch us and have only left once to get a quick bit of shopping. When I went to sprinkle the dogs with some water to cool them down, she came flying out of her van and started shouting at me that my hose fitting was leaking and I'm afraid I snapped and said 'I'll only be a minute'. I had to go for a walk one day just to calm down and get away from her. This morning she nearly reduced me to tears and my hands were shaking with stress! If you've seen 'Keeping Up Appearances' (Channel 2-6pm Saturday) you will understand why we call her Mrs Bucket (Bouquet). I now understand her neighbour, a normally rational person, who becomes a nervous wreck in her company!

We had new neighbours who, naturally, had a load of washing. They hung theirs out, then Mrs Bucket put hers out and I went and hung up a few hand-washed items. She came flying out of her van again and said 'What are you doing? I am using that' (meaning what space was left on the line). To cut a long tirade short, as luckily I can't recall most of it, she ended up saying 'You're a typical motor home owner'. I looked at her in astonishment and replied 'Oh, is that your problem'. I was stunned (and shaking like a leaf). Incidentally, when I went inside she moved my washing and put hers there! It is at least 30C here today and the washing is dry within twenty minutes wherever you put it! Unfortunately, since leaving the park, I have heard that our new neighbour has been too scared to hang her washing on the line since and apparently hangs it around her van!

The owner of the park tells me that I am lucky in not encountering the motor home versus caravan brigade before now and suggests I tell 'Mrs Bucket to 'get a life' but I'm certain that would not assist in making her more rational. I'd never heard of it and have never heard anything so stupid. It's beyond me. We went shopping and I bought two blueberry cakes and I was going to give her one and suggest she enjoys her neighbours, whatever they live in but when I saw her miserable face on my return I decided to freeze it! When I think of the problems those phone calls related and which were very serious, it makes me feel rather sick that I should get caught up in such mundane stuff like this. I can't handle it because I cannot understand how it can even arise.

Thanks to a friend of ours who suggested that I put name tags on the washing line because laughing relieved my tension and yes we got that second lot of forwarded mail from you today so now we are free to move south. Yes, we are lucky Paul - we can leave our neighbours if we don't like them! There are many advantages to being on the road and this experience has probably introduced us to the biggest!

We went to visit the Botanical Gardens but the dogs were not allowed, no doubt because there is a zoo there! We wondered what Callie would make of the monkeys as she's such an inquisitive dog.

Sunday

Well, we didn't leave until yesterday as we were suddenly befriended by so many people that it seemed silly to leave! Word had got around by people who had seen or overheard Mrs Buckets tantrums and one man called the attack on me as 'vicious'. One couple were particularly kind to us and we were soon sitting under their awning having drinks and chatting.

CHAPTER EIGHTY-ONE

We arrived here at **Calliope** yesterday to find the kind couple from the last park already here and waiting for us despite the fact that they had said 'No, not going there and 'Been there, done that'. They had the kettle on before we had parked the vehicles! However, they left this morning as they had run out of gas (for their cooking and hot water). We are hoping to catch up with them again. They have been teaching me more of the Australian language because I am still learning after twenty-three years here. I've already forgotten the two different terms that they used for what I term 'net curtains'.

We are on a huge off-road free camping area beside the Calliope River (pronounced Cal-I-pee) and Historical Village, 6ks north of Calliope itself. The dogs have settled down well as they do not need to be tied up any more and they are, therefore, much more relaxed. I understand it was 37C in Brisbane a couple of days ago and that was probably hotter than we have experienced but we do miss not being able to put on the air conditioner or jump in the pool when staying off site. We could run the generator of course and have air conditioning but with petrol the price it is it seems a bit expensive to run. Conversely, I feel far more relaxed with the dogs off site. It is a beautiful place to stay and when we arrived speed boats were towing kids on boards up and down the river, families and dogs were swimming and apparently no-one has ever seen any crocodiles despite the warning signs!

We nearly didn't stop overnight because we couldn't get our fridge to work. We checked fuses and all manner of connections but it was our new friend, who discovered that it worked on gas if the normal switch was on instead of the tropical switch. It works on tropical when we are on mains electricity but not on the gas apparently so that will have to be fixed. If you are buying a van in Australia it is imperative that you check that you have a tropical rated fridge if you want to travel to hot parts and also to check that it has good ventilation and insulation.

GLADSTONE

Today we went to look at Calliope (nothing much to see), then back across the highway and into Gladstone, first stopping at the Round Hill Lookout and then at the Auckland Hill Lookout, where there's a kiosk. The latter was well worth a visit. We went to look at the very pretty town centre and I can recommend visiting it on a Sunday as it was deserted, which is excellent for photographs! From there we drove to Tannum Sands which is very pretty along the Millennium Esplanade but dogs are not allowed there so we drove further along to the river inlet which was absolutely beautiful and we walked down the boat ramp into the water and onto the sands. We looped back to the highway to **Bororen** and turned off to **Lake Awoonga** which is another beautiful spot where dogs are not allowed as it is a nature reserve. As they were wet and cool, we left them in the Ute whilst we had lunch on the balcony of the restaurant which overlooks the lake and the waterfalls. The tranquillity was spoiled by there being a large screen showing the current car race, right there on the balcony! Surely people visiting a nature reserve are hoping for a bit of serenity! Anyway, instead of a week in Gladstone as planned, we will stay here for our second free night of camping (which is the limit) and we will move south tomorrow. Because we now have about five days to spare we are thinking of going back to see Bundaberg again, which we were originally going to skip as we've been there several times before. It's a long time since my son was studying there and I expect we will see many changes.

A point of warning though if coming to this beautiful free site - if you have a vehicle that is over five tons, you will not be able to cross the bridge over the river as there is a five ton limit. However, there is another access road further south between the Historical Village sign and the Calliope crossroads. If you are travelling north, look for a sign that says 'Stowe Park Brahman Stud' and go about 500m and you will see a road sign for 'River Ranch Estate' and 'Old Bruce Hwy'. Turn left there and immediately right where the 40kph sign is and continue down that road for about a kilometre (runs parallel to the highway) and you will see an unsigned entrance to the left and the river. Do not stay for more than forty-eight hours (your rego number will be noted each morning) or you will receive fines through the post. There are toilets but no showers and no drinking water. Another tip - don't stay there on a Friday or Saturday night as it seems a lot of local people come to camp and the teenagers were very noisy. Sunday night was blissfully quiet.

CALLIOPE BLISS

CHAPTER EIGHTY-TWO

About 63ks north of Gin Gin, on the right hand side of the road (just after the sign to Lowmead), there is a Driver Reviver rest stop and although unmanned during the week, there is a mobile pie van and there are barbecue tables and toilets etc. We grabbed the opportunity to stop for a coffee break. It was an easy, relaxed journey and when we entered Kolan Shire we at last found more overtaking lanes. It also became a little greener and hillier. We passed some major road works and since travelling along the coast, I have begun to realise just how much money is being spent on our roads in Queensland. We were eating up the miles and I was feeling quite excited because we are getting nearer home, which is kind of confusing as I am now enjoying the travelling! Just north of Gin Gin on the left there is a large rest area and there were a lot of caravans and motor homes taking advantage of it. You could probably walk into Gin Gin from there as it seemed very close to it although distances can be deceiving when travelling in a car!

We turned off the highway at the country town of **Gin Gin**, which was probably a stupid move as it is so pretty. I wouldn't have minded staying there for a couple of nights. In 2003 it won the 'Friendliest Town in Queensland' award.

BUNDABERG 11th October

Well after two wonderful days off road with the dogs unleashed we are now set up in a caravan park here. We needed water and power but have only booked in for a couple of days. There's nowhere to walk the dogs except for a grass strip opposite the park and there are too many dogs here for comfort but it's cheap and cheerful and we can get some washing done, recharge phones and have endless showers!

We set up before realising that we have forgotten to empty our black water tank yet again and to discover that we have mice again and having emptied and cleaned several cupboards we are ratty ourselves, which is why John just tripped over Jack outside the door and then shouted at him! Poor Jack is so fed up with being tied up again and he's picked up on our frustrations so he's been whining and trying to get in the door which is most unlike him. I think he wanted to find out what was going on and help in some way! The mice tried a couple of packets of soup mix but didn't like them, nor the sauce mixes but they were very partial to the pasta shells and we found a trail of them under the seats and in the cupboards. This time they have found new places and we have had to set up six traps!

Tuesday 12th

I congratulated a guy who lives in this park on what he'd done to his permanent site. An original, very large, caravan has obviously had the windows altered and attached is an extremely good (rigid) annexe. That is extended by a large covered patio with a fernery beyond. Surrounded by lovely gardens, it is fenced and it so attractive that I asked him if I could take some photos. He told us that he had moved to Bundaberg from Melbourne some years ago and had bought a Queenslander. He didn't do much to it and it cost very little to buy. Last year he collapsed with a heart attack and was clinically dead for a while and after extensive surgery he found out that this mobile home set up was on the market and they were only asking $22,000, including a new fridge and T.V. He reckons that he couldn't get to the bank quick enough. He sold his home for well over $300,000, is off to New Zealand shortly and then to Ireland, God willing, in 2009. He's a happy man and so grateful to be alive. I told him that I liked the look of Gin Gin and he answered with a grunt followed by 'They're all inter-related there'. There's no answer to that sort of comment, is there!

What a difference thirteen years makes. I wouldn't have recognised Bundaberg if someone had shown me photographs. Instead of a very wide and long, rather sad and neglected high street it is thriving and pretty with an abundance of trees, plants and gardens and the heritage buildings have all been cleaned up. I reckon it's one of the prettiest city centres that we've seen on our travels. Add to that the extensive parklands by the bridges with river walks and it really is a town now worth visiting. We were heading through town to go to Bargara beach but just had to stop and take some photos.

I knew that **Bargara** had changed but was pleased to see that it is still small. It is much prettier now though as the Council has landscaped the foreshore. We were delighted to find that the small motel that we had stayed at so many times before is still there, backing onto the golf course. There are now several apartment blocks along the front with more being built. We drove southwards along the coast, stopping at Innes Park, Coral Cove and Elliott Heads with its stunning beach. The dogs had a wonderful time as they were able to go into a couple of sea inlets, the sea and several parks. There was only one thing that we didn't like and that was a sign at Elliott Heads 'Beware of Stone Fish'! For my English readers they really do look like stones and you have no idea that they aren't unless you happen to step on one! I'm not sure whether there is an antidote or not! You are advised to go in the water with shoes on.

On our return we discovered a major retail centre slightly out of town, so Bundaberg is well serviced for retail shopping now. Everywhere we travelled new homes were being built and new land releases were being advertised. Instead of a sleepy town it is now a thriving and rapidly growing city.

p.s RIP two dead mice!

The street name and site number here in the park at Bundaberg are identical to the house we have rented out in Cabarita and I ponder the odds on that happening. The Jacaranda trees are turning from green to mauve and look so beautiful. In another couple of weeks Bundaberg will be a mass of purple because the council has planted so many of them along the streets.

We took another trip down to the coast, this time to visit **Burnett Heads** (north of Bargara), Oaks Beach and Mon Repos beach, where the turtles lay their eggs, so dogs definitely not allowed. We've been there before to see the turtles lay. I've never been to see them hatch out but have seen them on T.V frantically struggling to get into the ocean. Only one in a thousand survive to return to lay their eggs up to 25-30 years later. Apparently Mon Repos beach is one of the two largest loggerhead turtle rookeries in the South Pacific Ocean Region. It was a nice day out although we managed to take the wrong road when we came down The Hummock which is situated about half way between Bundaberg and Bargara. Although very small, it stands out because it is the only bit of land above ground level for miles and is surrounded by sugar cane fields.

On the way to Maryborough, which is our next stop, we will be leaving our rig at **Howard** (just off the Pacific Hwy) and will be going down to Burrum Heads to have a picnic lunch.

CHAPTER EIGHTY-THREE

BURRUM HEADS

Well Burrum Heads was lovely and there is a caravan park there opposite the parkland by the beach but it was so windy that I was scared to leave our thermos flask outside for fear it would blow away. Apparently it has been like this for three weeks and a local came down to check if his yacht was still in the same place. Apparently, earlier in the week all the boats went adrift. It is also windy further south apparently and it is these winds which are fanning the bush fires that we've been hearing about on the news. My son phoned me to assure me that only two homes burnt down at Cabarita Beach and ours wasn't one of them! Burrum Heads had a nice little town and we stopped to talk to a Real Estate agent. A three bedroom, two bathroom home on 800m of land on absolute waterfront is on the market for $595,000. That's pretty reasonable (in comparison to the Gold Coast it is as cheap as chips of course). It also seems cheap though in comparison to other homes in the area although you can buy a Queenslander near to the water for $285,000 (list price) with a waterfront Queenslander being $900,000.

MARYBOROUGH

We reached our van park at Maryborough to find our new friends already set up and waiting for us. They had been elsewhere whilst we were in Bundaberg. It's good to see Maryborough properly and we appreciate the Heritage buildings. Yesterday it rained - yes RAINED! In fact we had thunder last night and torrential rain overnight and it has rained for most of today!

A BEAUTIFUL SETTING – LAKE MC DONALD

The first European settler here was a guy called George Furber and in 1847 he built a wharf and store. Our park is next to the Mary River which was officially named in 1874 in honour of the New South Wales Governor's wife, Lady Mary Fitzroy. Between 1863 and 1901 nearly 21,000 immigrants first stepped on Australian soil here. 12,000 of them were South-sea Islanders who were to work on the sugar plantations. There's a steam train here called the Mary Ann, a replica of the original which was built in 1873, which was used for logging and it is still run by volunteers each Thursday in Queens Park and on the last Sunday of each month on a different route. There's also a cruise boat called the Proud Mary if you wish to take a cruise down the Mary River and if we didn't have the dogs with us we would certainly enjoy the morning tea cruise.

Maryborough has adopted Mary Poppins as a figurehead and has an annual Mary Poppins market day. The author of Mary Poppins, P.L. Travers was born here. This year the theme was 'Feed the Birds' apparently. A register is set up of females whose name is Mary (or is derived from Mary) and an annual get together is held during the Mary Poppins celebrations.

Yesterday we set off to explore the **Hervey Bay** area, most noted for its whale-watching tours and its proximity to Fraser Island. We started at Toogoom. Travelling south along the coast we came to Craignish and Dundowran Beach (beautiful and deserted) and if you have heaps of money, you too could live there! Then we went on to the main resort areas in Hervey Bay being Pialba, Scarness, Torquay, Shelly Beach and Urangan. We particularly liked the northern part of the coastline, probably because there are just deserted beaches and a few houses.

We enjoyed our lunch at the Arkarra Tea Gardens but didn't do the walks because of the rain. In the afternoon we visited the Sea Shell Museum and Gift Shop at Scarness with its collection of more than 50,000 sea shells from all over the world. They had a wonderful array of mother of pearl items, dating back 200 years. I couldn't resist picking out some shells to take home.

It's thundering again as I type this and I realise that if the power goes off we'll be fine as we have 12volt lights! That could come in useful if we are back home and have storms which cut the power off as we'll just move back into this van!

Hervey Bay surprised us as fellow travellers did not seem to want to hang around there but we found that it wasn't as commercialised as we had been expecting. There is so much acreage land there still and we never saw any main shopping centres all day although there are some there apparently. We set off fairly early and by 1.30pm had only seen three shops, two of which had been in Burnett Heads (a fish and chip shop and a general store which sold the necessities). We did see the beachfront shops and café strip along the front later in the afternoon but we had expected it to have changed more. It's good that it hasn't. We had also heard that it was expensive but for $800,000 there were two houses on the one block for sale on the beachfront and I think that is fairly reasonable. Acreage properties seemed very cheap to us too. Unfortunately, as we left the area, we saw an estate of brick and tile homes in the distance that looked like they were almost built on top of each other such was the lack of space to be seen anywhere. However, we had also seen some lovely streets just one or two roads back from the ocean with no two houses the same and with a mixture of old and new and the streets were tree lined and very attractive.

Today is a rest period and time to catch up on this and to research where we are going to go to next. We are about a week ahead of ourselves and may stay off road for a few days somewhere between here and Eumundi where we are booked in next week. I want to experience the Eumundi markets as I've heard so much about them and they are open on Wednesdays as well as on Saturdays and I intend to visit on Wednesday as I'm hoping that they will be a bit less crowded mid-week.

Our friends had been out all day and he just appeared and we said 'Where have you been all day? Come in and tell us all about it'. We teased him about 'being a dirty stop-out' because they've been gone for so long. His answer shocked us as he replied 'We've been at the hospital because she collapsed at the shops this morning'. It seems our plans could change.….

In answer to a couple of emails this week - we arrive home on Monday November 1st around lunchtime. However we may well carry on sleeping in the van for a few nights because we have to get all our furniture back out of the granny flat - not something to look forward to! Unlike when we move house, I did not label all of the boxes so have no idea what is where. Of course, we don't really need any of it because we have what we need in here - that's an odd thought. Why do we have so much 'stuff'.

We were due back on the Tuesday but its Melbourne Cup Day and I couldn't really haul the Real Estate agent out of a party to bring us the keys. For those abroad, it's like the Grand National in the U.K. but everyone stops work here and parties! You can't get any sense out of anyone except which horse have they picked out of the 'hat' in the office sweep and half the nation is tanked up on champers. It's probably the only day of the year that the cops don't seem to be around to breath-test anyone either so I guess they stop for the race too!

CHAPTER EIGHTY-FOUR

TAKEN FROM WILD HORSE MOUNTAIN

I had a glass of whiskey and lemonade this afternoon and before I was half way through it I fell down the van steps! I'm not very good with alcohol. It's just that we had a bitch of a day. First we had to go to the vets because Jack was obviously in pain. He's been poked, prodded and jabbed with anti-inflammatory and pain-killers and I now have to add a supplement to his food which cost us over $50 for a tub! I couldn't face the bill and left John to handle it! Anyway, at some time in his life his spine was hurt in the middle of his back, probably before we got him and he also has arthritis now in his lower back and legs. That is quite common for Shepherds (Alsatians). I tired to work out how old he is today because I have been saying he's the same age all year. He was at least a year old when we got him and I believe my daughter was 15. As she's 25 now that means he's maybe 100?. The vet told us he would live anything from 10-12 years. We came out rather shaken.

We then had to go to the hospital to see our friends. He had already gone back there by the time we got up this morning and we had no idea what was happening, or where the hospital was. Anyway, we spent a light-hearted forty minutes with her but I was very relieved to get out of there as hospitals depress me on principal.

Next we had to do the shopping but first we went down to the theatre café by the river to give the dogs a run and to have a coffee. That part was very pleasant and the rain ceased for about half an hour. However, it returned later with a vengeance accompanied by lightening and thunder and hail storms are forecast which doesn't do a lot for my peace of mind!

John has been buying the necessities but now we needed to do a major shop. That didn't enthral me much. We also had to find two banks, one of which seemed to elude us as we drove round and round Maryborough town centre, a chemist, a newsagent and a Post Office to send mail overseas. We went all over the place and then got so lost coming home that we've now seem most of the suburbs! John dropped me off with all the bags and went back into town to fill up the car with petrol and basically to find the garage that we had given up trying to find earlier which sells discount petrol. By this time it was after 3pm and we had missed lunch.

By the time we had got home our fiends had both just arrived back! She was very tired because the nurses kept waking her up all night to find out if she was awake. When she first arrived they asked her if she was allergic to anything and she replied 'mushrooms' so last night they brought her mushroom soup and a main meal which included mushrooms. He enjoyed her meal and she ate the roll he'd bought for himself some six hours earlier. Apparently she's had a small stroke and the 'panic attack' that her doctor had diagnosed last year was also a stroke. She needs an operation on her 'garrotte' or something and I cheerfully told her that means they are going to strangle her. She's also been told to lose weight and she was not amused to be given a piece of fruit instead of apple crumble and custard with lunch. After she's lost the weight she has to give up smoking and I've told her she needs to go to the gym. Despite all this very depressing advice from everyone around her she's still smiling, mainly I believe because he reckons she can't go shopping alone any more so she's told him he can do it all in future.

I wasn't smiling. I was exhausted and that was when the whiskey bottle came out. We've all decided to stay an extra night and have a relaxing last day together. We'll be going off-road for a couple of days but Sue and Greg are not sure where they'll end up.

Remember I said that she uses different words for net curtains? Apparently they are called 'scrims' or 'Terylene'. I was talking to her about the different highset and lowset houses and how a lowset is called a bungalow in England. 'What's a lowset?' she asked. I thought she was joking but she wasn't. So apparently Queensland uses different words to those used in Victoria! Sue tells me that one storey homes are just called houses and highset homes are called two storey homes in Victoria. I doubt I'll ever learn the Australian language, especially if it changes from state to state!

We heard later that they drove to a rest area south of Gympie which attracted a constant stream of trucks and by 5.30am were out of bed exhausted but desperate to leave. They were advised never to stop at that rest area on Tuesday and Thursday nights because of the trucks. We only travelled 25ks south of Maryborough today to stop at the **Tiaro** Shire Council rest area and it is fabulous. We had read about the Tiaro Meats and Bacon shop which sells such a wonderful selection of meat that people come from as far as Victoria once a year to stock up! I bought as much as I could get in our freezer and have now taken a loaf of bread out to get more in because I found the meat to be cheaper than that at the supermarkets. They cut me fresh lamb steaks, having taken the bone out first so I do not have to pay for the bone and I got some fresh veal and had it cut to my preferred thickness etc. You can also buy mutton, pig's trotters, lambs hearts and all manner of offal that we used to eat more of. We are surrounded by parkland and fields but close enough to the main road to walk to the Information

Centre, Council offices (they've told us where we can fill up our tanks with fresh town water), all the shops and two toilet blocks, one of which is new and provides free hot showers. It is spotless with soap and towels. In the park, near the main road, there is also a playground if you have children who need to let off steam.

In a leaflet on Tiaro it states that we could stay for two nights but the sign at the park said 'overnight' so the next morning John went into the Council office to clarify the situation. He tells me a lovely old lady told him 'You can stay another night as long as you behave yourself'. He assured her that he would be on his very best behaviour so after dinner I told him to 'Sit. Stay' and I have to admit that he was better behaved than the dogs!

We went to the Petrie Park Picnic Grounds (where you can also camp) and it was such a beautiful spot. A wonderful place for fishing too apparently and the dogs loved their swim in the Mary River. I find some of the names of the communities around here fascinating - Antigua, Miva, Gundiah, Tallagalla, Theebine, Curra and Bauple. The area used to have three groups of Aboriginal people, the Kabi, the Badjala and the Dowabara so perhaps some of the local names are of Aboriginal descent.

CHAPTER EIGHTY-FIVE

During our second evening we received a call from our travelling friends to say that they were at the park that we had already booked into at Eumundi and they loved it. They also said that if we arrived the following morning (a day early) and paid for a week, we would get a discount and it would only cost us $99. We did just that and parked opposite their van and whilst they watered and occupied the dogs, we set up camp, enjoyed the coffee Sue had ready for us and then jumped in the pool. Apparently the temperature was 37C but all we knew was that we were passed thinking straight and needed to cool down quickly.

We had stopped en route at **Windsong** at a Driver Reviver rest area and had gone over the road to visit the Windsong Tea House and Crafts. It was designed like a Thai village with a group of shops around a central area with outdoor (as well as indoor) dining. A sign invited us to help ourselves to free tea and coffee. There were all manner of arts and crafts, second hand books and jewellery. There were also internet facilities and an information room. When we got to **Gympie** we stopped at a park and I left John there with the dogs whilst I dashed into Woolworths to get some necessary items and the Saturday paper. It was lunchtime by the time we arrived at the caravan park.

EUMUNDI [SUNSHINE COAST HINTERLAND)

It's a lovely spot to spend our last full week and there is a lot of room for the dogs to play. It's also very relaxed and we haven't been given a list of park rules! The dogs do not have to be tied up as long as they behave themselves and the owner has filled up our gas bottle. On Wednesday I can walk to the famous Eumundi Markets. Another bonus is that there are no water restrictions here, so I've already washed the dogs and we'll do the van and the Ute before we leave as we cannot use hose pipes at the Gold Coast. The drinking water here is so pure that we don't need to filter it and I've noticed the difference with my hair and the dog's fur - we're all soft and fluffy!

And so I commence my final email. Had I known it was going to contain so many words I would never have started it.

TUESDAY

Having lolled about for a couple of days it was time to hit the road and go sightseeing. Having already seen most of the Sunshine Coast, we decided to head a little north to **Cooroy** and we really liked the town centre. The streets surrounding it didn't impress us that much though and that view was emphasised when we went on to Pomona because although the centre was much smaller the residential streets were delightful. **Pomona** boasts the oldest silent movie theatre in the world in the Majestic Theatre. Every year they have the 'King of Mountain' race where contestants run up Mt. Cooroora (and presumably back down!) Apparently it is a pretty steep climb and it certainly dominates the town. We then went to Boreen Pt. to see Lake Cootharaba which is a large salt water lake. It was a fabulous spot with tiny beaches and with a camping spot at one end. There is a shop which also sells hot food but we had taken our own picnic lunch.

On Wednesday I went to the markets and was very disappointed as the vegetables were not good and stalls were selling what was obviously prepacked broccoli by the floret rather than by the kilo. I couldn't find a Cos lettuce and the prices were stupid. John had dropped me off and by the time he contacted me on the two-way radio to find out where I was, I had had enough and asked him to bring the car back and pick me up!

On Thursday we went to **Noosa** via **Noosaville** and along the river. We parked with ease in the main street, unlike our friends who couldn't find a parking spot last Sunday and did a little window shopping. We had to be quick because it was so hot and although we had parked under a tree, we were worried about the dogs. We had a quick look at the beach and found that a little café that we have frequented often is still inside the arcade which pleased us immensely as it is very cheap! The arcade itself has been modernised and the town was awash with beautiful shops, buildings and trees. It certainly is very pretty and thriving. It is also too expensive for the average person to buy a property though. We went through to the parkland that abuts the river foreshore at the end and stayed there quite a long time. The dogs were enjoying the water and two children befriended them and endlessly threw Callie sticks. It was breezy and cooler and so pretty. We then returned to Eumundi as I hadn't seen much of it on market day. It is a pretty village and would be a nice place to live in my opinion. Needing lunch we checked out several places but John wanted fish and chips and we enjoyed the best cod, chips and salad that we have had for years at a small Thai restaurant. I was so impressed that I asked the proprietor where she purchases her salad vegetables and she said 'At the market'. I suggested that she doesn't buy them on a Wednesday and she said 'Goodness, no. You must go on a Saturday between 6.30am and 7am and go to the stall right at the back and you'll find the most beautiful home grown vegetables, but you must get there early'. I'm vaguely considering getting up at 6am on Saturday! John thinks I'm nuts but I keep remembering that salad.

Large markets and I are not really compatible though, firstly because they require me to get up early. As I am usually unable to do so, by the time I get to the markets they are either over or packed out with families and people browsing. I just want to find the fruit and vegetable stalls and get out but when I do eventually locate them, all the best produce has been sold and I stand there battered and bruised staring dumbstruck at the limp lettuce, overripe tomatoes, soft cucumbers and whatever fruit that is left being eaten by drunken flies. Then I have to find my way back out and try to recall where I parked the car. By this time I am not only battered and bruised by people's elbows, bags and the corners of market stalls, I am also ready to phone up the nearest child protection agency.

Why do people take their children to markets? Adults should try walking on their knees in a market for half and hour and find out what's it's like for them. Even babies and children in pushchairs are not immune from plastic bags full of apples thumping them across their heads and the distinct possibility of getting a broken nose from a swinging bag of potatoes. Whilst parents stand around the stalls their children are being battered by handbags, shopping bags, feet, people tripping over them and if that isn't bad enough, when they cry their parents tell them to shut up or 'be patient' and I look at them in sympathy and think that yes, they will be a patient any time soon and I'd better call the ambulance right away. The mothers touch everything and turn them over for a better look but when young Tom copies her his mother shouts at him 'Haven't I told you not to touch anything'. I feel like crying with them.

CHAPTER EIGHTY-SIX

Sunday

We said farewell to our lovely new friends yet again and John started washing the R.V whilst I got the washing out. He'd finished the awning and was on the roof when the phone rang and it was our friend who had just left. 'We're in Nambour'.

'Oh, that's good because we are going there to get our weekly shopping this afternoon so we'll come and see you again'.

'Um, yes but we're at Nambour hospital. I rolled the van and car and she started that funny breathing and she may have had another small stroke'.

We arrived at the hospital to find both of them shattered, her a bit battered and crying and him being his usual practical and stoical self. They were extremely lucky to be alive and shed reckons if it hadn't been for his having completed a defensive driving course they wouldn't have been. It was very windy and a semi-trailer passed and somehow the van blew out of control and the tow truck driver told them that there are many accidents with vans along that stretch of road so maybe there is something wrong with the camber of the road. They went down a ditch and were heading straight for two trees when he managed to swing the car so hard around that they ended up facing the way they were coming from and the huge tow bar is buckled and bent. The car was leaning over and the van still upright when he stopped and then the van turned over in slow motion. Apparently she asked him if he was alright but he didn't answer and she was too petrified to turn and look at him as she thought he was dead. She said that when she saw the trees she had been convinced that they were about to die.

The T.V channels turned up and we saw it on the news and in the papers. Apparently they had to get her out of the car before he could get out of her door and a lot of people had stopped to help. A lady suggested that she sit in her car and then added that she was on her way to a funeral!

It was thought that both vehicles would be written off but the car is driveable although it needs repairs. That has turned out to be a huge blessing. We all tried to be practical but I found that I felt quite exhausted and stressed by the events and couldn't have imagined feeling more drained, yet I knew that they would have felt the pressure tenfold. It is difficult to imagine their emotions. Our van park was fully booked so we all had to leave and as we had cancelled our next caravan park booking to stay with them we needed a van site and a cabin for them but everywhere we phoned was booked out whether motels or caravan parks. We did book into one place but it was way down the coast and John and I arrived there first and decided that none of us could stay there. In the meantime it was teeming with rain and even with the windscreen wipers on the fastest setting; it was difficult to see out of the windscreen. We ended up at a Gold Coast park and they managed to get a place back at Nambour late this afternoon because the blessed rain had caused a couple of people to cancel their villa bookings. The Managers told them that they had just seen photos of them in the paper! The doctors would prefer that she is home within the week to arrange for her operation but she wants to see us again before they go and may want to come and stay. I'll have to get cracking and find some beds just in case!

As we approached the Gateway Bridge I felt near to tears because I'm no longer used to the traffic! We eventually got our lunch at 5pm! So, having had a ten month holiday I have returned to the Gold Coast looking worn out and stressed out and when I saw myself in the mirror I said to John 'Good grief, I need a holiday'.

Friday

We arrived home to all sorts of problems, one them being that the Real Estate agency had not done the inspection report so we couldn't unpack anything! The tenancy employee eventually arrived around 3pm. The pool was filthy and the house has all sorts of faults but we found two mattresses and slept on the floor despite the fact that my son had turned up to help with the fridge, washing machine and had insisted on getting our king bed set up. Our friends rang and said they'd be with us the following day and they ended up in staying a couple of nights and helping us out so much that I wonder how we'd have managed without them. On the second afternoon other friends turned up and the lounge settee and my heavy coffee table are also in place.

Our friends eventually set off for their home State and my daughter arrived with her furniture the following day! I'm in the midst of absolute chaos and am surrounded by stuff out of the van, pictures, boxes and furniture! Did I ever say that I wanted to come home!!!

CHAPTER EIGHTY-SEVEN

I have kept a record of all the van parks we have stayed at and have included comments at times, to remind myself should I ever cover the same route again. I have hundreds of photographs, some of which I have printed out and which we have already referred to many times when people have mentioned places that we know we have visited but cannot immediately recall. We get muddled with names such as Burnett Heads and Burrum Heads and they are places that we have visited quite recently!

As you are aware, my feelings about this lifestyle have changed over the nine month period and I have enjoyed it much more since we have slowed down. Both John and I now detest towns and traffic, which is interesting as we are surrounded by both at the Gold Coast. For the first seven months we were doing so much sightseeing and travelling so often that we only had brief conversations with people but during our final three months we had started making friends with fellow travellers.

I'm glad that we didn't try to rush around Australia, albeit that we never actually have got around it yet, but I'm glad that we covered the New South Wales coastline in such depth. There are some places that we loved and that we can go back to for short holidays as they can be reached within a day or two of travel. Likewise, we discovered some wonderful places along the Queensland coast that we didn't know existed and I am certain that we will return to them. We have also noted places that we have missed seeing for various reasons, the dogs being one of them as it has made it difficult with so many National Parks that we would have liked to have visited but couldn't because of them. On the other hand we have had such joy with them that those memories will definitely last our lifetimes and this has been our first longish trip. We had a lot to learn and a lot of adjusting to do, such as slowing down! Obviously we did have time limits on this trip and we are now fully aware that you cannot see absolutely everything in one trip and it would be really rather silly to do so as there would be nothing left to see! So we didn't fret about being restricted by the dogs as they are both old anyway and won't be with us for many more years unfortunately. I also think that at some stage we will need a four wheel drive to really do the National Parks justice but I am certainly not prepared to trade in our Ute yet as I just love it and the dogs need it anyway.

I am overawed by the size of Australia and overwhelmed by how much we haven't seen. I cannot imagine how long it would take to cover the inland routes of Queensland and New South Wales, let alone the rest of this vast continent! Neither of us has ever been to any part of South Australia, the Northern Territory (Darwin/Alice Springs) or Western Australia (Perth) and we'd love to go back to Tasmania as our eleven day trip there years ago was just not long enough. We've seen a 'bit' of Victoria before, when we went to Melbourne and the Great Ocean Road and a little of the hinterland, which was very beautiful. We've been to Canberra in the ACT (or Australian Capital Territory for my overseas friends). During that tour we went to the Kosciuszko National Park (mountains/ski resort in New South Wales).

I have written many words about our mishaps, feelings and the weather because these are the things that we might later forget and I have tried to describe the places that we have visited to illustrate their uniqueness. I have kept in mind those of you who are thinking of doing 'the big trip' OR "THE BIG LAP" one day but I have little advice to offer as a place I love you might not think so amazing and a place that bored me you might find fascinating. We love the coastline; others prefer the outback or the National Parks. I adored the southern highlands but if you turned up there in July you would probably think I am nuts as it may well be freezing.

The biggest question is the type of 'home' you will be using as the homes we have seen have varied from tents and utility vans through to hard top and pop-top caravans, motor homes and huge converted buses. About half the people we have talked to are considering changing their form of transport and accommodation so you have to be prepared that you may not get it right the first time around. Unless you are absolutely certain, buy second hand because you will only know what your particular needs are after your first long trip. Everyone's needs are so different which is why experienced travellers design the interiors of their own vans in conjunction with the manufacturers. The cost factor is the only limit to your dreams but I would strongly advise you to travel first before deciding what those needs are. After nine months we have only recently decided that we would benefit from a small clothes rack as well as our rotary clothes hoist and the park washing lines because on wet days I could stand it in the shower recess to dry hand washing. However, it can get a lot more expensive than such trivial items if you buy a car and a new pop-top caravan and then decide that you would prefer to be in the National Parks and accessing areas via dirt road that are not accessible in a two wheel drive – another reason we missed out on seeing some things. There are now four wheel drive motor homes on the market but they are very expensive so you need to know that that is what you really need before buying one. So far we've managed well with our second-hand vehicles and I have been delighted with their practicality but I know that our needs will probably change in the future and we will be purchasing both a new vehicle and either a new motor home or caravan at some point.

There are things that I haven't written about such as the effect that the constant change in the quality of water, together with lengthy journeys has on ones bowel habits! The frustration when you suddenly need to dash to the loo, only to find that at that precise moment there is no way you can stop, such as during our approach and journey through Sydney which became a nightmare for me as I thought my bladder was actually going to burst! I cannot stress enough that you need your own toilet and there are many portable toilets these days that take up very little room.(porta potties] Our friends removed their fixed dining table and put in an extra kitchen cupboard which houses their portable toilet for emergency use and which added more work top for their microwave. They have a light-weight; fold up table which they bought for thirty odd dollars and which they like so much they bought a second one for outside use.

Many people do not travel continuously as we have done. They may travel via a different route each time to a set destination for the winter months. This could be another way to see Australia. We could say that we'll go to an Adelaide park for the spring and base ourselves there and just go out for day trips. Another year we could choose a destination for the autumn months, returning home between trips. You can travel vast distances very quickly with some determination as we did on our return trip from Melbourne to Cairns or as my daughter did from Melbourne to Brisbane – or perhaps her way is not such a good idea after all!

You can stay mainly off site or only in parks or vary it as most of the people we have met do. We are not good off road travellers. Last time, on our second day we were short of water and John was using a bucket to rinse the washed dishes in. Despite the size of our van, I promptly fell over it and we are still trying to dry the carpets out! We always love it the first day but by the third we want mains electricity, a swimming pool and commercial size washing machines! Many people say that they cannot stand being in caravan parks and I can understand that too as there are usually 'rules and regulations'. However, we have found parks where the owners/managers are so nice or the sites have such beautiful views that we want to go back to them. With experience you could build up a good list of parks that you love and that do not break the budget. My friend and I agree that it is often the two star parks that are the most relaxed or have the best views and that you cannot go by the ratings. My friend told me that if the roadways have kerbs, for example, they get an extra rating and who's bothered about that sort of thing! At the beginning I would only choose parks with ratings higher than three stars but although a pool is important to me in hot weather there is nothing that will limit me from looking at a park. We usually drive straight in and around the park in the Ute and look for ourselves but if there's a gate barrier we walk. We only ever book in for two night's maximum because the following day we will go and check out other parks in the vicinity.

I probably would advise that you make your first trip quite a long one like us because the odd week away is not going to give you any idea as to how you'd get along over a longer period. As you are aware, my feelings have changed over the nine months from wanting to go home after four months to loving it now. It was the same when we went back to England for ten months as it was so very different to going to England for a holiday. It takes a good while to really adjust and for life to become as 'routine' as it is going to become.

John had feared getting bored but he hasn't. John also thought that we'd be arguing over the T.V programs as we like different things but it hasn't been a problem. I thought I'd become super fit and instead I've become super flabby! I thought that John would never slow down and he has to the point that he really doesn't want to do anything! We thought we'd stay off road a lot and we didn't. I thought I'd find the washing a hassle but it's not a problem. We have got used to not knowing where to go to buy things and have learnt to stockpile necessities.

We still have a good meat or fish and vegetable meal most nights and rarely eat out. We have learnt to pack a flask as we have often found ourselves in some isolated and beautiful spot by a river bank for example, miles away from a café and don't want to leave the place we are at. John no longer worries if we skip lunch preferring to explore instead.

We have found that having the dogs has hardly limited our choice of van parks unless it is school holidays and we agree that it has been more fun having them with us than without them. To see their joy at the sight of a deserted beach still makes us laugh with delight. I doubt there is a human on earth that could beat Callie down to the water where she plunges in and sits down whilst she waits for us to join her. If we were to do another trip without them we would make a point of doing the things we haven't been able to do with them to justify their not being with us. We have seen cats on leads and pet birds accompanying their travelling owners and they seem to cope well. It has been such a wonderful trip and we absolutely love our motor home.

Will we do it again? Well we do have the rest of the Australian coast to get around – I'll think about it.

31/3/2005

CHAPTER EIGHTY-EIGHT

We have travelled for forty weeks and have driven just under 9,000ks in the motor home and over 20,000ks in the Ute. We have only spent 12 days off site and the average cost of caravan park accommodation has been $17.50 per night. A few more days off site would not be a hardship and would obviously reduce costs.

So now we are home at the Gold Coast, the weather is beautiful, we have a beautiful home with our own private swimming pool surrounded by tropical palms and plants. We have my daughter with us and my boys nearby and our friends down the road. We can walk to the beautiful Currumbin estuary and beach and we know where the shops are! The house seems even more enormous and we need some visitors to fill it up!

Of course, there is so much to do and so much to explore here and if we were visitors we would think we were in Paradise. I'm not just talking about the kilometres of stunning beaches, the theme parks (a few of which I have already mentioned) the water sports or aerial if you so wish, the canal or island excursions, the restaurants, the night life, the outdoor markets or the shops because there is too much to tell you about all of the above. (Mind you, if you are a visitor with an open wallet and fashion is your passion, do not miss visiting Elkhorn Avenue in Surfers Paradise where you will find Prada, Escada, Cartier, Gucci, Georg Jensen, Hermes and Salvatore Ferragamo as well as many other designers within walking distance.)

If, on the other hand, you are a bit strapped for cash yet need some luxury you should still be able to afford to go the Versace Hotel and enjoy a cup of some of the best coffee imaginable whilst sitting in the cafe beside the glorious lagoon pool. When you walk into the hotel you will be overwhelmed by what you see - it is an experience not to be missed especially if the pianist is playing or if you go in the evening and are surrounded by the hundreds of flickering candles. Ask if you can browse through the information on the construction of this 'palace' because the details are awe inspiring.

I'm really thinking about exploring inland such as the Springbrook National Park, a picnic by the Hinze Dam, explore Mt Tambourine where you can learn to glide as well as visiting the quaint shops or dig for thunder eggs! Travel to Ipswich, Brisbane or Toowoomba and northern New South Wales is certainly not to be missed. Take river cruises, sea cruises, go deep sea fishing or river and estuary fishing – it's endless here. I will leave you with this very brief example of what you can expect to sample in this part of Australia and I wonder again as I write this as to why we ever wish to leave the area.

Christmas is fast approaching and I am excited as I get the Christmas tree decorations back out of the storeroom in anticipation of our family get together. I would not have been so content if I had known that our home life was about to thrown into utter turmoil, but I'll tell you about that in my next letter.

I have already written 109,774 words to you all and I think that's quite enough for one letter, don't you!

You know, I do so wish that we'd seen Uluru and Alice Springs; I so wanted to see Adelaide and Perth. Should I or rather could I really go that far? If it took us nine months just to cover part of the east coast and fly through the inland route, could I tour the rest of Australia?

Trip One –The Route:

Queensland	Currumbin(Southern Gold Coast)	Continuation from bottom of the page:-	
New South Wales	Bangalow	New South Wales	North Avoca
!!	Clunes	!!	By-pass Sydney
!!	Lismore	!!	Mittagong
!!	Casino	!!	Bowral
!!	Ballina	!!	Moss Vale
!!	Wardell	!!	Burrawang
!!	Iluka	!!	Bundanoon
!!	Maclean	!!	Goulburn
!!	Yamba	!!	Penrose
!!	Ulmarra	!!	Wingello
!!	Grafton	!!	Tallong
!!	Woolgoolga	!!	Berrima
!!	Coffs Harbour	!!	Robertson
!!	Dorrigo	!!	Kangaroo Valley
!!	Bellingen	!!	Kiama
!!	Sawtell	!!	Gerroa
!!	Nambucca Heads	!!	Gerringong
!!	Macksville	!!	Nowra
!!	Telegraph Point	!!	Ulladulla
!!	Port Macquarie	!!	Manyana
!!	Taree	!!	Batemans Bay
!!	Manning Point	!!	Long Beach
!!	Old Bar	!!	Moruya
!!	Wingham	!!	Mogo
!!	Tuncurry	!!	Narooma
!!	Nabiac	!!	Dalmeny
!!	Forster	!!	Mystery Bay
!!	Pacific Palms	!!	Wallaga Lake
!!	Bulladelah	!!	Bermagui
!!	Hawks Nest	!!	Merrimbula
!!	Shoal Bay (Nelson Bay)	!!	Eden
!!	By-passing Newcastle	Victoria	Mallacoota
!!	Boat Harbour	!!	Orbost
!!	Swansea (Lake Macquarie Region)	!!	Lake Entrance
!!	Noraville	!!	Metung
!!	Wyong	!!	Bairnsdale
!!	Broken Head	!!	Paynesville
!!	The Entrance	!!	Eagle Point
!!	Toowoon Bay	!!	Stratford
!!	Toukley	!!	Yarram
!!	Belmont	!!	Welshpool

Trip One- The Route continued

‼	Croudace Bay	‼	Windmill Farm
‼	Woodrising	‼	Foster
‼	Buttaba	‼	Wilsons Promontory
‼	Shingle Splitters Point	‼	Sandy Point

Trip One- The Route continued

Continued from bottom of page:-

Victoria	Waratah Bay	Queensland	Black Mountains
!!	Walkerville North	!!	Cooktown
!!	Inverloch	!!	Mossman
!!	Wonthaggi	!!	Daintree
!!	Cowes (Phillip Island)	!!	Crystal Cascades
!!	Dandenong (Hume Highway)	!!	Gordonvale
!!	North Melbourne (Craigieburn)	!!	Yungaburra
!!	Wangaratta	!!	Kairi
New South Wales	Wagga Wagga	!!	Lake Tinaroo
!!	Ardletha	!!	Mareeba
!!	West Wyalong	!!	Kuranda
!!	Dubbo	!!	Lake Placid
!!	Gilgandra	!!	Mission Beach
!!	Coonabarabran	!!	Tully
!!	Gunnedah	!!	Innisfail
!!	Tamworth	!!	Kurrimine
!!	Armidale	!!	Flying Fish Point
!!	Ben Lomond	!!	Cardwell
+ !!	Llangothlin	!!	Hinchinbrook Island
!!	Glen Innes	!!	Ingham
!!	Casino	!!	Lucinda
!!	Murwillumbah	!!	Rollingstone
!!	Chinderah Lake	!!	Townsville
!!	Uki	!!	Bowan
Queensland	Tanah Merah(Brisbane Southside)	!!	Airlie Beach

Trip One- The Route continued

‼	Glass House Mountains	‼	Midge Point
‼	Landsborough	‼	Laguna Keys
‼	Beerwah	‼	Haliday Bay(Seaforth)
‼	Caloundra	‼	Cape Hillsborough
‼	Childers	‼	Ball Bay
‼	Gin Gin	‼	Mackay
‼	Marlborough	‼	Bucasia
‼	Bowen	‼	Eimeo
‼	Townsville	‼	Eungella
‼	Bluewater	‼	Pinnacle
‼	Mission Beach	‼	Sarina
‼	Innisfail	‼	Armstrong Beach
‼	Cairns	‼	Rockhampton
‼	Lake Placid	‼	Carmila Beach
‼	Trinity Beach	‼	Yeppoon
‼	Yorkey's Knob	‼	Calliope
‼	Palm Cove	‼	Gladstone
‼	Port Douglas	‼	Bororen
‼	Mareeba	‼	Lake Awoonga
‼	Mount Molloy	‼	Bundaberg
‼	Mt Carbine	‼	Bargara
‼	Lakeland	‼	Burnett Heads

Trip One:-The Route Continued

Queensland	
!!	Howard
!!	Burrum Heads
!!	Maryborough
!!	Hervey Bay
!!	Tiaro
!!	Windsong
!!	Gympie
!!	Eumundi (Sunshine Coast Hinterland)
!!	Cooroy
!!	Pomona
!!	Noosaville
!!	Noosa
!!	Currumbin (Southern Gold Coast)